# INDIGENOUS
# EFFLORESCENCE
## BEYOND REVITALISATION IN SAPMI AND AINU MOSIR

# INDIGENOUS EFFLORESCENCE

## BEYOND REVITALISATION IN SAPMI AND AINU MOSIR

EDITED BY GERALD ROCHE, HIROSHI MARUYAMA
AND ÅSA VIRDI KROIK

---

MONOGRAPHS IN
ANTHROPOLOGY SERIES

---

PRESS

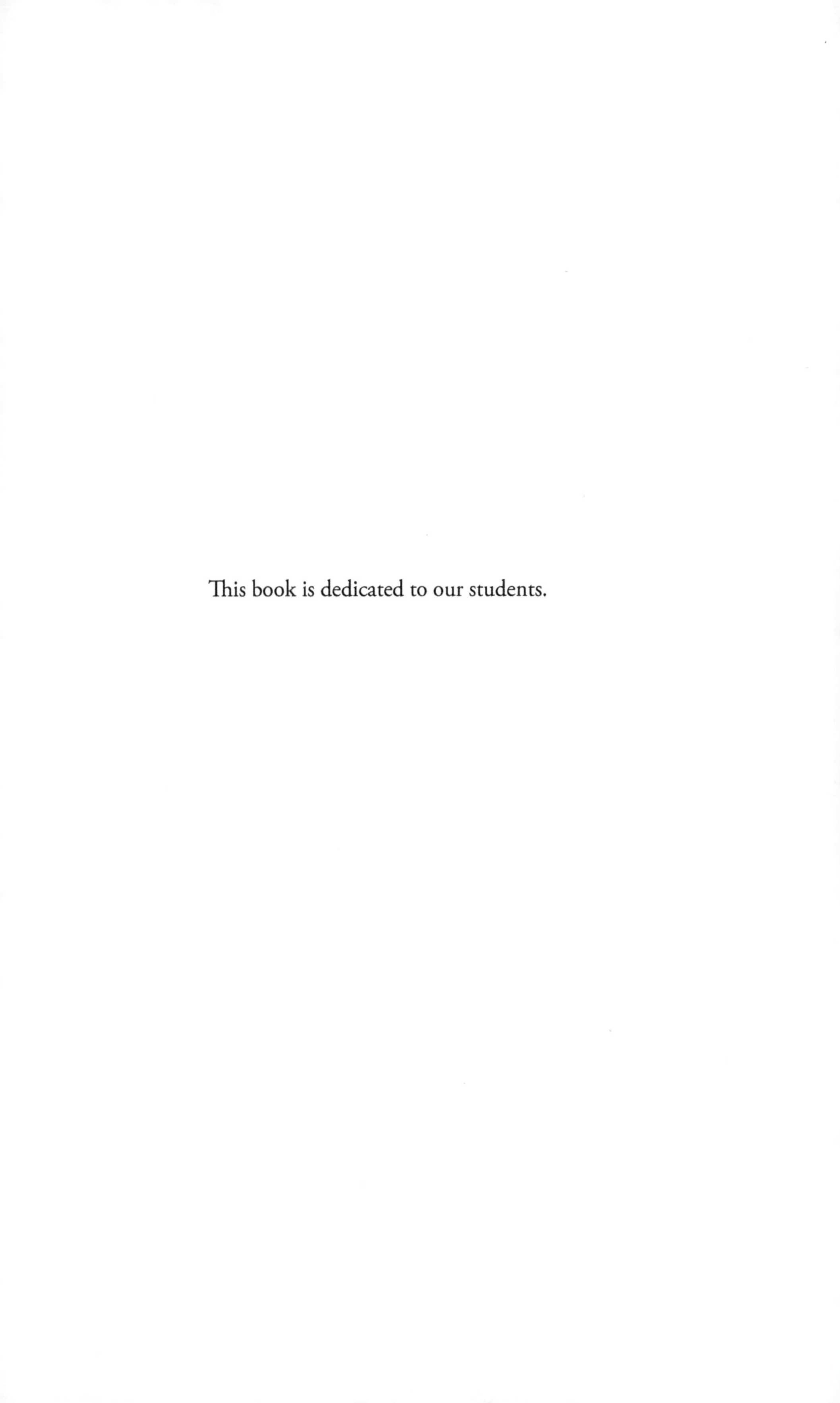

This book is dedicated to our students.

Published by ANU Press
The Australian National University
Acton ACT 2601, Australia
Email: anupress@anu.edu.au

Available to download for free at press.anu.edu.au

ISBN (print): 9781760462628
ISBN (online): 9781760462635

WorldCat (print): 1078701250
WorldCat (online): 1078701578

DOI: 10.22459/IE.2018



Cover design and layout by ANU Press. Cover illustration by Jenny Kroik.

# Contents



## Part One: Contexts of Efflorescence

## Part Two: Practices of Efflorescence

# List of Illustrations

## Map



## Figures

# Acknowledgements

The editors would like to express their gratitude, first and foremost, to the contributors to this volume for their hard work, and for their patience during the long process of bringing this book to fruition. Special thanks should also be given to the translators who helped make many of the case studies accessible to Anglophone audiences.

We also wish to thank Boska, Kulturrådet, and Konung Gustaf VI Adolfs fond för svensk kultur for their very generous funding towards the translation, copyediting and printing of this book. Thanks also to Matt Tomlinson for shepherding this publication through to completion, to Carolyn Brewer for her careful and patient editing work, and to everyone at ANU Press who helped make this volume a reality.

This book first began life in the corridors of the Hugo Valentin Centre at Uppsala University, and we would like to thank our colleagues there for their support: Leena Huss, Satu Gröndahl and Imke Hansen.

**Gerald Roche:** I would like to thank the Krampe family, Ilmari Käihkö, Jelena Spasenic and Jonathan Hall for their friendship and hospitality during my stay in Uppsala. Enormous thanks are also due to Elena and Arlo for their patience and support. I would also like to thank the countless people engaged in language revitalisation and other aspects of Indigenous efflorescence who have shared their knowledge and experiences with me over the years, and have thus helped to shape the ideas that went into this project. And finally, I would also like to express my gratitude to my coeditors for their dedication to this project through its many ups and downs.

**Åsa Virdi Kroik:** I would like to thank my family: my brother David and my daughter Jenny for their contributions in this book, my husband Harvinder for his support and patience and my father Arne Jonasson for teaching me so much that I need to know as a Saami—knowledge that

I want to pass on to the next generation, and to the world. I also want to thank all the people that participated in the revitalisation projects I arranged while working in Røyrvik and my colleague Anne Bjørg Evensen Svestad for her enthusiasm and support for that work. Thanks to my coeditors for inviting me to be part of this project. A very special thanks to Ian Stuart in Aotearoa/New Zealand for comforting me when in trouble, helping me to understand the concept of efflorescence, and for many fruitful intellectual discussions and friendship.

**Hiroshi Maruyama:** First of all, I am deeply grateful to all authors for having the patience to wait years for the publication of their papers. I would also like to thank volunteer translators Masumi Tanaka, Jeff Gayman and Miku Maeda for their efforts in carefully translating Ainu case studies into English. It is my great honour to have had the opportunity to be involved in this book project, including the documentation of Ainu case studies. I have learned a lot about Indigenous epistemology from contributions throughout the process of editing. Lastly, my special thanks go to my coeditors: Gerald Roche and Åsa Virdi Kroik. I contributed to the publication of this book much less than they did.

# Notes on Language: Locations in Sapmi – Land of the Sami

Sami authors are familiar with Sami language in various degrees from being fluent speakers to having some knowledge of the language. The most natural way for many authors is to name some places in Swedish/Norwegian/Finnish and others in Sami. The revitalisation of place names is currently ongoing and some place names, like the town of Staare (known as Östersund in Swedish), are increasingly heard. That said, many of our contributors feel more comfortable using Swedish, Norwegian or Finnish for certain place names. Despite the fact that this is a book in English we have encouraged our coauthors to use the place name they want as it is not for us as editors to decide the pace and extent of the Sami revitalisation process.

| Place name in Nordic language | Place name in Sami | Comment |
| --- | --- | --- |
| Amarnäs | Geavtse | |
| Ankarede | Åanghkerenjeeruve | |
| Buarkantjahke | Borgafjäll | |
| Gällivare | Jiellevárri | |
| Jämtland | | A colonial/administrative region on the Swedish side of Sapmi |
| Kiruna | Giron | |
| (Lake) Namsvatn | Nååmesjenjaevrie | |
| Lycksele | Liksjoe | |
| Nieden elva / Näätämö (River) | | A river in North Sapmi that flows through its Norwegian side and its Finnish side. Nieden elva is its Norwegian name and Näätämö its Finnish name |

| Place name in Nordic language | Place name in Sami | Comment |
| --- | --- | --- |
| Nord-Tröndelag | | A colonial/administrative region on the Norwegian side of Sapmi |
| Norrbotten | | A colonial/administrative region on the Swedish side of Sapmi |
| Röyrvik | Raavrevihke | |
| Sami/Sámi/Saami | | |
| Sapmi/Sápmi/Saepmie | | |
| Silisjaure | Sijliesjaevre | |
| Snåsa | Snaase | |
| Storuman | Luspie | |
| Tana elva | Deadtnu (River) | |
| Tärnaby | Dearna | |
| Umeå | Upmeje | |
| Utsjoki | Ohcejohka/ Uccjuuhâ/Uccjokk | |
| Vilhelmina | Vualtjere | |

# Note on spelling

Within the chapters dealing with the Sami context, the same word may be spelled differently in different chapters, depending on which Sami language the author is referring back to. The term Sami itself is a good example of this. It is spelled in three different ways: Sami, Saami and Sámi. Sami is most commonly used in the Anglophone literature; Saami is the preferred spelling in the South Saami context; whereas Sámi is preferred in the North Sámi context.

# Glossaries of Non-English Terms

A = Ainu; J = Japanese; LS = Lule Sami; NS = North Sami; S = Swedish;
SS = South Saami

## General glossary

| | |
|---|---|
| *aajja* (SS) | grandfather |
| Apefuchi kamui (A) | a deity; fire in the form of an elderly woman who mediates between humans and other deities |
| *apeoi* (A) | a sunken fireplace in the centre of the traditional Ainu house |
| *Asircepnomi* (A) | an Ainu salmon-welcoming ceremony |
| *attus* (A) | a traditional form of Ainu textile |
| *Aynupuri* (A) | 'the Ainu way' |
| *banya* (A) | a workshop and lodging for fishermen |
| *chinjiri* (A) | a type of traditional Ainu clothing |
| *chise* (A) | a traditional Ainu house |
| *Chise inomi* (A) | the ceremony to celebrate the building of a new house |
| *Chise koenomi* (A) | the ceremony of purifying a building site |
| *chitarpe* (A) | a rush mat |
| *chitatap* (A) | minced vegetables and fish |
| *cikornay* (A) | 'our river' |
| *cikoro-inaw* (A) | Ainu ritual wooden shaving stick, after being used for the house ceremony |
| *cipor don* (A, J) | rice bowl with salmon eggs |

| | |
|---|---|
| *citatap* (A) | pickles |
| *emusat* (A) | a cord used to hang a sword from the shoulder |
| *fu-ta-re-cui* (A) | an Ainu dance that expresses the movement of pine trees shaken by a strong wind |
| *fuchi* (A) | female elder |
| *gadniha* (LS) | invisible beings |
| *gåetie* (SS) | traditional Saami dwelling |
| *gáffevuostá* (NS) | 'coffee cheese' made from reindeer milk |
| *gáhko* (LS) | bread |
| *guksie* (SS)/*guksi* (NS) | a traditional cup |
| *heperay* (A) | an arrow with flowers used in *Iomante* (bear sending ceremony) |
| *Icarpa* (A) | ancestral remembrance ceremony |
| *ikupasuy* (A) | an Ainu folk stick used for prayer |
| *inaw* (A) | an Ainu folk shaved stick used for prayer |
| *iyairaikere* (A) | 'thank you' |
| *joik* | traditional Sami vocal art (written in English orthography), also spelled *yoik* |
| Kamuy (A) | deities, spirits |
| Kamuy-cepu (A) | the salmon god |
| *Kamuycepnomi* (A) | an alternative name for *Asircepnomi*, the Ainu salmon-welcoming ceremony |
| *Kamuynomi* (A) | reburial ceremony |
| *kofüe* (J) | embroidery technique revitalised by Shizue Ukaji |
| *kotan* (A) | community, village |
| *laevie* (SS) | relative, friend |
| *lavvu* | a traditional Sami dwelling (written in English orthography – *lávvu* in NS) |
| *mukkuri* (A) | a traditional mouth harp |
| *nomme*/*nïmme* (SS) | name |
| Okikirmuy (A) | a personal god of the Ainu |
| *pon saranip* (A) | a small, knitted basket |

| | |
|---|---|
| *potcheimo* (A) | dumplings made from fermented potatoes in winter |
| *rakko* (A) | sea otter |
| *rera* (A) | wind |
| *ru-i-be* (A) | a form of frozen sashimi |
| *ruunpe* (A) | a traditional Ainu dress |
| *Sameby* (S) | a Sami reindeer-herding community; recognised as a juridical person in law, and an economic association based on the traditional Sami community |
| *Samebyar* (S) | plural of *Sameby* |
| *seikatsukan* (J) | a community centre |
| *sirkap* (A) | swordfish |
| *sydisdans* (S) | 'southern dance', a new form of dance popular in Sapmi |
| *tar* (A) | a rope used to carry a load on the shoulders |
| *tonkori* (A) | an Ainu traditional instrument |
| *tonoto* (A) | raw sake |
| *torikabuto* (J) | a poisonous plant used by the Ainu for hunting big game |
| *ukoitaku* (A) | negotiation, discussion |
| *upopo* (A) | Ainu everyday songs |
| *utari* (A) | friends, companions |
| Wajin | ethnic Japanese who were settled in Hokkaido |
| *yoik* | see *joik* |
| *yukar* (A) | oral epic |

# Locations in Ainu Mosir – Land of the Ainu

| | | |
|---|---|---|
| Ainu Mosir | Biratori | Hokkaidō |
| Akan Lake | Chitose County | Ishikari River |
| Anecha | Chitose River | Kotoni River |
| Asahikawa | Hidaka District | Kurile Islands |

Kushiro

Matsumae Domain (former name for Hokkaidō)

Nibutani

Oshima Peninsula

Sakhalin Island

Sapporo

Saru River

Shiraoi

Usu

Yezo (former name for Hokkaidō)

## Locations in Sapmi – Land of the Sami

Amarnäs

Ankarede

Deatnu River

Gällivare

Jämtland

Kiruna

Lake Namsvatn

Lycksele

Neiden/Näätämö River

Nord-Trøndelag

Norrbotten

Røyrvik

Sapmi, Sápmi, Saepmie

Sijliesjaevrie

Snåsa

Storuman

Tärnaby

Umeå

Utsjoki

Vilhelmina

## Other locations

Ebisu, Tokyo — Japan

Hayama — Japan

Kantō (region) — Japan

Wajinchi — land of the ethnic Japanese, Japan

## Languages and ethnic groups

Aanaar Sami

Chukchi

Evenk

Kaurna

Khanty

Lule Sami

Mansi

Meänkieli

Michi Saagiig Nishnaabeg

Myaamia

North Sami

Romani

Sami/Saami/Sámi

Skolt Sami

Ume Sami

Wajin (ethnic Japanese)

Wôpanâak

Yukaghir

# Contributors

**Chisato Abe** worked for the Ainu Association of Hokkaidō for years. She has spared no effort in distributing accurate information on the rights of the Ainu and Ainu culture to the public through many channels, in cooperation with Ainu and Japanese peoples.

**Mattias Berglund** is my name and I have worked as a business developer, project manager and economist for 10 years. I have been an entrepreneur for many years now and I am driven by the objective to change and make society and industry more efficient, attractive and sustainable. For a long time in my professional life I have been working with the Sámi industries, in various forms such as web projects, investigations, accounting, business consulting, events and as a Sámi handicrafts consultant. My last big event was the Sápmi Awards in Jåhkåmåhkke/Jokkmokk in June 2014 and I also managed it the previous year.

Mu namma lea Mattias Berglund ja lean juo logi jagi bargan gávppašanovddideaddjin, prošeaktajođiheaddjin ja ekonoman. Mus lea fitnodat ja lean bargan entreprenevran máŋggaid jagiid ja jođihuvvon dáhtuin rievdadit ja dahkat servodaga ja ealáhuseallima beaktileappot, bivnnuhut ja guhkesáigásaččat bistevaš. Stuorra oasis mu ámmátdoaimmalaš eallimis mon lean bargan sámi ealáhuseallimis máŋgga hámiin nugo webbaprošeavttat, guorahallamat, rehketdoallu, fitnodatbagadallan, doalut ja sámiduodjekonsuleantan. Mu maŋemus stuorit doallu leai Sápmi Awards Jåhkåmåhkes geassemánus 2014 ja maid jagi ovdal.

**Coppélie Cocq** is an ethnologist and Associate Professor in Sámi Studies, Humlab, Umeå University, Sweden. Her research interests lie in the fields of folklore studies and digital humanities, with specific focuses on storytelling and revitalisation in Indigenous contexts.

**Jeff Gayman** has a Doctoral Degree in Education from Kyushu University, and is currently employed by Hokkaidō University, with a joint appointment in the School of Education and the Research Faculty of Media and Communication. Since coming to this post, he has devoted his efforts to strengthening the Ainu presence in Hokkaidō University research and education initiatives, including having held two international symposiums to address the issue of repatriating Ainu ancestral remains held by Hokkaidō University.

**Leena Huss** is Professor Emerita of Finnish at Uppsala University, The Hugo Valentin Centre, Sweden, and she has also worked at the Arctic University of Norway, Tromsø. Her main research interests are Nordic minority and minority language policies, Finno–Ugric minority languages, multilingualism, language maintenance and linguistic revitalisation.

**Kouichi Kaizawa** is founder of the Cikornay National Trust, former Visiting Professor at Muroran Institute of Technology, and the president of Biratori Ainu Culture Preservation Association. He was also one of two plaintiffs in the Nibutani Dam case and is currently a committee member of the Permanent Indigenous Peoples Committee for Forest Stewardship.

**Chris Kolbu** has more than a decade's experience in the coffee industry as a barista, coffee roaster and writer. Norwegian by birth, he now lives in Melbourne, Australia with his young family. He works as a software developer.

**Yōsuke Kosaka** is a Senior Editorial Writer at the *Hokkaido Shimbun*, a daily newspaper covering Hokkaidō, and former curator of the Ainu Museum. He has many publications on a range of topics from international relations, post-nuclear policies, to the Ainu in the Northern Kurile Islands.

**David Kroik** is a PhD candidate in Language Teaching and Learning at Umeå University and an assistant professor in South Saami at Nord University. His research focuses on South Saami as a language in school. He is involved in developing a teacher education program for Sámi language teachers. Kroik completed a Licentiate degree in Linguistics in 2016. He has a broad interest in language, which includes the structure of language as well as language revitalisation. Kroik learned South Saami, his heritage language, as an adult and he is dedicated to making the language available to others.

**Jenny Kroik** is a New York city-based illustrator. She was born in St Petersburg, Russia, and grew up in Israel. She received a BFA in illustration from the Art Institute of Boston, and an MFA in painting from the University of Oregon. She has been working as a freelance illustrator since 2007, and as a university art instructor for the last 10 years. Jenny has created two covers for the *New Yorker Magazine*, and has also exhibited paintings in galleries around the US.

**Åsa Virdi Kroik** is a South Saami woman who grew up in the small village of Buarkantjahke on the Swedish side of Saepmie. She took her academic education in Uppsala and Stuehkie (Stockholm). Writing is something she has spent much time doing and she has published books and articles, lyrics and poetry of all kinds. She has also worked coordinating local, regional and international projects and her motivation has always been to benefit her people and other Indigenous peoples all over the world, as she feels we have a lot to win by helping each other. Activism comes with being an Indigenous person with the motivation to survive, and she has been forced to learn activist methods to get her voice heard. She greatly enjoys spending time with Indigenous people and, without stress or other disturbances, to be able to listen to their stories and learn their knowledge, as well as sharing the same with them. She also likes to take whatever comes from that moment, and reshape it in a way to make it possible for others to get a part of it.

**Jenny Virdi Kroik** is a 15-year-old teenager. She is learning South Saami language in school and is still friends with the others who joined her on the trip to the mountaintop which her paper in this book is about. She lives in three worlds—urban, where her life is about school, friends and teachers; South Saami, where life is about relatives, dogs, reindeer and competences yet to get hold of; and India, where life is about her father's home in New Delhi, relatives and suits. This is her debut as an author but she has previously been a model in one of her mother's (Åsa) books.

**Ewa Ljungdahl** has a master's degree in archaeology and is employed by the South Saami centre Gaaltije in Östersund. She has documented the Saami landscape together with members of Saami villages in the south part of Saepmie over the course of many years. She currently spends most of her time writing and lecturing.

**Miku Maeda** is a master's student of Interpretation and Translation Studies at the Graduate School of Letters, Hokkaidō University. She facilitated conversation between international Indigenous and Ainu artists at the 2017 Indigenous Art Workshop in Sapporo as an interpreter.

**Tero Mustonen** is a fisher from North Karelia, Finland. He also works at the Snowchange Cooperative (www.snowchange.org) as a researcher. He is one of the lead authors of the Intergovernmental Panel on Climate Change (IPCC) 6th Assessment Report.

**Markus Nyström** has an academic background in sustainable development and environmental history. Though he lives in the south of Sweden, through his activism and academic works he has focused on issues concerning the Swedish north and its Indigenous population, the Saami. For the last few years, Markus has worked as a professional historical bowyer (someone who makes bows).

**Hanna Outakoski** is Senior Lecturer at Umeå University in Northern Sweden. She is Sámi from Finnish Sápmi and has been a North Sámi language teacher at Umeå University since 2001. Her main research interests lie primarily in the areas of multilingual literacy, Indigenous didactics and pedagogy, and augmented learning in heritage language situations. In her latest research project, Outakoski investigates how schools can support writing in Indigenous languages.

Filosofiija doavttir Hanna Outakoski lea vuosttaš amanueansa oahpaheaddji Ubmi universitehtas Davvi-Ruotas. Son lea sápmelaš gean ruohttasat leat Sámis Suoma bealde ráji ja son lea leamašan sámegieloahpaheaddji Ubmi universiteahtas jagis 2001. Su guovddáš dutkanberoštumit leat máŋggagielat čálamáhttu, eamiálbmot didaktihkka ja pedagogihkka, ja dasa lassin oahppama nanosmahttin eamiálbmot konteavsttain. Su maŋimuš prošeavttas son dutká mo skuvllat sáhttet nannet čállima eamiálbmotgielain.

**Nils-Jonas Persson** was born and raised in a reindeer-herding family in Geavtse (Amarnäs). He has worked at many different jobs. He was educated at the Sámij åhpadusguovdásj (Sami Training Centre) in Dálvvadis where he chose the program for craft in hard material (such as wood and antler) and has been practising those skills ever since, as much as possible. He slipped into dance during his time studying at the Sami Training Centre, and has participated in the Eurovision Song Contest as a dancer, and before that also held several minor dance courses for

Sami youngsters. He is passionate about reindeer herding and Sami rights. He occupies himself with test-driving cars during the winter season, and currently works in the timber industry. He has a general interest in outdoor activities, and enjoys being with his family, the mountains, and reindeer—this is what makes him feel whole.

**Chris Pesklo** is of Sami ancestry from the areas of Tromsø and Nordland in Norway, and Jämtland in Sweden. His family came to the USA in the 1930s. Chris is a member of the Norwegian–American Bygdelagenes Fellesraad and is the Lappmark Lag Genealogist for that organisation. He is also an active member and supporter of the Sami Siidda of North America, the Sami Cultural Center in Duluth, Minnesota, and a past contributor to the *Arran Newsletter* and *Báiki: The North American Sámi Journal*. Chris is a licensed social studies teacher, a beekeeper and an 'urban Sami' living in Saint Paul, Minnesota. He learnt *lavvu*-making from his Sami Elders and friends.

**Gerald Roche** is an anthropologist and Senior Research Fellow in the Department of Politics and Philosophy at La Trobe University. He was previously a DECRA Research Fellow at the University of Melbourne's Asia Institute, and a Post-doctoral Research Fellow at Uppsala University's Hugo Valentin Centre. His research focuses on the politics of language endangerment and revitalisation, with a regional focus on Tibet. Gerald previously lived on the northeast Tibetan Plateau from 2005 to 2013, working as an applied anthropologist, and also undertaking research for his PhD in Asian Studies from Griffith University. As an applied anthropologist, he has collaborated with people in Tibet on various educational and cultural initiatives, including the creation of the world's largest online archive of oral traditions from the Tibetan Plateau, and the publication of the first nationally distributed English language textbooks designed specifically for Tibetans. His academic publications have appeared in the *Asia Pacific Journal of Anthropology*, *Modern Asian Studies*, *China Quarterly*, *International Journal for the Sociology of Language*, *Anthropos* and *Asian Ethnicity*, amongst others. He recently coedited the *Routledge Handbook of Language Revitalization* with Leanne Hinton and Leena Huss.

**Oscar Sedholm** is a sociology master, politician, rock musician and writer. During the writing of this book he was employed as a project developer at Såhkie Umeå Sami Association and was actively working with finding new ways to preserve and teach Ume Sami. He is currently party secretary for the largest party in the Sami Parliament, the Party for Hunting and Fishing Sami (Jakt- och Fiskesamerna) and is also employed as political secretary for the Social Democrats of Umeå.

**Yuji Shimizu** is co-chair of the Hokkaidō University Information Research Disclosure Group, Chairperson of the Kotan Association, Chairperson of the Citizens' Roundtable for Ethnic Education and Special Advisor to the Citizens' Alliance for the Examination of Ainu Policy.

**Mana Shinoda** is a dancer in the Ainu tradition at Akanko Ainu Theatre 'Ikor' in Hokkaidō. In April 2015, she addressed the United Nations Permanent Forum on Indigenous Issues in New York, speaking about the emergence of hate speech against the Ainu and so forth.

**Sigrid Stångberg**, or Sagka, the Saami name she is more widely known under, has worked as a language revivalist, activist and a principal of a Saami school during her lifetime. She has also held many important positions in Saami society and continues to do so, despite being retired.

**Ryoko Tahara** is the deputy director of the Sapporo Ainu Association and founder and chief director of the Ainu Women's Association. She has been devoted to tackling Ainu women's issues, which were hidden prior to her campaign.

**Masumi Tanaka** trained as a museum curator. She previously worked for the Arctic Centre, University of Lapland, in Rovaniemi Finland. Currently, she works as an administrator at the Nibutani Ainu Cultural Museum.

**Nobuko Tsuda** is the first Ainu woman to receive a doctorate. At the age of 69, she wrote her dissertation on Ainu clothing culture. Before that, she had been engaged in Ainu embroidery as a curator at the Hokkaidō Ainu Center in Sapporo for more than two decades.

**Shizue Ukaji** is the founder and chief director of the Tokyo Ainu Association. She has taken the lead in campaigning for the rights of the Ainu in Tokyo, and has made a significant contribution to the maintenance and development of Ainu culture.

**Kanako Uzawa** is a PhD Candidate at the Arctic University of Norway where she focuses on urban Indigeneity in Ainu communities in Japan. Kanako is an editorial board member of *AlterNative* in New Zealand, a member of the Association of Rera in Tokyo, a former intern in the Project to Promote ILO Policy on Indigenous and Tribal Peoples (PRO 169) at the International Labour Organization, Geneva Switzerland.

**Anne Wuolab** was born just south of Narvik, in northern Norway. These days, she is based in Lycksele, Sweden, on a homestead where she lives with her husband, two children, a dog, a cat, and reindeer. Anne is a cultural entrepreneur with a wealth of local coffee knowledge.

# Summary of *Indigenous Efflorescence: Beyond Revitalisation in Sapmi and Ainu Mosir*

Summarised in South Sami by David Kroik

Daate gærja jealadehtemen bïjre. Gærjesne jïjnjh almetjh jïjtsh aamhtesi bïjre tjaelieh. Naakenh tjaelijh dotkijh, jeatjebh aaktivsth jïh naakenh kultuvretjiehpijh. Govlebe göökte aalkoealmetjijstie: saemieh jïh ajnuh, maam båeries, noere jïh geerve almejth saarnoeh. Jïjnjesh gïelen bïjre tjaelieh, dovne saemien gïelen bïjre jïh ajnugïelen bïjre, menh ij leah gærja barre gïelen bïjre; jienebh aamhtsh aaj artihkelinie jïjhtieh, v.g. dejpeladtje vuekieh, guktie jïjtsh maadtoej baalkah vaadtseme, guktie jieleme maadtoedajvesne lea. Jeatjebh buerkiestieh guktie åahpanamme aalkoealmetji vuekine stoerre staarine, dovne Saepmesne jïh Sveerjesne jïh Ajnu Moshirisne (ajnualmetji laante) jïh Japanisnie.

Maaje Ajnuj jïh Saemiej bïjre gærjesne tjaalasovveme; gåabpah aalkoealmetjh leah, jalhts dah fïereguhti bieline eatnamisnie jielieh. Jïjnjh tjaelijh tjåanghkenamme jïh buerkiestamme guktie barkeme gïelem jealadehtedh jallh guktie jeatjebigujmie ektesne aatskadamme jïjtsh jielemevuekiej mietie jieledh.

Hïehkehtallem gosse lohkem man jïjnjem dååjrehtalleme mij seammalaakan lea, dovne saemieh jïh ajnuladtjh. Gosse gærjam lohkeminie dle leara mij heannadamme vïellide jïh åabpide eatnemen dunniebielesne. Akte tjaelije, Ryoko Tahara, saerneste ajnu gujni bïjre, guhth joekoen vaejvies tsiehkiem åtneme. Nemhtie dam naakenh dejstie eah ennje åådtjeme l̈ieredh lohkedh j̈ih tjaeledh. Dannasinie tjuerieh garres barkoeh vaeltedh mejstie geerve b̈ierkenidh. Tahara vielie muana guktie tsiehkie maahta buaranidh.

Daan gærjan aamhtese aalkoealmetji tsiehkieh bueriedehtedh. Gærjan aalkoevisnie orre tearme buarkesåvva: *efflorescence*. Redaktööre Gerald Roche buerkeste mah goerkesidie sæjhta tearmine dijpedh. Aalkoealmetji *efflorescence* lea krijsetsiehkien mohte. D̈ihte baakoe edtja dijpedh maam heannede gosse aalkoealmetjh j̈ijtsh kultuvrh, aerpieviertien maahtoeh j̈ih g̈ielh jealajehtieh, gosse eajhnaduvvieh d̈ijpedh båeries jielemevuekieh j̈ih sj̈iehtesjidh daaletje ẗijjese j̈ih båetije biejjide. Redaktöörh digkiedieh tearme *efflorescence* daerpies, dannasinie hijven goerkesem vadta aellebe jaehkieh gaajhke barre nåake, gåarmoeh j̈ih vaejvie; vuekieh, åtnoeh, laanth j̈ih g̈ielh mah gaarvanedtieh, j̈ih ibie mijjieh aalkoealmetjh maehtieh maam darjodh. Gærjine redaktöörh j̈ih tjaelijh sijhtieh vuesiehtidh ij amma d̈ihte öövre staeries. Aalkoealmetjh: ajnuladtjh Ajnu Moshiresne j̈ih saemieh Saepmesne maaje g̈ielem j̈ih kultuvrem gorredieh, orrestehtieh j̈ih övtedieh. Ibie åadtjoeh barre goltelidh dejtie saernide mah nåake våajnoem mijjen åålmegidie buektieh, aellebe aelkedh vaajvehtovvedh jaehkedh ij gåaredh saemien j̈ih ajnug̈ielem j̈ih kultuvrem daaletje ẗijjese buektedh.

Gosse *efflorescencem* provhkedh dellie ibie barre bååstede vaeltieh dam mij kolonisasjovnen aalkoen åvtelen orreme; d̈ihte vielie j̈ih orre, veadtaldahkesne ẗijjese åvtelen kolonisasjovne, læjhkan daaletje ẗijjese sj̈iehtelovveme. *Efflorescense* heannede gosse aktine barkebe, abpe dåehkie, åålmege, fuelhkie jallh sl̈iekte. Vielie buerkeste fahkajahteme g̈ieli orre åtnoeh; eah govloeh j̈ih eah provhkesuvvh seamma laakan goh aerpieg̈ielh mestie tseagkanin.

Daennie gærjesne tjaelijh baalkah vuesiehtieh guktie saemien g̈ielem, ajnug̈ielem j̈ih jeatjah jealajehtedh. Naakenh tjaelieh guktie orre teknihke d̈irreginie sjædta dejtie jaksedh, guhth sijhtieh g̈ielide l̈ieredh. Dah tjaelijh Hanna Outakoski, Oscar Sedholm j̈ih Coppélie Cocq fiereguhte teekstesne dan b̈ijre saarnoeh. Sedholm prosjekten b̈ijre tjaala maam ubmejensaemieh stuvrin; sijhtin ubmejensaemien raajesh j̈ih baakoeh tjöönghkedh j̈ih vedtedh gaajhkide g̈ieh gaskeviermiem jeksieh. D̈irregem gaskeviermesne provhkin man nomme Memrise. Cocq såårne guktie dejpeli saemien vaajesh orrestovveme j̈ih jeatjahtovveme gosse gaskevearman sj̈iehtesovveme. Cocq tjaala daaletje vaajesh jeatjhlaakan båeries vaajesi muhteste. Mearan båeries vaajesh jienebh åtnoeh utnin, akte dejstie maanah bijjiedidh, daaletje vaajesh gaskeviermesne edtjieh luste årrodh guktie maanah sijhtieh goltelidh. Outakoski tjaala guktie barkeme gïelekuvsjigujmie gaskeviermesne mah edtjieh sjïehtedh saemide, gïeh dan bårran årroeh. Kuvsjen gaavnedimmiesijjie viermesne vihkielommes sijjie gusnie learohkh gïelem pruvhkieh. Outakoski buerkeste guktie maahta sijjiem haamoehtidh guktie edtja dagkeres learoehkidie sjïehtedh gïeh eah saemien lïerh desnie gusnie årroeh.

Gærjesne akte teekste åarjelsaemien gïelen bïjre. Leena Huss jïh Sagka Stångberg tjaeliejægan guktie åarjelsaemien gïeletsiehkie Vualtjeren jïh Luspien raedtesne. Dah guakah lægan goerehtalleme maam skuvlemaanah, eejtegh jïh lohkehtæjjah saarnoeh gïelen bïjre, gåessie gïelem pruvhkieh, gåessie jïh gusnie tuhtjieh gïele vïhkeles maehtedh jïh man jïjnjem maehtieh saemiestidh. Gaajhkesh debpene gïelem dasseme, men hijven utnieh åadtjodh dam bååstede vaeltedh. Jalhts eah skuvlh gïelem nænnosth, læjhkan maanah jïjnjem lierieh dannasinie tuhtjieh vihkele sijjide.

Naakenh tjaelijh ajnuladtjh. Båeries ajnuladjen gujne man nomme Shizue Ukaji jïjtse teekstesne tjuarma: vedtede ajnualmetjidie bååstede aktem loesejeanoem Ajnu Moshirisne, gusnie maehtieh gööledh. Nuerebe ajnugujne Kanako Uzawa buerkeste guktie maahta ajnun gïeline jïh kultuvrine åehpenidh gosse stoerre staaresne byjjene, mij guhkede Ajnu Moshiriste. Tjaala man vihkele åålmegem jïjtse almetjijstie gaavnedh desnie gusnie byjjene jïh desnie gusnie biejjeste beajjan jeala. Jïjtje tjaala dagkeres sijjien bïjre: akte ajnu-beapmoesijjie Tokyosne. Desnie jeatjebigujmie sov almetjijstie åahpanadteme. Uzawa tjaala eah edtjh aalkoealmetjh barre årrodh aerpielaantine goh vuesiehtimmie gaavhtan Saepmie jallh Ajnu Moshiri, vaallah aaj stoerre staarine.

Chris Pesklo, saemien aerpieguedtije noerhteamerikasne, tjaala guktie barkeme altese aerpiem buektedh daaletje aajkan. Låavthgåetiejgujmie barka; dejtie dorje jïh duaka. Pesklo buerkeste magkere joekehts låavthgåetiej jïh amerijhken aalkoealmetji tijpij gaskem. Dïhte vielie buerkeste guktie sïeltem tseegkeme juktie beetnegh dienesjidh gosse låavthgåetieh dorje jïh duaka. Beetnegh aevhkie gosse kultuvrem nænnoestidh saemiej luvnie debpene amerijhkesne. Dah voeres almetji maahtoe debpene Atlanten dunniebielesne vihkele sjïdteme gosse edtjin vïht aelkedh låavthgåetieh darjodh.

Gærjam edtjh lohkedh ihke lïeredh guktie jieleme orrestahta göökte aalkoealmetjh luvnie jïh guktie kolonisjasjovne dejtie tsavtseme, tsavtsa jïh edtja tsevtsedh båetijen biejjine. Baalkah vuesehte guktie kolonisasjovnen vööste barkedh, dellie jïjtse vuekieh, åtnoeh, gïelh jïh jienebe provhkedh, guktie tjievliesvoetem saemine jallh ajnujne årrodh.

# Introduction: Indigenous Efflorescence

Gerald Roche with Åsa Virdi Kroik
and Hiroshi Maruyama

In thousands of communities, amongst hundreds of nations around the world, an Indigenous revolution is currently taking place, transforming the lives of millions of people. In Australia, the Aboriginal scholar Marcia Langton (2013) has referred to a 'quiet revolution' in the lives of Aboriginal people, a dramatic increase in economic well-being and political control that has largely gone unnoticed by mainstream Australia. Māori scholar Ranginui Walker (2004: 10) describes a 'cultural renaissance' amongst the Indigenous population of Aoteoroa, accompanied by 'exponential' demographic increase. In the USA, Joane Nagel (1995) has pointed to similar trends amongst Native Americans, referring to an 'ethnic renewal' and 'resurgence of identity'. In Canada, John Ralston Saul (2014) has spoken of a 'comeback' of Aboriginal peoples, a demographic upsurge, coupled with growing political assertiveness and cultural confidence. The anthropologist James Clifford, focusing on the Americas and the Pacific, has meanwhile declared our era as a moment of global *Indigènitude*, in which Indigenous people have 'emerged from history's blind spot' to 'renew their cultural heritage and reconnect with lost lands' (2013: 13). In what follows, I introduce the concept of 'Indigenous efflorescence' as a way of both describing and analysing this situation, before moving on to introduce the contributions to this book, which explores Indigenous efflorescence in two very different contexts: Japan and northern Europe.

I have borrowed the term 'efflorescence' from sociologist and political theorist Jack Goldstone, who originally deployed it in a study of early modern economic history, as a necessary but lacking binary opposite to 'crisis'. He defines efflorescence as 'a relatively sharp, often unexpected upturn in significant demographic and economic indices, usually accompanied by political expansion, institution-building, cultural synthesis, and consolidation' (2004: 252). The term therefore carries several implications: of economic prosperity, human flourishing, cultural creativity and surprise. This sense of surprise in efflorescence is embedded in the term's usage in another field—chemistry—where it refers to the sudden emergence of crystals formed by materials previously suspended, invisibly, in water, and which emerge on surfaces after the water has seeped through them and evaporated.

Perhaps nothing demonstrates the surprising nature of efflorescence more than the revitalisation of Indigenous languages (Hinton and Hale 2001; Grenoble and Whaley 2006; Jones and Ogilvie 2013; Hinton, Huss and Roche 2018). Dozens of languages once declared 'extinct' or pronounced 'dead' are now being spoken again. The Wôpanâak language of northeastern USA, not spoken since the mid-nineteenth century, is now being taught to hundreds of students.[1] The Myaamia language of Ohio tells a similar story (Leonard 2008). In Australia, the Kaurna language (Amery 2016) is just one of many Aboriginal languages that have been reawakened (Hobson et al. 2010; Troy and Walsh 2010). In Finland, a revitalisation program successfully recreated a lost generation of speakers of the Aanaar Sami language, thus helping to heal the wound of ruptured intergenerational transmission (Olthuis, Kivelä and Skutnabb-Kangas 2013). Due to the success of these and many other programs around the world, activists and scholars working in language revitalisation now no longer speak of dead, extinct, or lost languages, but of dormant or sleeping languages, waiting to be reawakened, to spring back to life (Leonard 2008).

The efflorescence of languages contradicts in very concrete terms the sense of crisis that often surrounds conversations about Indigenous peoples, not only today, but also in the past, in the era of high colonialism. Past visions of the present future were replete with prophecies of 'vanishing savages' and 'doomed natives' (Brantlinger 2003). Such prophecies were the very foundation of colonial and modernist civilising projects (Wolfe 2006; O'Brien 2010). The prescriptive nature of these declarations is revealed by the reality of Indigenous 'survivance', the 'active sense of presence over historical absence' (Vizenor 2009: 1). Two of the most dramatic cases of

---

1    For more, see the *Wôpanâak Reclamation Project*. Online: www.wlrp.org/ (accessed 16 June 2018). For an overview of language revitalisation in the Americas, see the edited collection by Serafín M. Coronel-Molina and Teresa L. McCarty (2016).

survivance can be seen in the Caribbean and Tasmania, both canonical examples of 'vanished natives'. In the Caribbean, Maximilian Forte (2005, 2006a, see also his 2006b edited collection) has drawn attention to the enduring presence of Indigenous Amerindian peoples in the region, supposed to have vanished in the violence that opened our present era of colonial globalisation. Another case in point is the Aboriginal people of Tasmania, the Palawa. Often touted as a classic case of colonial genocide and the lamentable passing of the native, the Palawa persist (Ryan 2012). Such continuities should not diminish our awareness of the violence and genocidal intent of colonialism, but rather, deepen our respect for Indigenous survivance, and heighten the significance of exploring and explaining Indigenous efflorescence.

In this context, the term Indigenous efflorescence is, on the one hand, a descriptive one, which refers to the under-studied phenomenon of the multi-sited demographic and cultural flourishing of Indigenous peoples. As a coinage, the term helps us to talk about a previously diffuse set of events and trends, to bundle them together and slot them seamlessly into sentences, and thus start new conversations. It is, furthermore, a concept that gives us critical purchase on the present—the historical moment in which 'the native' was supposed to have disappeared—and provides leverage against simplistic narratives of both decline and progress. Beyond being a descriptive term, however, Indigenous efflorescence is also an analytical frame that provides new ways of looking at the contemporary Indigenous situation, as explored in the next section.

## Orienting efflorescence

This focus on Indigenous efflorescence is designed to both augment and provide alternatives to other approaches to the contemporary Indigenous moment based on various (re)work: *revitalization*, *resilience*, *resurgence*, *return*, *renaissance*, *resurrection*, *revival*, *resuscitation* and *renewal* (Amery 2016). 'Efflorescence' is distinct from these approaches, first of all, in being *process-oriented*. It draws attention to the creative, dynamic nature of the contemporary Indigenous moment, and sees it as involving something exceeding the recreation of the past, the return to a former state of being. Efflorescence is not simply about the resumption of stable cultural practices, of picking up where Indigenous people left off before the long colonial interruption, of a return to a precontact utopia. Revitalised languages are not the same as the ancestral languages on which they were based; they are built differently, sound different, inhabit new contexts, and serve entirely different functions (Bentahila and Davies 1993). James Clifford (2013) captures this well when he speaks about twenty-first-century indigeneity as being rooted in *translation* and *generativity*: to be Indigenous is not to reproduce precolonial ways of being, but to translate them into the present, to draw on them as inspiration and authority for generating Indigenous ways of living in the twenty-first century. Or, as Leanne Simpson puts it, efflorescence means

> reclaiming the fluidity around our traditions, not the rigidity of colonialism; it means encouraging the self-determination of individuals within our national and community-based contexts; and it means re-creating an artistic and intellectual renaissance with a larger political and cultural resurgence (2011: 51).

In drawing attention to processes of creativity and generativity, rather than on the social forms, cultural and linguistic products and so on which are generated, an emphasis on efflorescence is also *future-oriented*. This involves, first, an alertness to what Appadurai calls the 'trap of trajectorism'—a deeply ingrained 'epistemological and ontological habit' which assumes that 'time's arrow always has a teleos' (2013: 233), and thus that the future is knowable by extending a trajectory from the past, through the present and into the future. Our current moment of Indigenous efflorescence, and the way it makes patent failures of colonial and modernist trajectories as both explanatory models and ideological projects, recommends an orientation to the future as radically other, as 'imaginable but unknown' (Pink, Akama and Fergusson 2017: 133). We should therefore interrogate acts and aspects of Indigenous efflorescence for the multiple futures they may make possible, the 'states of emergence' and the many 'about-to-be-present[s]' (Tsing 2005: 269) with which they are pregnant.

In order to reject trajectorism and engage with multiple possible futures, we can look at (at least) three different types of future. First is the simple future—that something will (continue to) happen. It may be tempting to see individual incidents of efflorescence in temporal isolation, as aberrant blips with no future, or worse, as misguided, futile attempts to resist the inevitable logic of this or that trajectory, and therefore to erase projects from consideration of the future. We therefore need to imagine a future where projects of efflorescence, some taking place now, many unimagined, not only occur, but develop, grow and expand. This, in turn, enables us to imagine in terms of the future conditional—if this happens, then what will/might/could happen? And finally, we can also look at the future perfect, or what Judith Butler (2016) calls the 'future anterior', a stance looking back to the present from some unknown point in the future—'something will have happened'. This stance, of inhabiting a future replete with current and as yet unimagined works of efflorescence, and their multiple, contingent outcomes, gives us imaginary purchase on the many futures that are emerging in the present.

Finally, whilst being distinguished from (re)work approaches in being future and process oriented, what an Indigenous efflorescence approach shares with these other ways of exploring the contemporary Indigenous moment is a commitment to anticolonial engagement and intervention. That is, an approach focused on Indigenous efflorescence seeks to extend beyond the descriptive and explanatory to the constructive and constitutive. It seeks to not only explore possible Indigenous futures, but to help create them. This is done in at least three ways. First, by exploring conditions that enable or create barriers to efflorescence. Second, by pursuing new theoretical insights from anthropology that might help in understanding and promoting Indigenous efflorescence. And third, by increasing the horizon of possible futures by helping to foster and multiply Indigenous future imaginaries.

## Grounding Indigenous efflorescence: Ainu and Sami

This book explores Indigenous efflorescence in two specific Indigenous contexts: amongst the Ainu of Ainu Mosir (in present-day northern Japan), and the Sami of Sapmi (in Norway, Sweden, Finland and Russia). Our focus on these two groups aims to draw attention to activity taking place outside the more well-known CANZUS (Canada, Australia, New Zealand, and the US) settler states, which dominate the Anglophone literature in anthropology and Indigenous studies. Although the Sami have been important in the development of international Indigenist theories, networks and practices (Merlan 2009), they still remain somewhat peripheral within Anglophone academic discussions; the Ainu are perhaps even more marginalised in this literature, due, in no small part, to the general resistance against applying concepts of indigeneity in Asia

(Baird 2016). Focusing on the Ainu and the Sami thus helps us expand the circle of paradigmatic Indigenous case studies beyond the CANZUS group and towards the vast number of under-represented Indigenous groups around the world, a topic we return to in the conclusion of this book.

The Ainu are the Indigenous people of northern Japan and southern Sakhalin and Kuril islands (Russia), a territory they refer to as Ainu Mosir (the land of the Ainu, or more literally, the land of humans). The colonisation of Ainu Mosir by the Japanese took place over several centuries, beginning with asymmetrical trade relations in the fifteenth century, which evolved into economic dependency in the seventeenth and eighteenth centuries (Walker 2001). Colonisation intensified particularly after the Meiji Restoration (1868) with the establishment of the Colonial Office in Sapporo in 1869, and the formal annexation of the island of Hokkaidō in 1872 (Maruyama 2013a). The late nineteenth and early twentieth centuries saw the implementation of a range of assimilatory policies, which began by defining the Ainu as 'former aborigines' (Maruyama 2013b, 2014). These policies dispossessed the Ainu of their land, deprived them of their traditional livelihood, and outlawed numerous Ainu cultural practices. Meanwhile, immigration of ethnic Japanese into Ainu Mosir was actively promoted. Furthermore, assimilationist, monoglot language policies aimed at creating a linguistically homogenous Japanese nation, and implemented primarily through the formal schooling system, had disastrous impacts on the Ainu language (Heinrich 2012).

The other perspective this book draws upon is that of the Sami of northwestern Europe, a territory they refer to as Sapmi, now divided between Russia, Finland, Sweden and Norway. As with the Ainu, the story of Sapmi's colonisation has two phases, a long, gradual diminishment of territory and steady growth in asymmetrical relations (Rydving 2004; Broadbent 2010; Roche 2017), and a final attempt at complete annihilation during the high tide of Romantic nationalism. For the Sami, the first phase dates back almost a thousand years, with south Scandinavian populations gradually moving farther and farther north. The intense phase of colonisation, meanwhile, lasted from the mid-1700s until the middle of the twentieth century. This period saw Sapmi divided between the nation-states of Norway, Sweden, Finland and Russia, fragmenting the Sami into several populations, all under different assimilatory regimes (Sergejeva 2000; Minde 2003; Lantto and Mörkenstam 2008; Axelsson 2010).

In addition to these shared histories of colonisation and assimilation, the Ainu and the Sami also share a recent past characterised by efflorescence. This has involved, in both cases, the termination of deliberately assimilative policies and the implementation of liberal, democratic multicultural orders, coupled with improved economic standing in both relative terms (within the state) and on absolute terms, globally. The contributions to this book document these developments and the ways in which Sami and Ainu people have made use of them, whilst engaging in ongoing struggles for decolonisation.

## About the book

This volume emerged, originally, in the wake of an Indigenous people's conference held at Uppsala University, from 14–19 October 2013. The conference was titled 'RE: Claimings, Empowerings, Inspirings: Researching and Exploring by, for, and with Indigenous Peoples, Minorities, and Local Communities' and brought Indigenous experts, both academic and otherwise, to discuss issues of relevance to the contemporary challenges of global indigeneity. Although taking inspiration from this conference and its approach to Indigenous issues, the materials collated here bear little resemblance to those presented in Uppsala. Rather, this conference served as a launching pad for conversations between the three editors, drawing on our work with and for the Ainu (Hiroshi Maruyama), Sami (Åsa Virdi Kroik) and Monguor and Tibetans (Gerald Roche).

Our book draws inspiration from the work of Indigenous academics in creating spaces where Indigenous concerns and achievement are acknowledged and advanced. The last 40 years have seen the emergence of a generation of scholars who have not only pushed back against the implicit colonial agendas of academic research, but have devised new research paradigms for research by, with, and for Indigenous peoples. We were inspired in this book by the work of such scholars as Linda Tuhiwai Smith, Shawn Wilson, Rauna Kuokkanen and Leanne Betasamosake Simpson, amongst others. The volume is offered in an 'Indigenist' spirit—an inclusive research paradigm that emphasises indigeneity as a philosophical orientation and political project, and thus acknowledges that non-Indigenous academics have a role to play in supporting the pursuit of Indigenous goals (Adams et al. 2015).

In the spirit of the original conference that began the conversations which launched this book, we have adopted a supra-disciplinary approach (Gärdebo, Öhman and Maruyama 2014) in collating the contributions, and have thus included articles written by academics, and case studies written by both academic and nonacademic practitioners of Indigenous efflorescence. Criteria for inclusion in this volume involved not only typical academic standards of rigour ensured by peer review processes, but also the acknowledgement and recognition of contributors within the communities they were writing about. Therefore, whilst some authors hold the academic qualifications typical of contributors to scholarly volumes, others were considered qualified by virtue of their contribution to the Ainu and Sami communities, and their participation in Indigenous efflorescence.

The contributions to this book are organised into two main sections, looking at *contexts* and *practices* of efflorescence. Each of these sections is opened with a brief introduction exploring the broader context and providing information on the specific contributions. 'Part One: Contexts of Efflorescence' explores the political, economic and technological circumstances that have scaffolded the emergence of contemporary efflorescence. The case studies and articles in this section therefore look at developments within both mainstream settler societies and Indigenous societies. Thematically, they deal with settler epistemologies, digital technologies, land and sovereignty, and Indigenous social movements, and explore their role in Indigenous efflorescence. 'Part Two: Practices of Efflorescence' provides case studies and articles that explore how people *do* efflorescence, and what their subjective experience of it is.

In addition to explaining the origins and organisation of the book, we also feel that it is important for us, as editors, to explain our role in the volume, and our approach and motivations to its creation.

## Hiroshi Maruyama

My current research topic has been focused on policies towards Indigenous peoples, or Indigenous policy. It was in 2007 that I started studying the construction of huge dams in the Saru River in Hokkaidō, which is called the cradle of Ainu culture. Then, I was aware that the Ainu are still trapped by colonialism. They were in poverty and totally excluded from decisions about the construction affecting their community. However, the majority population does not recognise that the Ainu should be especially protected by international human rights law for the reparation of historical and existent injustices imposed on them. Since then, I have been critically analysing Japan's Ainu policy in accordance with international human rights standards. In order to know more about the situation faced by the Ainu, I have been collaborating with Ainu Elders who are still fighting against the Japanese Government for their Indigenous rights and dignity. In the process of studying policies towards the Ainu, I came to know that comparative studies between Indigenous peoples are needed. I happened to meet Marie Persson, Sigrid Stångberg and Tomas Colbengtson in Tärnaby, Sweden. Marie Persson is a human rights defender with a focus on Indigenous peoples' and children's rights, a member of the Sami Parliament, founder of the organisation Stop the Rönnbäck Nickel Mining Project, and a graphic designer. Sigrid Stångberg is a long-time South Sami language expert and revitalisation leader. She was also a former principal at the Tärnaby Sami School, and was the first person to take 40 credits in South Sami at Umeå University. Tomas Colbengtson is a resident artist at KTH Royal School of Technology, where he has been working on visual arts. He is also a lecturer in fine printmaking at Konstfack National College of Art, Craft and Design, Stockholm. My encounter with these people has inspired me to study the situation faced by the South Sami in Tärna with Leena Huss, Professor Emerita, Uppsala University. My aim in studying Indigenous policy is to support Indigenous peoples' struggles for the right to self-determination, which is related to Indigenous rights and dignity as a people, based on scientific findings.

## Åsa Virdi Kroik

My reason for writing and editing this book is that I have participated in many revitalisation projects where I have gained knowledge and experience that has been important for my development as a Saami, but also as a human being. There are a few things that have been striking about those projects. One is their low status. Although the participants often enjoy the work and think it is important, it is usually not considered as important as their 'ordinary' or 'real' work or hobbies. Revitalisation projects are also very enjoyable and the participants often laugh a lot. People participating in revitalising process are oppressed—and their history of oppression stays as a sorrow in their souls. I initiate and participate in revitalisation projects because I think they have something very important to contribute. I have learned a lot about methods and methodology that I can take with me into other fields, but I also have learned that the moments of joy and laughter binds people more tightly to each other. To discover that other Indigenous people also are dealing with the same threats against their language and culture, and to see the similarities in what we protect and the ways we protect it, also binds us together. Researchers are also protectors of knowledge. While Indigenous peoples' languages and cultures have been neglected in the past, an increasing number of researchers are now finding the value of, and joy in, the revitalisation process, and even participate in the laughter. My hope is that Saami and Ainu people will be able to share inspiration and the joy of revitalisation in this book, and to do so together with we editors and with you—the reader.

## Gerald Roche

At one point whilst writing this introduction, I found myself reading two books side-by-side: Judy Atkinson's (2002) *Trauma Trails, Recreating Song Lines: The Transgenerational Effects of Trauma in Indigenous Australia*, and James Clifford's (2013) *Returns: Becoming Indigenous in the Twenty-First Century*. Both books were erudite, nuanced and eloquent, but their tone and voice set them miles apart. The first was written by an Indigenous author, and dealt with the intergenerational trauma inflicted on Indigenous peoples as the result of colonisation, resulting in the horrific violence and substance abuse (violence against the self) seen in many Indigenous communities in Australia today. The tone is forceful, the rhetoric strong. Clifford's book, on the other hand, is far more detached. He adopts an approach of 'lucid ambivalence' (2013: 18), characterised by 'an alert receptivity and willingness not to press for conclusions' (2013: 23). It is whimsical, almost playful, and in lacking 'the emotional convulsions of identification and memory' (Pearson 2017: 23) that Indigenous researchers experience, is therefore also devoid of hope and has no need of optimism. On the one hand, as an engaged anthropologist, I identify strongly with Atkinson's search for certainty. I admire the strength of her rhetoric and share her belief in the importance of knowledge as a tool for justice and healing. However, like Clifford, as a non-Indigenous person, I have the luxury of deferring certainty in order to inhabit peripheral nuances and contradictions. In addition to my intellectual positioning, my work on this book was also influenced by physical position. At the time we started work on this book, I had just left China, where I had lived for several years, and I was thinking about the volume in relation to the Monguor and Tibetan communities I had worked with there, in comparison to what I was learning about in Sweden. I was also thinking about how communities in China, and elsewhere around the world, might use materials like those we have collated here. By the time we were finishing this volume, I had returned home to Australia after an absence of 10 years, and was thinking about what the concept of Indigenous efflorescence could tell me—and couldn't—about the Indigenous context here.

## Conclusion

By way of conclusion, we, as editors, wish to jointly express our hope that, in addition to starting a discussion on Indigenous efflorescence as a topic of anthropological analysis—a possibility we discuss further in the conclusion—we also hope the materials presented in this book help inspire new projects, and perhaps even new collaborations, amongst people working towards efflorescence. We particularly hope that they demonstrate the ways in which efflorescence can take place in all aspects of life: from watching films, to drinking coffee and dancing. We hope that the articles raise issues and offer solutions that are helpful in navigating the complex terrain of efflorescence. We hope that the materials presented here help those working towards efflorescence to see their individual and collective efforts as part of a movement that is a dynamic, growing field of activity that is expanding and will likely continue to do so. And finally, we hope that this volume can offer a source of respair—the return of hope after a period of despair—to activists, scholars, and others working to bring about Indigenous efflorescence.[2]

## References

Adams, Dawn Hill, Shawn Wilson, Ryan Heavy Head and Edmund Gordon. 2015. *Ceremony at a Boundary Fire: A Story of Indigenist Knowledge*. Longmont, CO; Sydney: Sydney eScholarship Repository. Online: hdl.handle.net/2123/13689 (accessed 16 June 2018).

Amery, Rob. 2016. *Warraparna Kaurna! Reclaiming an Australian Language*. Adelaide: University of Adelaide Press. doi.org/10.20851/kaurna

---

2    On the term 'respair', see 'Why words die: How to keep lexical treasures from keeling over', 2017.

Appadurai, Arjun. 2013. *The Future as Cultural Fact: Essays on the Global Condition*. London: Verso Books.

Atkinson, Judy. 2002. *Trauma Trails, Recreating Song Lines: The Transgenerational Effects of Trauma in Indigenous Australia*. North Geelong: Spinifex Press.

Axelsson, Per. 2010. 'Abandoning "the Other": Statistical enumeration of Swedish Sami, 1700 to 1945 and Beyond'. *Ber. Wissenschaftgesch* 33(3): 263–69. doi.org/10.1002/bewi.201001469

Baird, Ian G. 2016. 'Indigeneity in Asia: An emerging but contested concept'. *Asian Ethnicity* 17(4): 1–5. doi.org/10.1080/14631369.2016.1193804

Bentahila, Abdelâli and Eirlys E. Davies. 1993. 'Language revival: Restoration or transformation?' *Journal of Multilingual & Multicultural Development* 14(5): 355–74. doi.org/10.1080/01434632.1993.9994542

Brantlinger, Patrick. 2003. *Dark Vanishings: Discourse on the Extinction of Primitive Races, 1800–1930*. Ithaca and London: Cornell University Press.

Broadbent, Noel. 2010. *Lapps and Labyrinths: Saami Prehistory, Colonization, and Cultural Resilience*. Washington: Smithsonian Institute Scholarly Press.

Butler, Judith. 2016. *Frames of War: When is Life Grievable?* London and New York: Verso Books.

Clifford, James. 2013. *Returns: Becoming Indigenous in the Twenty-First Century*. Harvard: Harvard University Press. doi.org/10.4159/9780674726222

Coronel-Molina, Serafín M. and Teresa L. McCarty (eds). 2016. *Indigenous Language Revitalization in the Americas*. London: Routledge. doi.org/10.4324/9780203070673

Forte, Maximilian. 2005. *Ruins of Absence, Presence of Caribs: (Post)Colonial Representations of Aboriginality in Trinidad and Tobago*. Miami: University of Florida Press.

Forte, Maximilian. 2006a. 'Introduction: The dual absences of extinction and marginality—what difference does an indigenous presence make?' In *Indigenous Resurgence in the Contemporary Caribbean: Amerind Survival and Revival*, edited by Maximillian Forte, 1–18. New York: Peter Lange.

Forte, Maximilian (ed.). 2006b. *Indigenous Resurgence in the Contemporary Caribbean: Amerindian Survival and Revival*. New York: Peter Lang.

Gärdebo, Johan, May-Britt Öhman, and Hiroshi Maruyama (eds). 2014. *Re: Mindings. Co-Constituting Indigenous/Academic/Artistic Knowledge*. Uppsala Multiethnic Papers 55. Uppsala: Hugo Valentin Centre.

Goldstone, Jack. 2004. 'Neither late imperial nor early modern: Efflorescences and the Qing formation in world history'. In *The Qing Formation in World-Historical Time*, edited by Lynn A Struve, 242–303. Cambridge, MA: Harvard University Asia Center. doi.org/10.2307/j.ctt1tfj908.11

Grenoble, Lenore A. and Lindsay J. Whaley. 2006. *Saving Languages: An Introduction to Language Revitalization*. Cambridge: Cambridge University Press.

Heinrich, Patrick. 2012. *The Making of Monolingual Japan: Language Ideology and Japanese Modernity*. Toronto: Multilingual Matters.

Hinton, Leanne and Kenneth Hale (eds). 2001. *The Green Book of Language Revitalization in Practice*. Leiden: Brill. doi.org/10.1163/9789004261723

Hinton, Leanne, Leena Huss and Gerald Roche. 2018. *The Routledge Handbook of Language Revitalization*. London: Routledge.

Hobson, John Robert, Kevin Lowe, Susan Poetsch and Michael Walsh (eds). 2010. *Re-awakening Languages: Theory and Practice in the Revitalisation of Australia's Indigenous Languages*. Sydney: Sydney University Press.

Jones, Mari C. and Sarah Ogilvie. 2013. *Keeping Languages Alive: Documentation, Pedagogy and Revitalization*. Cambridge: Cambridge University Press. doi.org/10.1017/CBO9781139245890

Langton, Marcia. 2013. *Boyer Lectures 2012: The Quiet Revolution: Indigenous People and the Resources Boom*. Sydney: HarperCollins Australia.

Lantto, Patrik and Ulf Mörkenstam. 2008. 'Sami rights and Sami challenges'. *Scandinavian Journal of History* 33(1): 26–55. doi.org/10.1080/034687 50701431222

Leonard, Wesley Y. 2008. 'When is an "extinct language" not extinct?: Miami, a formerly sleeping language'. In *Sustaining Linguistic Diversity: Endangered and Minority Languages and Language Varieties*, edited by Kendall A. King, Natalie Schilling-Estes, Lyn Fogle, Jia Jackie Lou and Barbara Soukup, 23–33. Washington, DC: Georgetown University Press.

Maruyama, Hiroshi. 2013a. 'Japan's post-war Ainu policy. Why the Japanese Government has not recognised Ainu indigenous rights?' *Polar Record* 49(2): 204–07. doi.org/10.1017/S003224741200040X

Maruyama, Hiroshi. 2013b. 'Revitalisation of Ainu culture and protection of their right to culture: Learning from Norwegian Sami experiences'. *The Yearbook of Polar Law Online* 5(1): 547–70. doi.org/10.1163/22116427-91000136

Maruyama, Hiroshi. 2014. 'Japan's policies towards the Ainu language and culture with special reference to North Fennoscandian Sami policies'. *Acta Borealia* 31(2): 152–75. doi.org/10.1080/08003831.2014.967980

Merlan, Francesca. 2005. 'Indigenous movements in Australia'. *Annual Review of Anthropology* 34: 473–94. doi.org/10.1146/annurev.anthro.34.081804. 120643

Merlan, Francesca. 2009. 'Indigeneity: Global and local'. *Current Anthropology* 50(3): 303–33. doi.org/10.1086/597667

Minde, Henry. 2003. 'Assimilation of the Sami: Implementation and consequences'. *Acta Borealia* 20(2): 121–46. doi.org/10.1080/08003830310002877

Nagel, Joane. 1995. 'American Indian ethnic renewal: Politics and the resurgence of identity'. *American Sociological Review* 60(6): 947–65. doi.org/10.2307/ 2096434

O'Brien, Jean M. 2010. *Firsting and Lasting: Writing Indians Out of Existence in New England.* Minneapolis: University of Minnesota Press. doi.org/10.5749/ minnesota/9780816665778.001.0001

Olthuis, Marja-Liisa, Suvi Kivelä and Tove Skutnabb-Kangas. 2013. *Revitalising Indigenous Languages: How to Recreate a Lost Generation.* Ontario: Multilingual matters. doi.org/10.21832/9781847698896

Pearson, Noel. 2017. 'A rightful place'. In *A Rightful Place: A Road Map to Recognition*, edited by Shireen Morris, 5–117. Carlton: Black Inc.

Pink, Sarah, Yoko Akama and Annie Fergusson. 2017. 'Researching future as an alterity of the present'. In *Anthropologies and Futures: Researching Emerging and Uncertain Worlds*, edited by Juan Francisco Salazar, Sarah Pink, Andrew Irving and Johannes Sjöberg, 133–50. Sydney: Bloomsbury.

Roche, Gerald. 2017. 'Linguistic vitality, endangerment, and resilience'. *Language Documentation and Conservation* 11: 190–223. doi.org/10125/24733

Ryan, Lyndall. 2012. *Tasmanian Aborigines: A History Since 1803.* Sydney: Allen and Unwin.

Rydving, Håkan. 2004. *The End of Drum-Time: Religious Change among the Lule Saami, 1670s–1740s.* Uppsala: Uppsala University Press.

Saul, John Ralston. 2014. *The Comeback: How Aboriginals are Reclaiming Power and Influence.* Toronto: Penguin Canada.

Sergejeva, Jelena. 2000. 'The Eastern Sámi: A short account of their history and identity'. *Acta Borealia* 17(2): 5–37. doi.org/10.1080/08003830008580509

Simpson, Leanne. 2011. *Dancing on Our Turtle's Back: Stories of Nishnaabeg Re-Creation, Resurgence and a New Emergence*. Winnipeg: Arbeiter Ring Publishing.

Troy, Jakelin and Michael Walsh. 2010. 'A linguistic renaissance in the South East of Australia'. In *Endangered Austronesian and Australian Aboriginal Languages: Essays on Language Documentation, Archiving and Revitalization*, edited by Gunter Senft, 175–82. Canberra: Pacific Linguistics.

Tsing, Anna. 2005. *Friction: An Ethnography of Global Connection*. Princeton: Princeton University Press.

Vizenor, Gerald. 2009. *Native Liberty: Natural Reason and Cultural Survivance*. Lincoln and London: University of Nebraska Press. doi.org/10.2307/j.ctt1 dgn41k

Walker, Brett. 2001. *The Conquest of Ainu Lands: Ecology and Culture in Japanese Expansion, 1590–1800*. London: University of California Press.

Walker, Ranginui. 2004. *Ka Whawhai Tonu Matou: Struggle Without End*. Auckland: Penguin.

'Why words die: How to keep lexical treasures from keeling over'. *The Economist*, 4 March 2017. Online: www.economist.com/news/books-and-arts/21717802-how-keep-lexical-treasures-keeling-over-why-words-die (accessed 21 June 2018).

Wolfe, Patrick. 2006. 'Settler colonialism and the elimination of the native'. *Journal of Genocide Research* 8(4): 387–409. doi.org/10.1080/14623520601056240

*Wôpanâak Language Reclamation Project*. Online: www.wlrp.org/ (accessed 16 June 2018).

# Part One: Contexts of Efflorescence

# Introduction: Contexts of Efflorescence

Gerald Roche

Why has Indigenous efflorescence occurred more-or-less simultaneously, in parallel, in so many different contexts? What shared conditions and circumstances have enabled it, and what changes may enable efflorescence to continue and expand in the future? Before looking at the answers suggested by contributions to this section of the book, we first draw on the literature to suggest how political and economic developments since the mid-twentieth century have created the conditions for contemporary Indigenous efflorescence.

Indigenous efflorescence has been facilitated, in part, by incremental changes in the political and economic spheres that have gathered momentum since the mid-twentieth century. Politically, the Canada–Australia–New Zealand–United States (CANZUS) bloc has experienced increasing Indigenous enfranchisement, first through the abolition of aggressive, explicitly assimilatory policies, and then through the legal and political measures that recognised the rights of Indigenous peoples within settler colonial states, supported by a framework of international mechanisms focusing on Indigenous peoples (Merlan 2009). International landmarks in Indigenous rights include the establishment of the Indigenous and Tribal Populations Convention, International Labour Organization (ILO) 107, in 1957; growth in the global Indigenous civil rights movement, exemplified by Red Power in the USA and Black Power in Australia during the 1960s and 70s (Merlan 2005); the transformation of ILO 107 into ILO 169, the Indigenous and Tribal Peoples Convention, in 1989; the founding of the Permanent Forum on Indigenous Issues at the UN in 2000; the declaration of two UN decades of the World's Indigenous People (1995–2004; 2005–14), and; the creation of the UN

Declaration on the Rights of Indigenous Peoples in 2007. Since the mid-twentieth century, there has been constant feedback between national Indigenous movements and the global Indigenous network (Johnson 2016), which has established a supportive political environment in which Indigenous efflorescence can take place.

Indigenous efflorescence has also been facilitated by economic changes, under the conditions of 'late capitalism' or neoliberalism. James Clifford describes how this new economic order supports the proliferation of 'zones of exception, niche markets, and commodified cultural exchanges' where 'Indigenous cultural resurgence and political self-determination can find room for maneuver' (2013: 17). Not only has the neoliberal era been one of increasingly diverse economic relations, spaces, and livelihoods, but it has also seen the emergence of a more complex, pluricentric economic and political order. This has been accompanied by a cultural crisis in Anglophone settler societies—'a moment of acute public uncertainty' as these countries 'dissolved economic and cultural ties to Britain and sought out new postcolonial identities' (Johnson 2016: 3). During this same time, economic historians have identified a Great Convergence—an ongoing, global levelling of income and standards of living, the reversal of economic inequalities that date back to the nineteenth century and the apogee of the colonial era (Korotayev, Goldstone and Zinkina 2015). John Wendel and Patrick Heinrich (2012) have described this contemporary moment of increasing decentralisation, prosperity, mobility and rising equality as constituting a 'glocalising' language ecology, characterised by language revival and nativisation.

The contributions in this section explore how these political and economic developments, amongst others, have created an enabling context for Indigenous efflorescence. We also consider contextual factors that continue to *constrain* efflorescence. The first contribution, by Markus Nyström, looks at how the narrative practices of settlers, in this case mainstream Swedes, act to constrain Indigenous efflorescence. Nyström examines Swedish parliamentary debates for evidence of colonial masterplots—easily recognised, oft-repeated story templates that frame understandings, interpretations, and retellings of events. In Swedish parliamentary debates, Nyström finds evidence for several colonial masterplots, including the Terra Nulius, Robinson Crusoe and Noble Savage masterplots, and argues that these serve to justify the continuing colonisation of Sapmi and the oppression of Sami people. He concludes by reflecting on the importance of counter-narratives in bringing about critical insights that help problematise privilege, build settler-Indigenous solidarities, and support efflorescence. Nyström's article is a reminder that there is still much to be done in creating political contexts that support Indigenous efflorescence.

The next series of case studies examines land as an important context for Indigenous efflorescence. These studies suggest that access to and control over land, which have both increased in postassimilationist multicultural societies as the result of political struggle by Indigenous people, are important contexts for efflorescence; later in the volume we will see that this continues to be the case even when Indigenous people move away from their land and into cities. In these case studies we see not only the struggle to access and gain stewardship over land, but also the important role that interacting with land plays for identity. Kouichi Kaizawa writes on the Cikornay National Trust, an Ainu organisation that works to acquire and rehabilitate forests that have been devastated by industrial forestry. The second case study in this section comes from Tero Mustonen from the Snowchange organisation in Finland. Mustonen describes distinctly Sami ways of interacting with seen and unseen elements of the landscape, and ways of being with the land, which are essential for not only maintaining local environments in the face of climate change, but also for fostering other aspects of local culture, in a holistic relationship between land, people and culture.

Whilst Mustonen's contribution shows how the land can be a resource that enables Indigenous people to adapt to the future, Ewa Ljungdahl's contribution demonstrates how land connects them to their past. Claiming that 'Sami history is a fairly quiet history' because it is unwritten, Ljungdahl shows how subtle traces in the landscape—overgrown hut foundations, bone deposits, cairns, ancient pathways—provide evidence of ongoing relationships with the land. As climate change and economic development erode these records, the South Sami community is faced with difficult decisions about how to preserve records of this knowledge whilst remaining control and a sense of intimacy with these facts once they become public records. The final two contributions on land, from Yōsuke Kosaka and Shizue Ukaji, both focus on *water* as land. These authors take, respectively, a past- and future-oriented approach to the issue of the Japanese state's denial of Ainu people's access to rivers and salmon. Yōsuke Kosaka explores the importance of rivers and salmon to the Ainu, and how Japanese colonisation denied Ainu people access to these, and then discusses the revival of a 'salmon welcoming' ceremony in the early

1980s. Shizue Ukaji continues this trajectory of loss and recovery into the future, asking what might happen if the Ainu had a river—just one river—in which to hunt salmon and practise their traditional livelihood.

Whilst Shizue Ukaji's speculations suggest that the future may, in some sense, entail a return to the past, the next series of contributions look at one way in which the future will be radically different from both the past and the present: technology. These case studies examine how the development of new technologies can provide another context that supports Indigenous efflorescence, particularly the revitalisation of language. As with developments in politics and economics, many of the activities taking place within the broader field of Indigenous efflorescence would not have been possible without developments of new, particularly digital, technologies. The first case study looks at a project to provide support for the learning of an endangered language, Ume Sami, which has less than 50 speakers, through a partnership between the community and the online learning platform, Memrise. Following, Hanna Outakoski's contribution examines the use of virtual learning space for language teaching and learning, particularly in contexts where communities are small and dispersed, and learners highly mobile. A third case study in this section, from Coppélie Cocq, introduces *Tjutju*, an online, multimedia narrative in the Lule Sami language, which demonstrates how traditional narratives can be adapted to new, digital contexts.

The fourth and final group of contributions in this section all address the topic of social movements for Indigenous efflorescence. They demonstrate how the affordances for social, cultural and political mobilisation within the context of postassimilationist multicultural societies have been crucial to the emergence of Indigenous efflorescence. These social movements take a variety of forms and scales, but all enable individuals to collectively or independently pursue their visions of Indigenous flourishing. Chisato Abe describes starting the 'Ainu Indigenous People's Film Society' and other activities to bring together the Ainu community in Sapporo and promote greater understanding of Indigenous issues amongst the wider public. Mattias Berglund introduces the Sápmi Awards, which provided recognition of excellence in Indigenous cultural pursuits, whilst also employing and promoting Sami languages. Åsa Virdi Kroik, meanwhile, discusses an effort to promote language revitalisation work through the formation of a children's choir, which also introduced students to traditional South Sami music. The final case study in this section, from Yuji Simizu, discusses efforts by Ainu Elders to have Ainu remains, previously seized by Hokkaidō University, returned to the community. All of these case studies deal with the numerous ways in which Indigenous people can mobilise to pursue shared goals and create efflorescence.

Collectively, these contributions remind us that the emergence of Indigenous efflorescence is over-conditioned by a variety of political, legal, economic and technological developments. Rather than serving to mystify how Indigenous efflorescence takes place, this multiplicity of supports, sources and conditions should encourage anthropologists to think about the many ways we may intervene in support of individuals and communities engaging in projects of efflorescence.

# References


Clifford, James. 2013. *Returns: Becoming Indigenous in the Twenty-First Century*. Harvard: Harvard University Press. doi.org/10.4159/9780674726222

*Indigenous and Tribal Peoples Convention*, adopted 27 June 1989, ILO 169 (entered into force 5 September 1991).

*Indigenous and Tribal Populations Convention*, adopted 26 June 1957, ILO 107 (entered into force 2 June 1959).

Johnson, Miranda. 2016. *The Land is Our History: Indigeneity, Law, and the Settler State*. Oxford: Oxford University Press. doi.org/10.1093/acprof:oso/9780190600020.001.0001

Korotayev, Andrey, Jack A. Goldstone and Julia Zinkina. 2015. 'Phases of global demographic transition correlate with phases of the Great Divergence and Great Convergence'. *Technological Forecasting and Social Change* 95 (June): 163–69. doi.org/10.1016/j.techfore.2015.01.017

Merlan, Francesca. 2005. 'Indigenous movements in Australia'. *Annual Review of Anthropology* 34: 473–94. doi.org/10.1146/annurev.anthro.34.081804.120643

Merlan, Francesca. 2009. 'Indigeneity: Global and local'. *Current Anthropology* 50(3): 303–33. doi.org/10.1086/597667

Wendel, John and Patrick Heinrich. 2012. 'A framework for language endangerment dynamics: The effects of contact and social change on language ecologies and language diversity'. *International Journal of the Sociology of Language* 218: 145–66. doi.org/10.1515/ijsl-2012-0062

# 1

# Narratives of Truth: An Exploration of Narrative Theory as a Tool in Decolonising Research

Markus Nyström

## Introduction

This anthology is about cultural and linguistic revitalisation. Narratives, or stories, are, I believe, the perfect middle ground between these two concepts, between culture and language. It is difficult to imagine a culture without shared language and stories, and it is probably inaccurate to call the existence of shared language and stories anything other than a culture. As part of the Sami revitalisation of culture and language, I believe stories are central. But as a white, Swedish man brought up in the south of the country, I firmly believe it is not my role to tell or analyse Sami narratives. My role, instead, has to be to turn my critical eye towards those in power, towards my own culture—towards myself. I was raised in a country whose colonial past (and present) is most often absent in the narratives told about the country, and first came into contact with this history as an adult and never in school. This chapter is as much about me as it is about the political discourse in which I exist. This chapter is therefore an attempt— to some degree—to 'unsettle the settler within' (Regan 2010: 11) by trying to expose colonial mindsets towards Sami and Sapmi in Swedish political discourse, the discourse I was brought up in.

I believe that for Sami, especially young Sami, creating new and holding on to old narratives and understandings might be crucial in the revitalisation process. But, in that process it is also important to have tools to see through and criticise the dominant narratives, as well as form counter narratives. My hope is that this chapter will make available one such tool by showing how concepts from narrative theory can be used to analyse political discourse.[1] My claim, or hope, is that narrative theory, and especially the concept of a masterplot, can function as a means to expose that which may not be explicit, but assumed, in a discourse. As a master's student in Environmental History, at the time of writing, researching the Swedish discourse on mining in Sapmi, it became, and still is, quite clear to me that there are dispositions, attitudes and knowledge formations in the political discourse which stem from colonial relations, but which are difficult, or even impossible, to positively pinpoint when analysing the discourse. The concept of a masterplot may be, in some cases, a way of doing just that—a way of pinpointing where and how a covert colonial 'mindset' is present in a discourse. By exposing how colonial mindsets are infused in a discourse, it is my hope that it will be easier to oppose and resist them, and thereby support a revitalisation or decolonising process.

I will attempt to explain my method in detail and then apply it to a selection of debates in the Swedish parliament relevant to Sami affairs. Before getting into the method, and before beginning the analysis, I need first to establish what I regard as colonialism and what, in this article, I call colonial mindsets.

---

1    In this chapter, 'political discourse' refers to *mainstream* political discourse, the political hegemonic discourse. More specifically, the way people in political power, in the parliament and government, speak and construct their world view.

# Colonialism and colonial mindsets

Colonialism can be a rather imprecise concept, spanning various phenomena and methods of domination, and definitions available through dictionaries are often vague or even misleading.[2] The problem with a succinct definition is that it easily becomes either too narrow or too vague to be of much analytical use. A well-functioning analytical definition must be rather elaborate and sensitive to variations in colonial methods. There is simply not enough space to create such an elaborate definition here, but my work so far has resulted in an understanding of colonialism as functioning in two main categories: the ordering of physical/political reality on the one hand, and the ordering of ideological/ontological reality on the other.

The ordering of physical/political reality includes domination of a territory and/or a people by an external power (a nation state, empire, corporation). Military force or police violence is often present, or at least the threat thereof. Domination is a key concept because it denotes the inequality of power and control between the colonisers and the colonised. Colonialism includes the permanent settlement of significant numbers of colonists, or the establishment of strong enough institutions, or large enough industries, on the colonised land against the will and/or interests of the colonised people. Imperialism—a closely related concept—refers mainly to domination without significant numbers of permanent settlers, and refers to a larger degree to the ideological backdrop of colonialism. Imperialism can be seen as the idea that a country/polity/corporation has the right to expand at the expense of others; colonialism is that idea's most spectacular expression (Smith 1999; McLeod 2000). It is also important to note that the driver of colonialism (and imperialism) is the economy— access to resources, expansion of markets, cheap labour. Even though other

---

2    The Oxford online dictionary, for instance, defines colonialism thus: 'The policy or practice of acquiring full or partial political control over another country, occupying it with settlers, exploiting it economically'. Note that there is no subject doing the colonising, but it can be read implicitly (since it is 'another country' being colonised) that colonialism is something countries do, not corporations, federations, or other units of power. Furthermore, it says nothing of the 'colonisation of the mind', of colonial discourses, or ruptured identities. Many former colonies were not technically countries at all at the time of colonisation, but were constructed as countries by the colonisers. With this definition, colonialism cannot occur within the borders of one country, as in Sweden. Sapmi has thus not been colonised for two reasons: it was not 'another country' and it was (and is) technically within the borders of Sweden.

'well-meaning' reasons for the expansion of empires has been proposed—'the white man's burden', or saving the souls of not yet baptised heathens, for instance—the main driver remains economic gain.

The second category, the ordering of ideological/ontological reality, refers to the psychological violence which shatters identities and creates new ones. This has aptly been called the 'colonization of the mind' (Thiong'o 1986). Colonial discourses are naturalised that posit the colonisers as *righteously* dominant, and through religious, educational, scientific, moral, legal and bureaucratic institutions, colonial discourses are maintained and internalised by the colonised people themselves. This internalisation is central because colonialism does not work merely by a colonising power imposing itself on a society which actively resists it. Instead, colonialism functions by the colonised people internalising the *narratives* of the colonisers—in a word, the colonised are forced, through various means, to see the world and themselves in the same way as the colonisers do. The internalisation of colonial discourses is a key instrument of power. This is why narratives are so central in a revitalisation or decolonisation process, because they can entail rejecting the internalised colonial discourses and regaining narratives, identities and pride that were lost.

A definition focused only on the ordering of physical/political reality must necessarily regard colonialism as past and over the day the native flag is raised instead of the flag of the colonial power. But this is not how colonialism works. Colonialism lingers in the minds of people; it is passed down through generations, by means of the psychological violence of the colonisation of the mind. Just because the wording in political discourse or some nationalistic formalities change does not mean that the (former) colonising power regard the (former) colony differently, or that the (former) colonised people regard themselves or the (former) colonisers very differently either. It is easier to change a flag than the world views, narratives and identities of people who have suffered for centuries under the yoke of colonialism. Colonialism cannot be regarded as an on/off-practice. Despite formal decolonisation, colonial practices can still be in place. This is often referred to as neo-colonialism.

And this leads to the subject of this article, because not since the beginning of the twentieth century has the political discourse in Sweden included an explicitly colonial perspective on the north. The debate around the turn of the twentieth century concerned whether this colony of Sweden ought to be an agricultural or industrial economy (Sörlin 1988). For roughly a hundred years, therefore, Sweden has officially or explicitly *not* colonised Sapmi. Yet, during this same period, enormous increases in industry in Sapmi have occurred, a number of divisive and ill-advised laws have been passed with relevance to Sami livelihoods, reindeer herders have been displaced, racism toward Sami has been and is still widespread, and large numbers of Swedish settlers have migrated to Sapmi, to give just a few examples. In many ways, the colonial efforts of the Swedish state have increased simultaneously as the word colonialism has all but disappeared from the political discourse and agenda (Lundmark 2008). So, in short, during the same time as the physical/political reality has been ordered to exploit Sapmi to an ever higher degree (physical/political reality), and during the same time as Sami livelihoods, identities and languages have been systematically degraded through state actions (ideological/ontological reality), the narratives describing the relationship between Sapmi and Sweden have been transformed to virtually give the opposite view.

This lack of explicitness in the Swedish political discourse concerning the relationship between the state and Sapmi brings two distinct problems. The first is that it is difficult for a researcher (or anyone) to find actual and explicit colonial statements in current political discourse. In a positive research tradition, where one analyses what is actually said—not what is not said—this makes for a difficult methodological problem. Finding ways to circumnavigate this problem is important since silencing and rendering invisible are highly effective instruments of power, common in colonial relations—and analysing power structures ought to be an important goal for academic work. At the same time, there is a methodological problem with leaving it entirely up to the individual researcher to 'speculate' as to what is not said, to 'read between the lines'. Investigating the invisible and untold, or rather the implicit and assumed, therefore, needs stringent methods and theory in order to work well.

The second problem that arises from this lack of explicitness is that even the proponents of further exploitation of Sapmi and further delimiting of Sami rights (for instance, Sweden's former minister of commerce, Annie Lööf) do not regard themselves as proponents of colonialism. Instead, they may regard themselves as proponents of, for instance, economic growth and equality. In other words, without access to the explicit terminology of colonialism in the political discourse, colonial actions are cloaked not only from researchers but also from the colonialists themselves. In effect, they cannot be colonialists because colonialism does not exist in their discourse. This is where I choose to introduce the concept of *colonial mindset.* Simplified, one has a colonial mindset if one's actions and rhetoric (or narratives) have colonial outcomes and/or origins without explicitly using a colonial vocabulary. A politician, for instance, reveals a colonial mindset when arguing for a continuation or increase of colonial policies and practices, or subscribes to and uses colonial narratives and masterplots to describe reality at the same time as his/her rhetoric hides colonial aspirations. The term colonial mindset is thus closely tied to neo-colonialism. I choose this term because it is my understanding that politicians who actually promote colonialism, but call it something else, sincerely believe themselves not to be promoting colonialism.

## Narrative theory

The word *narrative* is often used synonymously with *story*. We like to think of narratives as art, however modest, and we think of writers, filmmakers and playwrights as good storytellers. They are people who master the art of narrative. But narrative is a larger concept than story. Narrative is something we all engage in all the time: it is our species' 'principal way' of organising our understanding of time (Abbott 2008: 3). Paul Ricœur wrote his three-volume opus titled *Time and Narrative*, where

> one presupposition commands all the others, namely, that what is ultimately at stake in the case of the structural identity of the narrative function as well as in that of the truth claim of every narrative work, is the temporal character of human existence (1983: 3).

But what does it mean to organise the 'temporal character of human existence'? A quick answer could run something like this: when we tell of something—let's say, how our day at work was—we do not tell of everything that happened during the day. We *choose* to convey certain *events* that make the listener understand our day; events that exemplify and explain, in other words, create meaning. Compare this kind of narrative to a story dictated by clock-time, a so-called 'pure chronicle' (Cronon 1992: 1351), an objective story, as it were, where no interpretation of meaning is made. This would be a story in which clock-time—not meaning or importance—would dictate our telling of our day. Every event that occurred during the day would receive the same amount of attention, given that it took the same amount of clock-time.

This is why Ricœur says that narrative is the method we humans use to create an understanding of 'human time'. By narrative, we make our telling of our work day 'human'. Narrative is *the* way for us to make sense of things. A pure chronicle does not make sense to us, no matter how 'objective' it might be. That it does not explain things sufficiently is, at a first glance, rather ironic since it seems to offer an unbiased representation, which ought to be attractive to the rational mind. But this sense of irony probably comes from the idea (or ideal) that humans are primarily rational beings, while we in fact are at least as much, if not more, *narrative* beings. In this perspective, narrative is a central human trait. Indeed, it has been argued that the propensity for narrative is what distinguishes humans from other animals; that narrative is 'the central function or *instance* of the human mind' (Jameson 1981: xiii). We cannot avoid engaging in narrative activity.

There are four more concepts that need further examination in this article. They are *plot, masterplot, type* and *plotline*. These concepts have more to do with what are usually referred to as 'stories' than the more instinctual or reflexive narrative thinking described above.

A *plot* is, according to Ricœur and his reading of Aristotle, an operation, not a static structure, which creates a 'synthesis between heterogeneous elements'; a plot 'serves to make *one* story out of … multiple incidents' (Ricœur in Wood 1991: 21). A plot has a wholeness to it, a beginning, a progression and an end, and events are more than just occurrences— events are what contribute to the progression, beginning and end of the plot. This has some interesting repercussions, namely that events are to some degree chosen to belong to a narrative insofar as they contribute to the (preconceived) plot. In other words, a plot is never neutral but constructed with particular goals in mind—whether the narrator is conscious or not that he/she is doing so.

This brings us to the idea of *masterplot* and *type*. A masterplot is a plot that is easily recognised by members of a culture and oft-repeated in various forms. Sometimes referred to as *master narratives* or *story skeletons*, masterplots are plots that we hear and see over and over again within a specific culture's narrative tradition (Abbott 2008). When we start watching a movie and have a pretty good idea after three minutes how the story will progress and end, there is a good chance we are dealing with a masterplot. Classic masterplots for western culture are for instance the Quest (*Exodus, Lord of the Rings*), the Escape (*The Count of Monte Cristo*,

*Midnight Express*), the Sacrifice (*Jesus Christ, Saving Private Ryan*), the Forbidden Love (*Romeo and Juliet, Titanic*). See, for instance, Ronald B. Tobias's list of masterplots, *20 Master Plots and How to Build Them*.

Masterplots are more than just stories we know. This is important. They are operations by which we interpret reality; they are 'mental maps' onto which we try to fit the reality we see outside ourselves *even if it does not fit very well* (Abbott 2008: 46). Masterplots are, as it were, culturally sanctioned templates for interpreting reality around us.

What constitutes a masterplot exactly is hard to say. But they often, if not always, come with specific *types*. A type is a recurring kind of character (Abbott 2008: 49). The troubled but daring seeker of the Quest masterplot and the tormented and wise martyr from the Sacrifice masterplot are examples. When a type is too shallowly described, and appears too predictable, we often call the character a *stereotype*. Masterplots can also be rendered stereotypically, in which case the narrative appears as too simple, shallow and clichéd.

A *plotline*, finally, denotes the development within a plot, whether it ends better or worse than it starts. It's a rather vague concept academically perhaps, but a concept nonetheless that I find quite intuitive. Are things better in the end of a plot than in the beginning? Are the characters (the types) wiser, richer, more mature—or the opposite? The characters in a Quest masterplot are often wiser and richer in the end than in the beginning, even if the quest has its toll, while one or both of the lovers are dead in the Forbidden Love masterplot.

So how can this framework, this terminology, be used in order to highlight colonial mindsets? How can it be used to investigate the invisible and untold, the implicit and assumed? By drawing two conclusions. First, we can assume that the history of colonialism and racism has generated a number of colonial masterplots, or masterplots with importance for colonial mindsets. I will try and list a few of these below that I believe I can identify. These colonial masterplots are 'mental maps' which people repeatedly put to use in order to interpret and describe the world around them.

Second, narrative activity is a central human trait; we reflexively organise our understanding in the form of narratives, and masterplots are almost instantly recognisable to us. This means that a speaker does not have to tell the entire masterplot narrative in order to activate the rhetorical leverage, the force, of that masterplot. A single phrase can turn the listener's mind in the direction of a familiar masterplot, encourage him/her to interpret the narrative in that light, and in turn also try to fit the characters of the narrative into the types of that masterplot. A proud 'I'm going on a mission' as one heads out to the supermarket comically draws on the Quest masterplot; a concerned 'She's your Juliet' from a friend can draw attention to the hopelessness of a relationship you are in by drawing on the Forbidden Love masterplot.

And conversely, and maybe more importantly, these masterplots, being part of our cultural metaphoric vocabulary as it were, can frequently be expressed unintentionally. Saying, for instance, that Norrland is 'wild' and 'desolate' are such standard expressions they usually pass us without much notice (even though what today is called Norrland has been populated since the last ice age (see Hagström Yamamoto 2010). These words, I would argue, are all expressions of a masterplot about Norrland— or possibly colonised lands in general—that render the Indigenous population invisible and portray the land as 'up for grabs'.[3]

Masterplots can sometimes even be woven into the discourse on a linguistic level, that is, into the words themselves. Above I wrote about 'Norrland', but I did so partly ironically. Norrland (literally, 'North Land') is what constitutes roughly half or more of Sweden's landmass, and it is obviously named so because the people who defined and named it were to the south if it. 'Norrland' is north of whatever and whoever is important enough to define the world. Within that word—Norrland—an entire masterplot could arguably be read.

## Colonial masterplots

I try here to list a few colonial masterplots that I can identify. Masterplots are arbitrary in the sense that there is no formula to easily demarcate them. They often overlap (the Escape and the Quest masterplots described above could, for instance, be said to belong to an even larger masterplot going back to ideas of Purgatory). Someone else making a list like this would

---

3    An obvious example of this was when the CEO of Beowulf Mining, a company that is planning to start a mine in Gállok outside Jokkmokk, Sapmi, answered the question of what the local people would think of the mining project with a rhetorical question, 'What local people?' I call this masterplot the Terra Nullius masterplot (elaborated below) from the Roman expression for 'no man's land'—which goes to show how old this masterplot is in colonial relations.

possibly end up with a different categorisation than I. I mainly make this list to exemplify to the reader what I mean by masterplots, since I believe this list makes the theoretical talk above more concrete. This list is not exhaustive.

## The Terra Nullius masterplot

The land is empty, up for grabs, and the plotline suggests that the land not only can but *deserves* to be 'improved' (Cronon 1992: 1351). The land is of course not really empty at all but is generally perceived as such, as the original occupants are lacking the rights to the land for one reason or another (they are not organised into nation states, they are not Christians, they are not farmers). The land itself is an important type in this masterplot. The land is what is developed by a nation, an industry or a people, who make it—in their eyes—better. (Narratives: countless westerns, *Star Trek*, colonial historiographies, Columbus 'discovering' the 'new world'.)

## The Robinson Crusoe masterplot

This shares a lot with the Terra Nullius masterplot but is more individualistic. A lone survivor, an adventurer, a settler or entrepreneur leads the way in this 'empty' land. The focus is on toil and hardships, (western) ingenuity to solve problems and discovery of 'strange lands'. The protagonist (most often a man) can get to know the Indigenous people, but if he does, it is the Indigenous who are changed most dramatically by the encounter. The focus is on character development of the protagonist who most often returns to civilisation or is saved. (Narratives: *Robinson Crusoe*, Amundsen and Scott's competition to reach the South Pole, Meriwether Lewis, *Lars Monsen: Kanada på tvers* (Lars Monsen: Across Canada)).

## The Lost Culture masterplot

A romantic or nostalgic masterplot seems to pay homage to the nobility of lost (or about-to-be lost) cultures, neglecting that many of these cultures still exist but *do not fit the romanticised ideal* of Indigenous people. This masterplot brings relief to the colonialists because the progression of 'civilisation' is regarded as more or less unavoidable. With unavoidability comes freedom from responsibility. The masterplot can end in roughly two ways. It can end with 'civilisation' progressing (as in *Dances with Wolves*) or with the resistance to it being too strong (as in *Avatar*). The plotlines can therefore vary. Types include the 'Noble Savage', the 'evil colonialist', and a westerner who is changed, who 'goes over to the other side'. (Narratives: *Pocahontas*, *The Last Samurai*, *Lawrence of Arabia*.)

## The Noble Savage masterplot

In this version, the Indigenous peoples are portrayed as part of nature rather than culture. Their nobility, their inherent ecological savvy, is peaceful, harmonious and infantile. The influence of western culture is seen as harmful and the fragile 'children of nature' need protecting. The Indigenous person is not someone who makes much noise, does not drive a snow mobile, have a cell phone, or live in the city. When civilisation comes around, the Noble Savage slowly shakes his/her head and shies away, opting for the peacefulness of nature instead. This is a masterplot where the Indigenous do not change much, do not want change, and where indigeneity is something more or less fixed. It is up to benevolent colonialists to 'protect' them. Ultimately, however, this protection is futile as the progression of 'civilisation' is unavoidable. (Narratives: *The Mission*, Jimmy Nelson's *Before They Pass Away*.)

## The Development/Industrial Production/White Man's Burden masterplot

I lump these together because they have much in common, and they could be seen as representing more of a thought structure, a red thread, common in many masterplots rather than a single masterplot in itself. The idea where 'raw materials' are transformed into 'finished products' is the linear production apparatus of modern industrial production; it is the masterplot of industrialism, as it were. This is not necessarily colonial, but the structure recurs in colonial masterplots. For instance, in the Terra Nullius masterplot, the 'raw material' is developed by colonial forces into a better state, and into a finished product. Obviously, the word 'development' is central here, involving change supposedly inherently for the better. This development is good, something everyone ought to want, but it is also exclusively defined as westernisation. In this sense, this masterplot is closely related to the idea of the 'white man's burden', justifying colonialism as a noble cause. Compare the white man's burden idea to the idea of 'developing countries' being thankful for the introduction of western technology and their inclusion into western institutions and economic systems.

## The Nation State masterplot(s)/narratives

A similar linear development can be found in narratives about nation states, born out of dim and/or cruel beginnings, as they are often pictured, developed over time into glorious, powerful and naturalised institutions. Narratives about nations can take a number of forms and plots—Rise/Fall, David/Goliath, Good/Evil—but what makes nation state narratives important to bring up is that they work to unify, in some sense to make, a homogenous 'people', no matter what masterplot(s) the narratives employ. Not infrequently, this is done through the reminiscence and nostalgia over a more or less imagined lost past (Lahtinen 2012). A 'national history functions like a "story of the tribe", providing the people with a sense of shared origins, a common past and a collective identity in the present' (McLeod 2000: 70).

# Masterplots and narratives used in political debate

Using masterplots, types (and stereotypes), and plotlines can be done in a number of ways for a number of purposes. Their use is rather flexible. They can be employed sarcastically, earnestly, sympathetically—intentionally or not. Going through text—especially rule-bound, dry parliamentary debates, as I do below—in the hope of finding clear-cut and obvious uses of colonial masterplots can be difficult. In this dry genre, stories, as we usually think of them, are largely missing. Instead, 'statements of fact' (descriptions of how the world is or ought to be) dominate the genre. Of course, what is regarded as 'statements of fact' are political and ideological and the 'matter-of-factness' way of speaking is a rhetorical device aimed at making the speaker appear more convincing and thus making counter arguments more difficult. Very little hedging is done and expressions of feelings are rare in parliamentary debates. Quite a substantial amount of effort is spent by politicians bashing opposing parties, throwing numbers and statistics at each other, and other devices aimed at specific parties and alliance formations between parties. There is a lot of election strategising going on that is not directly tied to the issues discussed.

A narrative analysis of this genre has to try to find what 'story' or 'stories' are told 'behind' the statements of fact; what are taken for granted and shared as common understandings of reality? There are narratives there, behind the facade of matter-of-factness, there are masterplots, there are types; this is what narrative theory applied in this fashion has to seek.

All this taken together probably makes rule-bound political debate one of the most difficult genres to apply this method to. I expect the method to be more successful on other genres, like debate articles, journal articles, Facebook posts and fictional works. But it is also exactly because of the parliamentary debate genre's apparent impregnability that I choose to try.

## Analysis: Parliamentary debates

The Swedish Parliament has 349 members from eight different political parties. The sample of debates I have gone through—somewhere between 20 and 30 hours in total—is no more than a snippet of the total amount of information this institution produces. I have sought those debates where Sami issues, in some way, are debated; for instance, debates around hunting and wildlife management, interpellations about the legal status of the Sami population and Sami Parliament, minority and language issues, and debates around the mining industry. The debates were from 2010 to 2015.

Generally, the members of the Swedish Parliament agree and restate that the Sami are an Indigenous people in Sweden and, as such, have special rights (with the exception of the Sweden Democrats who, with their nationalistic perspective, do not accept Sami as entitled to Indigenous peoples' rights). Sapmi, on the other hand, seems to be used rather ambiguously as a word to describe the traditional Sami land, best exemplified perhaps by the former Minister of Rural Affairs, Eskil Erlandsson, who called this land 'that which the Sami Parliament calls Sapmi' (Erlandsson 2013). Thereby, he emphasises that calling it Sapmi—a land that is not *Sweden*—is a Sami idea, not a Swedish one, and in the process discredits its use in national political discourse. In other words, Erlandsson thereby reinforces a narrative of national unity.

Indeed, the minister is more admitting here than most other MPs. Many refer to this land, if they feel the need, as the 'reindeer-herding territory'. This is interesting because it has historical roots. For a long time, since the first Reindeer Herding Act from 1886, and especially since the Reindeer Herding Act of 1928, the state's perspective was that a real Sami was a reindeer-herding nomad. It ascribed rights to wildlife, forests and water to reindeer herders organised in Sami villages (Ryd and Cramér 2012). This caused a rift within the Sami population, between the reindeer herders and non–reindeer herding Sami, that still exists today. Speaking of this land as 'the reindeer-herding territory' instead of Sami Land (Sapmi) reveals, I believe, the continuation of this understanding of Sami identity—an identity which is difficult to distinguish from the livelihood of reindeer herding.[4] I would argue that equating Sami people and their interests with reindeer herding is part of a masterplot about Sami culture.

'Sapmi', just like 'Norrland', or indeed 'Sweden'—all these names come with their own narratives, their own perspectives, on this area. Geographically, they do refer to slightly different areas, but choosing to call the lands where Sami have traditionally lived 'Sweden', 'Norrland' or 'Sapmi' reveals different perspectives and thus different narratives, even if the three technically overlap. (Yet another name, especially at the European Union level, is 'the Barents Region'.)

Saying that the Sami are an Indigenous people *in Sweden* tells a specific narrative too. As an example, one could try reversing it, saying that Sweden is one of the four nations that conquered Sapmi, or even more sharply, that Sweden is one of four states that colonised the Sami people and their lands. The different versions of phrasing are all 'true' depending on perspective, and the different versions come with a certain narrative baggage and thereby a certain understanding of reality.

Regarding the history of colonialism, there are large differences. Some argue that 'Sweden as a great power … does not have a pretty history' in regards to the Sami population (Skånberg 2012), and some urgently call for ratification of ILO 169. At the other end of the spectrum, history is reversed by MPs claiming that the state 'invented' the south Sami language

---

4    For an historical view on how the Sami 'race' was equated with reindeer herding as a livelihood, see Lundmark (2008: 141).

and is trying to expel the true Indigenous people, the mountain farmers and cattle owners in south Sapmi, to unjustly benefit the cherished reindeer herding (Larsson 2013).

One example is especially interesting in this regard, where an MP (Tuve Skånberg, Christian Democrats) shows that he is aware of the 'centuries-old failure of Swedish Sami politics', while at the same time he states, 'It is thus not possible to let a third of the country go to the Sami, even if they have legitimate demands for such a large area' (Skånberg 2012). It is a comparatively honest and knowledgeable speech, but narratively, a number of interesting things happen here. First, the centuries-old Swedish Sami politics are claimed as having failed, which is of course true on some levels, but the way it is said naturalises that Sami politics have been and are part of *Swedish* politics. Why is it regarded as a natural thing that the Swedish state should have decisive power, throughout the centuries, over Sami and Sapmi in the first place? The underlying premise, the Swedish 'ownership' of this land, is not in question; this 'ownership' is thus part of a shared understanding of reality. The conflicts Skånberg then goes on to describe, where 'by the kitchen table' when he lived in Kiruna 'land owners and Sami even fought', is not understood as a colonial tension between groups, but as a Swedish problem of law, of balancing different interests.

Second, Skånberg's speech is a good example of something I see as a general tendency, namely to regard Sami rights to land and water as a privilege given by a kind Swedish state when historically the order should be reversed—the rights Sami today have are mere scraps of what they ought to have had if the state had not stolen the land.[5] Letting 'a third of the country go to the Sami' is a narrative where Sweden *gives* Sami their rights, not a narrative where Sweden has taken a third of what is today 'the country' from the Sami. Add to this the honesty of admitting that the Sami do have legitimate demands for the land and we end up with something that inadvertently comes as close as it gets to formally admitting to present colonialism, or at least unlawful occupation.

In fact, this narrative could be regarded as a form of Swedish masterplot, with the Sami and Sweden (its self-image) as types: Sweden as the giver of rights, the careful balancer of conflicting interests, rather than the

---

5    'Stolen' might appear as a harsh way of putting it, but it is a paraphrase of Lundmark's 2008 book title, *Stulet Land* (*Stolen Land*).

enabler of continued colonialism. The Sami are seen as being not that bad off, since they can still herd their reindeer, and the reindeer herders still have special rights in relation to average Swedes. Discussions regarding the possible ratification of ILO 169 often have this tendency too, where a continued stalling of the process is not seen as a continued theft of rights from the Sami, but where the possible ratification is seen as an act of generosity. As a generous giver, you are not necessarily compelled to give a gift quickly, so it is more dangerous to hasten into ratification without thoroughly investigating its consequences, than to let the receiver of the gift wait a little longer. Meanwhile, Sweden allows (so to speak) the Sami to continue their reindeer herding, and points of conflict—like the advancement of the mining industry in Sapmi, for example—are defused with dialogue between industry and reindeer herders (even though the legal framework around mining grants reindeer herders no rights to veto mining projects). This masterplot is thus connected to the idea of Sami as reindeer herders, as it is generally understood that as long as reindeer herding can continue in some fashion, Sami culture is not under immediate threat. Another way of putting it is that, from the state's perspective, the plotline of the masterplot is really not that bad. It can get better, but it is not negative. That there is no immediate threat to Sami culture (since reindeer herding is still going on, Sami = reindeer herder) is, in my opinion, one reason why the two-decade long stalling of the ratification of ILO 169 is not seen as particularly disgraceful. Slowness is rather seen as taking responsibility.

I have stated that masterplots are 'mental maps' which we use to interpret reality. An unusually clear example of this (for the genre) is the MP Sven-Olof Sällström (Swedish Democrat) who shapes his narrative like a fairy tale to more clearly evoke the power of colonial masterplots:

> Once upon a time there was an explorer who we can call Sven, who together with his crew sailed north along the coast in three ships … They sought a new and closer road to India. Instead, they found an undiscovered piece of land populated by people with strange clothes, strange habits, and who lived close to nature. During a few centuries, the native inhabitants were banished, their land was stolen, and they were put in reservations. And so ends the story (Sällström 2012).

Sällström then concludes that this was, of course, not how it happened in the Swedish north. The Sami have been subject to atrocities by the state, admits Sällström, but many people, not only Sami, were historically subject to atrocities by the state. The message is that no appropriation or colonialism has occurred. 'The wish,' Sällström continues, 'that we in Sweden should have our own "Indians" who need protection from all the misfortunes of the world has overshadowed a correct historiography' (ibid.). The correct historiography, according to Sällström, is that 'the reindeer-herding territory' has been multicultural for centuries, maybe millennia, and therefore the Sami should not receive any special legal treatment or support. He also claims most of the modern reindeer herding in the Scandinavian mountains originated as a result of the war between Sweden and Russia in 1809, and shakes his head in disbelief as he utters the words 'custom immemorial' (ibid.).

The fairy tale narrative is a caricature, not only of the Terra Nullius masterplot (finding 'undiscovered' but still populated lands) but also of the many counter plots and counter narratives to that plot. Sällström also ridicules the Noble Savage masterplot, in that he claims the wish for Sweden to have its own '"Indians" who need protecting' has hindered a correct historiography. Interestingly, he ridicules both these colonial masterplots so that he can argue for a legal framework (in hunting and wildlife management) which dispossesses Sami further of their rights as an Indigenous people. *Exactly because* Sweden's history does not fit the masterplots of colonialism, according to Sällström, Sweden *cannot be* a colonial state, and thus Sweden should not have a legal framework which in any way treats differently this group of people. In short, the reality does not fit the 'mental maps' of colonial masterplots and therefore the reality must not be colonial. The masterplot that is most fitting to describe the situation in 'Norrland', the way Sällström thinks of it, is the Nation State masterplot—Sällström even makes a point of highlighting that the Sami are also Swedes.[6]

Of the parliamentary debates that I have listened to, I believe this to be one of the most interesting examples of how flexibly masterplots can be deployed as rhetorical tropes; and an interesting example of how narrow the understanding can be of what forms colonialism can take. By sarcastically disproving the colonial masterplots as not fitting to

---

6    In December 2014, Sällström's party colleague Björn Söder completely reversed this and caused a scandal when he, in an interview, said that Sami (and Jews) are not 'Swedes'. Mainstream media was outraged at Söder's statement, but Sami representatives argued that he was right, and that it was exactly because of this that the Sami have special rights to land and water.

the Swedish context, Sällström can argue for not only a continued but a radically increased dispossession of the Sami in the name of the nation state—that is, a continuation of colonialism.

One thing I see clearly in the material is that the political discourse on Sami issues in the Swedish parliament in general leans heavily on the Nation State and Development masterplots. Sällström is one example, but another is Ingela Nylund Watz (Social Democrats) who opens a debate about mining with this unifying remark:

> There is a broad consensus in Sweden about the importance of the mining industry. It has in the past, and will in the future, constitute an important foundation for our ability to maintain employment and welfare (Nylund Watz 2014).

No eyebrows are raised. This is a 'statement of facts' common to all political parties' understanding of the mining industry, repeated in various forms by many. That is why it works well as an example of a common narrative understanding of reality, part of a masterplot. The narrative here is one of national unity, of a common history and a common future.

Mining especially, closely followed by hydropower and forestry, are raw material industries primarily established in Sapmi, with resources and money flow going pretty much one-way from Sapmi to Sweden. Of all the ore produced in Sweden, over 90 per cent comes from Norrbotten, from Kiruna and Gällivare municipalities (Hedström 2012). These mines are undisputedly in ('what the Sami Parliament calls') Sapmi. The large dammed rivers and the vast felled forests of Sapmi are routinely cherished as primary industries foundational for Sweden as a state and/or the welfare state (Persson 2014)—though, just as routinely, the Sapmi part is missing from the narrative. It is extremely rare to find explicit references to Sapmi or even to Norrland when speaking of these industries. The national narrative, of Sweden rising to become a modern nation, veils the fact that this ascent was largely accomplished by resources appropriated through colonial means in Sapmi. Nylund Watz does, however, slip a little when saying that the renaissance in the mining industry *actually* is a concern for the whole country' (Nylund Watz 2014).[7] It might appear petty to focus on that word—'actually'—but it does reveal that this is not

---

7    In the address, Nylund Watz emphasises 'actually', though in the written records there are no italics.

normally the case; normally, mining does not concern the whole of the country. Normal, historically, is that mining belongs to a certain area of the country, particularly the north, that is, Sapmi.

I would like to point out that I do not doubt the minerology, that Sapmi is rich in mineral and other natural resources. What I do question is the basically undisputed, self-appointed right of the Swedish state to directly exploit, or enable others to exploit, those resources without even granting the Sami the right to veto or dispute. Such organisation, especially combined with the continued stalling of the ratification of ILO 169, and coupled with an overtly nationalistic rhetoric surrounding the mining industry (or extractive industries in general), are all part of a narrative about the mining industry which distinctly underplays its colonial structure and operations. The existence of this narrative, and the virtual absence of dissent to it in the discourse, is an example of a shared colonial mindset.

## Summary of analysis

Constructing one concise masterplot which shapes the narratives surrounding the relationship between the Swedish state and Sapmi could be summarised as follows. The state has done bad things to Sami in the past, but, exactly what that was, is rather vaguely described most often. In the material I have gone through, I cannot recall a single instance of the word 'colonialism' actually being used, even when describing the past. Sweden, as a type in a masterplot, is pictured as kind, a giver rather than a taker of rights, an upholder of equality, democracy and responsibility. The stalling of the ratification of ILO 169, for instance, is seen mainly as a sign of taking responsibility in a delicate situation of conflicting interests rather than a continuation of withholding human rights from the Sami. I believe the state, as a type, downplays its own actions that enable modern colonialism, and do not sufficiently acknowledge historical acts of colonialism. Indeed, those historical acts of colonialism are pictured as national success stories which everyone within the borders of the country ought to be thankful for and proud of. The extractive industries, which in my opinion (and doubtless that of many Sami as well) embody and act as the motivation for Swedish colonialism, are what 'built' the country. The narratives around these industries thus serve a nationalistic function. Particularly—it seems—the narratives around mining get to carry this nationalistic, unifying function. These industries have been and still are located to an extensive degree in Sapmi, drawing wealth from Sapmi to Sweden. At the same time, Sami communities are not given the possibilities to oppose them or benefit from them. This unequal relationship, in the material I have gone through, is never acknowledged.

The Sami as a type are often equated with reindeer herders, and Sapmi is 'the reindeer-herding territory' (in other words, an area within Sweden where some have this 'job'). Since the reindeer herders are still going about their business, there is obviously no immediate danger to Sami culture. Indeed, many times it seems that Sami issues literally translate to reindeer-herding issues. For instance, this is seen in discussions about ILO 169, which are relevant for more Sami than just reindeer herders. Constructing Sami as a type in this fashion diminishes Sami culture (which is more diverse), ignores the non–reindeer herding Sami population to a large degree, and draws attention away from the state's maintaining of policies which make the Sami effectively powerless, and which cause division within the Sami population.

The plotline in this masterplot is thus a progressive one. It was worse before but it is getting better, even if it takes some time to get there. The plotline seems to follow closely the idea of progression of the Swedish state as a type, from feudal and oppressive to capitalistic, democratic and modern. The plotline thus follows the modernistic assumption of linear development, that things always get better, more evolved, developed and just over time.

## Concluding remarks

When working with my master's thesis, I ran into problems. What I wanted to explore and expose was not there to be found in the material I wanted to analyse. No one in decision-making institutions in mining affairs in Sweden expressed anything remotely colonial, at least not on the surface of it. In the parliament, in government reports, in agency decisions and historiographies—everything seemed so very nice and rational. At the same time, looking at what decisions were actually made, hearing Sami friends and colleagues describe a completely different reality (counter narratives), and having experiences from being an activist protesting mining operations on site in Sapmi, it was painfully obvious to me that there existed a discrepancy between the narratives in mainstream politics and the actual practices those narratives brought about. I needed to find a way to pry open what appeared as a closed box within the Swedish political discourse on Sami issues.

In narrative theory, I believe I have found one such leverage tool. Part of the advantage of this method is that it helps a reader to ask and critically examine what is excluded from descriptions of reality (narratives) instead of looking only at what is included. That is a key difference, as I see it, between what I try to do with narrative theory and what is commonly done in discourse analysis more broadly. It is also a method which is easier to apply to larger sets of text and full arguments, rather than to the meaning of individual words or short sentences, to examine how meaning changes over time and in different contexts. It is far from a finished, complete methodology, but it is a start—at least for my own thinking and writing.

My method demands an understanding of counter narratives, and that one is flexible enough to question what is taken for granted and objective in a discourse. My understanding of counter narratives is theoretical. It comes from friends and literature, not from my own personal history. With personal experiences of having lived through, and still being threatened by, colonial practices and racist attitudes, even greater credibility and quality could most likely be lent to academic works applying this or similar methods.

Had I not, by chance, come into close contact with counter narratives half a decade ago, I would most certainly still subscribe to a masterplot which diminishes Sami culture, glorifies colonial industries and portrays the perpetrator/enabler as wise, righteous and fair. Because I heard counter narratives, met and befriended people who lived with the heritage of colonialism, I changed my perspective. My 'world' changed. I am therefore an example of the importance of counter narratives, of the telling of Sami narratives and world views. I cannot speak or do research from the perspective of the colonised, but I can speak and do research from the perspective of one who has lived most of his life benefiting from colonialism without being aware of it. I can try and combat that widespread unawareness, in academia and as an activist. That is what my contribution can and should be in revitalising Sami culture.

# References

Abbott, Porter H. 2008. *The Cambridge Introduction to Narrative*. Cambridge: Cambridge University Press.

Cronon, William. 1992. 'A place for stories: Nature, history, and narrative'. *The Journal of American History* 78(4): 1347–76. doi.org/10.2307/2079346

Erlandsson, Eskil. 2013. 'Interpellation 2012/13:488'. *Sveriges Riksdag*, 15 August. Online: www.riksdagen.se/sv/Debatter--beslut/Interpellations debatter1/Debatt/?did=H010488 (accessed 21 August 2018).

Hagström Yamamoto, Sara. 2010. *I gränslandet mellan svenskt och samiskt: identitetsdiskurser och förhistorien I Norrland från 1870-tal till 2000-tal* [In the borderland between what is Swedish and what is Saami: Discourses of identity and pre-history in Norrland from 1870 to 2000]. Uppsala: Uppsala Universitet, Institutionen för Arkeologi och Antik Historia.

Hedström, Jan-Olof. 2012. *Igenom gode Ordningar och flitigt uppseende: Bergsstaten 375 år* [Through good order and diligent attention: Bergsstaten 375 years]. Uppsala: Bergsstaten, Sveriges geologiska undersökning (SGU).

Jameson, Fredric. 1981. *The Political Unconscious: Narrative as a Socially Symbolic Act*. Ithaca and London: Cornell University Press.

Lahtinen, Sara. 2012. 'A valuable void: How nostalgic reminiscence and grief over a lost past constitutes part of cultural identity'. MA thesis, Stockholm University. Online: su.diva-portal.org/smash/record.jsf?pid=diva 2%3A584359&dswid=3340 (accessed 23 August 2018).

Larsson, Olle. 2013. 'Interpellation 2012/13:488'. *Sveriges Riksdag*, 15 August. Online: www.riksdagen.se/sv/Debatter--beslut/Interpellationsdebatter1/Debatt/?did=H010488 (accessed 7 September 2018).

Lundmark, Lennart. 2008. *Stulet land: Svensk makt på samisk mark* [Stolen land: Swedish power in Saami land]. Stockholm: Ordfront.

McLeod, John. 2000. *Beginning Postcolonialism*. Manchester: Manchester University Press.

Nylund Watz, Ingela. 2014. 'Betänkande 2013/14:NU14'. *Sveriges Riksdag*, 19 March. Online: www.riksdagen.se/sv/Debatter--beslut/Debatter-och-beslut-om-forslag/Arendedebatter/?did=H101NU14 (accessed 22 August 2018).

Persson, Kent. 2014. First speech in *Debatt och beslut: Mineralpolitiska frågor*, 19 March.

Regan, Paulette. 2010. *Unsettling the Settler Within: Indian Residential Schools, Truth Telling, and Reconciliation in Canada*. Vancouver: University of British Columbia Press.

Reindeer Herding Act, 1886, Svensk författnings samling [Swedish Code of Statutes], SFS 1886: 38.

Reindeer Herding Act, 1971, Svensk författnings samling [Swedish Code of Statutes], SFS 1971: 437. Online: lagen.nu/1971:437 (accessed 11 September 2018).

Ricœur, Paul. 1983. *Time and Narrative*. Chicago: University of Chicago Press.

Ricœur, Paul. 1991. 'Life in quest of narrative'. In *On Paul Ricœur: Narrative and Interpretation*, edited by David Wood, 20–33. London: Routledge.

Ryd, Lilian and Tomas Cramér. 2012. *Tusen år i Lappmarken – Juridik, skatter, handel och storpolitik* [A thousand years in Lapland – law, taxes, trading and politics]. Skellefteå: Ord&visor förlag.

Sällström, Sven-Olof. 2012. 'Betänkande 2011/12:MJU13'. *Sveriges Riksdag*, 28 March. Online: www.riksdagen.se/sv/Debatter--beslut/Debatter-och-beslut-om-forslag/Arendedebatter/?did=GZ01MJU13 (accessed 21 August 2018).

Skånberg, Tuve. 2012. 'Betänkande 2011/12:KU17'. *Sveriges Riksdag*, 23 May. Online: www.riksdagen.se/sv/Debatter--beslut/Debatter-och-beslut-om-forslag/Arendedebatter/?did=GZ01KU17 (accessed 21 August 2018).

Smith, Linda Tuhiwai. 1999. *Decolonizing Methodologies: Research and Indigenous Peoples*. London: Zed Books.

Sörlin, Sverker. 1988. *Framtidslandet: debatten om Norrland och naturresurserna under det industriella genombrottet* [The land of the future: The debate about Northern Sweden and its resources through the industrial era]. Stockholm: Carlssons.

Thiong'o, Ngũgĩ wa. 1986. *Decolonising the Mind: The Politics of Language in African Literature*. Nairobi: East African Educational Publishers.

Tobias, Ronald B. n.d. *20 Master Plots and How to Build Them*. Online: www.writersdigest.com/wp-content/uploads/Master-Plots-Exclusive.pdf (accessed 21 August 2018).

# 2

# Cikornay National Trust: Emancipation of Our Ainu land from Colonial Land Use and for the Enjoyment of Ainu Culture

Kouichi Kaizawa (translated by Masumi Tanaka)

Nowadays, it seems many people are trapped in the misperception that the way to conserve forests is just to plant seedlings. But, in truth, this is not the way. I recognise that all plants grow in the most suitable place by themselves. It would be best to just let the forest be. So, why do we do planting in our forest? Planting seedlings receives a lot of attention and is seen by society as symbolic of our efforts to revitalise forest. Through Cikornay's activity, society should be able to recognise the historical facts of the colonisation of our Ainu land, as well as our hope and practice of maintaining our Ainu culture based on a balanced human–nature relationship into the future.

Figure 1. Kouichi Kaizawa at his home, Nibutani, Hokkaidō.
Source. Photographed by Miwako Kaizawa, 23 July 2013.

The name 'Cikornay' means 'our river' in Ainu language. When we asked the late Dr Shigeru Kayano, who devoted his life to preserving Ainu language and culture, to give a name to our organisation, he named it based on the Ainu way of thinking—that forests are always tied to rivers. Shigeru and I were the two plaintiffs for the Nibutani Dam trial, which defined the illegality of the dam and was the first official sentence to clarify the indigeneity of the Ainu. Cikornay was started in 1995, just two years before the Nibutani court decision was announced. I consider these two actions as parts of one effort to revitalise Ainu culture—opposing the Nibutani Dam construction on one hand, and conserving forest on the other.

When the Nibutani Dam construction plan was announced by the then Ministry of Construction in the 1980s, my father, Tadashi Kaizawa, and Shigeru were the only two locals who opposed the plan with legal action. When my father and Shigeru were in the legal process of opposing the dam, my father was hoping that the Japanese Government would finally listen to our Ainu voice and allow us to claim our Ainu rights. He had been taking an active political role in the then Hokkaidō Ainu Association for a long time. One day, he asked me to succeed him in opposing the dam, in case he died before the case was settled. He had never requested anything of me before that. When my father passed away in 1991, I succeeded him in the struggle, and in 1993, Shigeru and I filed the case in court.

Cikornay's forest is located in the Nibutani community in Biratori Town of Hokkaidō, where the majority of people are Ainu. Nibutani has been my family's home place for generations. My main occupation has been farming, while also doing many other kinds of work. In the past, Ainu people were basically hunters and gathers. In the case of the Biratori area, it seems that some millet and vegetables were also grown, even before colonial policies began to coerce the Ainu into doing modern farming. At the beginning phase of the Cikornay National Trust, Cikornay's land in Nibutani was bald, with almost no trees, due to modern industrial forestry, which had operated there since after colonial imperial Japan let the big company Mitsui & Co., Ltd exploit the local forest. When Dr David Suzuki came to Cikornay's land, he said that it looked just like a war zone.

Now, the Cikornay National Trust has registered 28 hectares in Nibutani as our land (Figure 2). In addition, in January 2015, we finished registering 2.3 hectares of donated land in Furano, around 150 kilometres from Nibutani. During the first year of Chikornay's operations in 2001, 7,500 seedlings were planted by students and volunteers. Recently, we have changed the main agenda from expanding the land by purchasing (though we still receive ceded lands) to focusing on growing, planting and caring for the seedlings of local tree species which are intensively and regularly used in the Ainu way life.

Figure 2. Cikornay National Trust's activity – planting local tree species in Nibutani.

Source. Photographed by Akemi Ooae, Nibutani, Hokkaidō, 4 May 2018.

We are especially trying hard to produce elm tree seedlings. Elm is used for making the traditional Ainu textile called *attus*. In Nibutani and its surroundings, only a small number of elms are old enough to provide material for weaving. We started to grow elm trees from seeds in 2001, and finally we succeeded in growing elm seedlings after six years. However, although we have kept planting elm seedlings, almost none of them have survived so far. As one misfortune followed another, Ezo deer, which are overpopulated in Hokkaidō and which like to eat elm trees, have provided the biggest pressure on elm trees in my home area.

Cikornay is a registered nonprofit organisation under the law. It is required to have an annual general meeting, and thus we set the day of planting and the annual general meeting in early May. We schedule a two-day program. On the first day, we plant seedlings on Cikornay's lands, have the annual meeting, and also hold a get-together party at our log house. On the second day, we enjoy picking local edible plants on my family's land, while I teach about local plants and animals, and how we humans should behave in relationship to them. For example, I teach that we have to leave some of the plants at one spot, which plants are edible or poisonous, their Ainu names with meanings and related stories, and so on.

All species, including human beings, live together on the Earth. When we Ainu go to the forest, we send a prayer to tell the land that we are sorry for the disturbances caused by us taking the animals and/or plants that we need. We also apologise and ask forgiveness for taking the life from those creatures. By listening to the local Ainu Elders' experiences, I have come to understand that, traditionally, the Ainu have tried to become good friends with all beings in nature. Based on this idea, we Chikornay members try to nurture and maintain our forest. The Chikornay National Trust's future plan is to make its forest become a place where all coming to Cikornay can experience, practice and enjoy Ainu culture. For example, we could pave a footpath, set plates on each tree to show the trees' Ainu names, their meaning, and how they are used in the Ainu context, and so forth.

If we think of Ainu language revitalisation, it would be necessary to establish an Ainu territory in which the Ainu language is officially used. In 2007, the Japanese Government became a signatory to the UN Declaration on the Rights of Indigenous Peoples, so Ainu policies should be implemented based on the declaration. I do recognise that it is possible to say all the land in Hokkaidō is Ainu territory, however, I have no intention of claiming Ainu land rights for all of Hokkaidō, because of the reality that many non-Ainu people are living in Hokkaidō, and the land area of Japan is so tiny. Instead of that, I hope for the establishment of Ainu self-government and an area where our Ainu cultural right is fully recognised and can be enjoyed by all. If this can be realised, our culture and language will survive, even if our territory exists inside Japanese territory.

The Japanese Government and even those in the world of Japanese academia have not yet understood well the results of Indigenous studies and Indigenous policies in the international arena in terms of Indigenous peoples' collective rights. We seem to be 50 years behind places such as the Nordic countries or Canada. In the past, the country of the Ainu existed at least on Hokkaidō Island, although it was not fitted into a modern nation-state system. Since 2009, the traditional Ainu dance has been on UNESCO's Representative List of the Intangible Cultural Heritage of Humanity. It was even listed as part of Japan's intangible cultural heritage in 1984. Ainu traditional dance is normally enjoyed by a group in a community. This shows one example of the collectiveness of Ainu people. Therefore, the Japanese Government should officially recognise the collectiveness of the Ainu as a people. In addition, Ainu culture and language should be in the Japanese school curriculum, since we Ainu people have Japanese citizenship and we have a right to enjoy our Ainu culture.

# 3

# 'He Might Come Back': Views on Sámi Cultural and Linguistic Revitalisation from Finland

Tero Mustonen

One of the Sámi traditional knowledge holders of his time, the late Jouni Antti Vuomajoki (1917–99) from the Deatnu River area in Utsjoki, Finland, was walking in the forest close to his home community.

He saw a stone object resembling, and most likely it was, an ancient stone axe on the ground.

Upon returning home, he mentioned this discovery to his son, Niilo. Niilo suggested that they contact the authorities or the National Board of Antiquities to register this Stone Age archaeological find.

Jouni Antti refused.

Niilo asked, 'Why not?'

Jouni Antti replied, 'Because one day … he who left the axe there … one day he might come back looking for it at the spot where he left it'.[1]

---

[1] The author is grateful to Niilo Vuomajoki for passing on this oral history, and allowing it to be published here. The Vuomajoki family has reviewed the draft of the article and approved it.

The Sámi are constitutionally recognised Indigenous peoples in Finland. There are three Sámi ethnolinguistic groups in Finland, each with specific territorial engagements to their places—the North Sámi, numbering the most; the Inari Sámi, who only live in the territory of Finland; and the Skolt Sámi, who belong to the larger Eastern Sámi cultural sphere.

While Finland is, at the time of writing, in December 2014, contemplating the ratification of the International Labour Organization (ILO) 169 Convention on Indigenous rights to the lands and waters, there are many issues which are still in need of urgent solutions. The Snowchange Cooperative, a Finnish cultural and scientific organisation, has been working with Sámi communities for 15 years. The partnerships with the Sámi have contributed to the governmental Arctic Council assessments such as the Arctic Biodiversity Assessment and Arctic Climate Impact Assessment in addition to authoring several scientific papers and monographs about the situation in these communities. While these scientific reports have made the Sámi situation in Finland more visible, the most central challenges, which are at the same time the most urgent, remain. These challenges have to do with cultural and linguistic revitalisation.

The opening story of this article conveys part of the oral history of the Vuomajoki family, where the old man Jouni Antti sees a stone axe and leaves it to be. Younger generations challenge this, calling for a report to the authorities. Jouni Antti, being immersed in the Sámi tradition, decides otherwise. No matter how we interpret the decisions and choices of the elder Vuomajoki, we are left with a realisation that the Sámi have their own senses of the world, of time, place and events that can be challenging to understand from outside the culture.

However, these stories also convey a profound and sensitive engagement with the landscape and all of its elements—seen and the unseen—and more importantly, ways of being with it. In essence, they result from decisions flowing from and guided by Sámi tradition. Furthermore, the Sámi language, traditional mind, livelihoods, culture and life itself exist in a deep and holistic engagement with its places—each to their own respectively. Therefore, the revitalisation efforts need to reflect this realisation—a view the nation-state governments in their compartmentalised categories of decision-making often fail to understand.

Across the Finnish Sámi areas a successful model of linguistic revitalisation has been built on the Māori language nests. The idea behind this action is that children, from the earliest age possible, are fully immersed in their Indigenous languages as much as possible. Often parents, who are also (re)learning the Sámi language, join the nests while children are learning, to boost their own skills. A struggle that remains is that funds for these language nests are negotiated on a yearly basis and, every year, major cuts are proposed, leaving it to the Sámi Parliament to defend and repeatedly justify why the annual funds are needed.

The strategically most advanced and deepest-reaching effort underway in Finland in terms of cultural and linguistic revitalisation amongst the Eastern Sámi is the *Neiden/Näätämö River Collaborative Management Process* (Mustonen and Feodoroff 2014). It is located, with various manifestations, in the Neiden watershed. This project began as cooperation between the Skolt Sámi and other Eastern Sámi communities, the Sámi Council, Indigenous Peoples' Climate Change Assessment (IPCCA, at United Nations University - UNU) Traditional Knowledge Initiative, and the Saa'mi Nu'ett cultural organisation.

The project has been a part of the international IPCCA initiative that is being developed and coordinated by a Peru-based Indigenous nonprofit organisation, Asociación ANDES, and supported by UNU. By applying the IPCCA methodology of community-led self-reflection, evaluation and future visioning based on local world views and traditional knowledge, the Sevettijärvi Skolts developed a community-based climate change adaptation plan. Out of this process, a collective consensus has emerged that the climate change challenges faced by the reindeer, while significant, are manageable given the present-day nature of reindeer herding. Instead, the Skolt Sámi identified their customary salmon fishery, the other half of their traditional subsistence and cultural identity, as a much greater concern.

As a result, the Snowchange-Skolt partnership has chosen to focus their climate change adaptation efforts on enhancing the resilience of the Skolts' traditional salmon fishery along the Näätämö River. Scientists have also identified that the stocks of Atlantic salmon have diminished in the past 30 years, mostly due to fishing and human alterations in the habitats of the fish. Therefore the focus on the salmon is justified as concern is shared both in Indigenous societies and the scientific community. Now in its fifth year, the comanagement activities have spread to another Eastern

Sámi home river, the Ponoi, in the Murmansk region, Russia. A major cultural-linguistic digital database and maps have been developed with international partners across the world. Earlier in 2014, the Skolts released a short film about the all-encompassing efforts underway, as part of the process of registering the Skolt Archives into the UNESCO Memory of the World Register (SAKK Medialinja 2014). Materials from the river project have been actively used in the language nest work of the Skolts.

Most profoundly, the Sámi have invited others to join. The collaborative management plan and project along the Neiden River includes local knowledge of the Kven Finnish minority living on the Norwegian side of the river, as well as scientists, local Finnish peoples and authorities. Therefore, it has emerged as a potential vehicle for a peace process between the state and the Skolts, to address decades of a colonial rule, leaving them behind and exploring a future of joint management of the river, so that all cultures, all ecosystems, and the landscapes, can survive the twenty-first century. As recently as September 2014, the Skolts hosted a major international 'Festival of Northern Fishing Traditions' (Mustonen and Raygorodetsky 2014; Pecl et al. 2017), another success and a demonstration of how traditional culture, language and peoples can make a powerful comeback when all of these elements work together in the same direction.

When Jouni Antti Vuomajoki found the stone axe in the forest, it became a crucial *event* for him. This is a key concept in many Indigenous societies of the Eurasian North from the Sámi to the Kolyma River and the shores of Chukotka in northeast Siberia. These events, which are often documented, as 'Indigenous observations' should be read in the context of a many-layered spherical reality. An event, when it occurs, is often interpreted in the Indigenous culture against the immediate surroundings, but also against the mythical–spiritual deeper layers of Indigenous mind and memory. An event can be reflected on in many ways; it may contain links and repetitions to mythical times, which are passed down as oral narratives and histories. It may even exist simultaneously in myth-time and the present.

Listening to the voices of the Snowchange community work across Eurasia in 2014, from Swedish Sámi to the Skolts, to Murmansk, onwards to the Khanty and Mansi in Western Siberia, all the way to the Evenk, Yukaghir and Chukchi of Sakha-Yakutia, northeast Siberia, a common realisation is emerging—*now* is the event, now is the hour of change, now is the moment when the future of these societies, languages and cultures is decided.

If the Indigenous leaders across the world fail now in their efforts, and the nation-states and corporations infringing on their lands continue their relentless assault, we will witness a massive collapse of both natural and cultural diversity in the imminent future. Therefore, the time has come to act today, for the elders of tomorrow, to make sure these peoples, their lands and communities, and their distinct societies survive this century.

# References


Mustonen, Tero and Pauliina Feodoroff. 2014. 'Report on the Collaborative Management Workshops in Kola Peninsula, Russia and along the Näätämö River Catchment Area, Finland – Working Report from 2013–2014'. *Snowchange Report #3*. Online: www.snowchange.org/pages/wp-content/uploads/2014/05/Snowchange-Ponoi-and-Neiden-2013-Report.pdf (accessed 2 July 2018).

Mustonen, Tero and Gleb Raygorodetsky. 2014. 'Fishers of Eurasian Arctic come together in a time of war'. *Our World*, 10 July. Online: ourworld.unu.edu/en/fishers-of-eurasian-arctic-come-together-in-a-time-of-war (accessed 2 July 2018).

Pecl, Gretta, Miguel Aroújo, Julia Blanchard, Timothy C Bonebrake, I-Ching Chen, et al. 2017. 'Biodiversity redistribution under climate change: Impacts on ecosystems and human well-being'. *Science* 355(6332): eaai9214.

SAKK Medialinja. 2014. *The Skolt Sámi Archive*. Online: www.youtube.com/watch?v=qI2J-qQRUrs (accessed 2 July 2018).

Snowchange Cooperative. 2018. Online: www.snowchange.org (accessed 2 July 2018).

4

# Documenting Sami Cultural Landscapes

Ewa Ljungdahl

'Over there, it looks like it has been something, maybe a hut-foundation.' It is Sigrid who first responds that the vegetation within a defined area looks different from the surrounding area.

We are several people, walking in the mountains in order to document the Saami cultural landscape in a Sami village, in the south part of Sápmi. There are five of us: Sigrid, a woman who is about 70 years old; her daughter Inga; her grandchildren Ante and Silje; and I, an archaeologist (Figure 3). It is not the first time that Sigrid and I have documented Sami cultural heritage. We have spent several days in the mountains, both in rain and sunshine. Sigrid is well acquainted with the landscape, with hut-foundations and other important old sites. Her *aajja*—her grandfather—and other elderly relatives told her about their old places. But her grandfather did not tell her everything. Sigrid remembers a time when she was young and she and her grandfather were herding reindeer together with her father. They passed a collection of stones, like a cairn, next to the path, and Sigrid understood that the stone collection was something that people had built up, but she did not understand why. Could it be a grave? But both her father and grandfather were quiet and mumbled that people should not ask about everything. The best thing to do was to walk past and not worry so much. This approach has been common among old Sami.

Sami history is a fairly quiet history. We have no written sources of our own, and when the Sami are found in Swedish and Norwegian archives, it is mostly in connection with baptism, trials and paying taxes. The South Sami language was not written until around 1900, and therefore knowledge, stories, and history have mainly been disseminated orally, from one generation to the next, from father to daughter, in the same manner that Sigrid's father had told her. But such living memories rarely survive more than two or three generations. Therefore, Sami history is almost unknown. You can still see the old fireplaces from the huts and the sacrificial sites, but the names of the old places have usually been forgotten. For previous generations, this was no problem, because in old Sami tradition, buildings and other things that were no longer used would be returned to nature, like the abandoned hut whose birch bark and turf lay like a ring around the hut, slowly being handed back to Mother Earth. You should not interfere with the ancestors, they should be allowed to rest in peace. In this way, Indigenous peoples around the world manage their history, and for this reason, the traces from previous Sami settlement are weak and difficult to discover. Climate change now means that vegetation hides the traces of ancient settlements at a faster pace.

Today, there is a need for the Sami people to demonstrate their existence. There are many conflicting activities and parties who are interested in their landscape, for example mining, wind-power parks, large-scale tourism and forestry industries. Such activities can destroy the traces of the ancient Sami settlements forever.

There are different views among the Sami people. Some want to show their history, and are proud of restoring huts, building up old reindeer pens, and putting up information boards, while others feel strong aversion to marking ancient settlements as dots on a map, because this is contrary to the old ways of thinking, and is merely a concession to modern society. But, if the old places are not marked on a map there is nothing that actually says they exist, and they cannot be protected from exploitation. Sami ancient monuments such as hut foundations, bone deposits, and graves are protected by the Culture Heritage Act in Sweden, like all other ancient sites, but it is difficult to protect sites that are not marked on maps. There is generally a well-founded fear of leaving out the old traditions and knowledge. Many persons have had bad experiences of researchers and authorities digging up graves and other relics, collecting bones and drums, and taking them to museums far away, sometimes in completely different parts of the world.

Figure 3. Undertaking survey work. Ewa Ljungdahl is standing to the left. Sitting beside her is the archaeologist Bernth Ove Viklund. To the right of them are reindeer herders Lasse Kuhmunen and Magnus Kristoffersson.

Source. Photographed by Åsa Virdi Kroik, between Voernese and Vilhemina Södra Saami villages, June 2010. Used with permission.

Sigrid has given much thought as to how she should relate to her own history. She is proud of her history, but she feels ambivalent. While she is deeply involved in searching for and documenting her history, she is afraid that the same history will end up in the wrong hands. But she would like to bring her knowledge to her children and grandchildren. If she does not show them the important old places that her grandfather showed her, those places will soon be forgotten. Sigrid is the last person who knows where her family's hut sites and bone deposits are. When she is dead, her knowledge will also go away, and her grandchildren will never get to know who lived in the hut on the hill over there.

5

# Revival of Salmon Resources and Restoration of a Traditional Ritual of the Ainu, the Indigenous People of Japan

Yōsuke Kosaka

## How Ainu people have traditionally regarded salmon

Among the Ainu gods' tales compiled and translated into Japanese by the young Ainu woman, Yukie Chiri, two stories out of 13 were on the theme of salmon. Yukie died at the age of 19 in 1922; however, her work has been well-known in Japan through her beautiful poetic translations, such as the following: 'Silver droplets falling, falling all around, golden droplets falling, falling all around' (Chiri 1978: 11). One of the tales about salmon begins with a scene in which, 'A vicious man changed a clear stream into poisonous water by setting up walnut tree trunks in the river' (Chiri 1978: 135). As a result, the salmon could not come back to the headwaters. Having discovered such a malicious act, a son of Okikirmuy, a personal god of the Ainu, fights against the spiteful man and finally defeats him in order to recover the clean water and salmon. This tale, I think, reminds us how important it is to protect the river environment for the salmon.

The Ainu people regarded famine as being caused by the misconduct of humans. An Ainu oral tradition tells of the God Who Controls Hunting Lands being informed that a human village was suffering from famine. When the god inquired the reason from another god whose spirit possesses the salmon, and from yet another god whose spirit possesses the deer, the God of Salmon answered that humans had forgotten to use a particular wooden stick when killing the salmon, which allows their souls to return to the gods' world. Meanwhile, the God of Deer replied, 'Humans have forgotten to worship the soul of deer, so I stopped supplying them to the human land' (Nabesawa 1998: 83). Following the counsel of the God Who Controls Hunting Lands, humans resumed abiding by their traditional protocols for taking wildlife, and both gods came to forgive humans and supply salmon and deer again. We can conclude that the Ainu people have had their own traditional protocols in making use of natural resources and that these protocols played a role in the Ainu's sustainable maintenance of their surroundings.

In transcribing interviews with Ainu Elders, I often came across the caution, 'Don't collect wild plants exhaustively. You must preserve them for future generations and wild animals' (Kosaka 1994: 190). This way of thinking must come from the Ainu people's concept of not possessing natural resources exclusively. In this context, to catch all salmon for humans to breed artificially would be a perverted deed and one that their gods would not forgive.

## The dawn of the modern era and the prohibition against catching salmon in rivers

Among the four major islands comprising the Japanese Archipelago, Honshū, Kyūshū and Shikoku were territories of Japan during the feudal period. The ethnic Japanese who lived there were mainly engaged in agriculture, especially the cultivation of rice. On the other hand, Hokkaidō, together with the southern part of Sakhalin, and the Kuril Islands were the lands of the Ainu people, who supported themselves by hunting, fishing and gathering. Throughout the feudal period, the ethnic Japanese gradually came to exercise control over the Ainu through trade, and by exploiting the Ainu as labourers in fishery camps. Then, Japan's modern era started 150 years ago in 1868, with the Meiji Restoration.

The Meiji Government annexed Hokkaidō and designated Sapporo as the capital of Hokkaidō prefecture because the presence of a vast alluvial fan there made the site suitable for building a city. The government chose a wide hollow, blessed with a number of springs as the city centre, and placed the Hokkaidō Colonial Commission there. The area designated in this way as the downtown was the very place where the Ainu people had already formed four villages, where they lived subsisting off the salmon coming up the Kotoni River system, a tributary of the Ishikari River, in autumn.

In 1877, in order to make use of such rich fishery resources for industrialisation, the Hokkaidō Colonial Commission established a hatchery at the spring waters beside one of the Ainu villages, and introduced artificial salmon breeding there. Simultaneously, the commission prohibited the Ainu people from catching salmon in all tributaries of the Ishikari River.

In the process of making this decision, the head office of the commission in Sapporo resisted the strict regulation policy that the Tokyo office was willing to carry out. The Sapporo head office insisted, 'The Ainu of Chitose County [along the Chitose River, another tributary of the Ishikari River] live in a mountainous area, so it is difficult for them to subsist other than by fishing salmon' (Yamada 2011: 166). Instead of prohibition, the Sapporo office proposed an alternative plan to introduce a licence system and impose taxes on harvests.

However, the Tokyo office, having the real power, rejected this proposal, stating their position as follows,

> We expect artificial breeding will bring about economic benefit in the future. When you take total gains and losses into account, the damage to the minority can be ignored. You should not adhere to residents' welfare. They may be driven to be farmers (Yamada 2011: 168).

The prohibition also targeted Japanese settlers; however, Japanese fishermen usually caught salmon offshore or around the mouth of rivers. So, this policy in actuality affected only the Ainu.

Figure 4. Salmon at the headwaters of the Chitose River.
Source. Photographed by the author, 17 January 2017.

I can point out that this policy, especially the attitude of the Tokyo office, demonstrates the standpoint of colonialism of the Japanese Government, which prioritised industrialisation and the national project in Hokkaidō over the right of an Indigenous people to exist. Moreover, it cannot be overlooked that government officers had an assimilationist view that included converting hunter-gatherers to farmers. Later, the government expanded the prohibition of catching salmon to all rivers in Hokkaidō and this, combined with a sharp decrease in the deer population, caused widespread starvation amongst the Ainu people.

The inhabitants of the four Ainu villages in Sapporo, which had existed at the beginning of the Japanese modern era, dispersed before long and the villages disappeared in the early 1880s (Katō 2017: 56).

To replace the Ainu villages, the official residence of the Hokkaidō Governor, the Hokkaidō University campus and the Hokkaidō University Botanical Gardens were constructed on spring-water sites. As the development of the valley of the Kotoni River system as a residential area for homesteaders proceeded, the springs and rivers went dry.

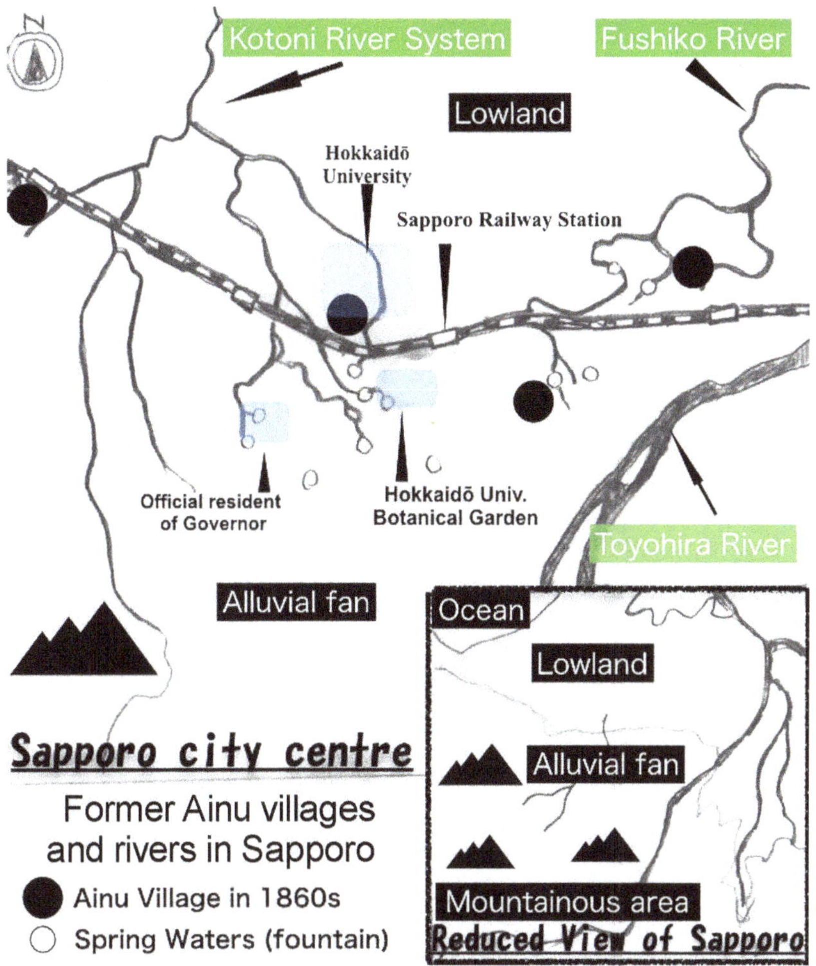


Map 1. Former Ainu villages and rivers in Sapporo.

Source. This map was made by the author based on information provided by Yoshio Katō.

# The period when Ainu 'poachers' were arrested

Amidst such severe living conditions, a number of Ainu men could not help but poach for salmon in the rivers.

Shigeru Kayano, who became the first member of Ainu origin of the House of Councillors, retraced the day in the 1930s when his father was arrested on a charge of poaching for salmon, in his book *Ainu no Ishibumi* (Monument of the Ainu) (1990):

> Before I enrolled in elementary school, a serious event happened to my family. One day, a policeman entered our house. Just after, the patrol officer asked my father, 'Seitarō, will you go out with me?' My father prostrated himself and replied, 'Yes, I will.' Though my father had lost one eye, I found tears flowing out of both his eyes. I was surprised to see tears pouring from the lost eye. My father was arrested on a charge of salmon theft. He caught salmon every night for my brothers, for old women in the neighbourhood, and for the Gods. However, it was prohibited to catch salmon (Kayano 1990: 74).

Kayano also represented the inner voice of the Ainu people with the following words:

> According to a document 120 years ago, the departure of a herd of deer looked as if an enormous brown carpet, covering a slope of a mountain, had moved. A run of salmon looked as if the surface of the river swelled. *Wajin* [ethnic Japanese], surged into Hokkaidō and pressed 'law' one-sidedly on us. Based on such 'law', the Ainu were arrested on charges of theft, when we cut a tree. We have also been arrested, when we catch salmon. My father was one such man (Kayano 1994: 111).

> It is our common understanding that we have neither sold nor rented *Ainu Mosir* [land] to the country of Japan (Kayano 1990: 79).

As the word '*Ainu*' has two meanings, one a self-designation and the other, 'humans', '*Ainu Mosir*' can be translated in two ways; one is 'the land of the Ainu people', indicating their settled areas in Hokkaidō, Sakhalin and the Kuril Islands. The other translation can be 'the land of Humans', an antonym to '*Kamuy Mosir*' (the land of the gods). In Kayano's context, it obviously means 'the land of the Ainu people'.

Kayano was indignant that the government and ethnic Japanese deprived them of their traditional food resource. And the law prohibiting them from catching salmon was unreasonable.

Even ethnic Japanese Government officials also held antipathy toward government policy. Kanzō Uchimura, an employee of the Hokkaidō Colonial Commission, insisted from a humanitarian perspective that the Ainu people should be treated more generously. He reported in an official document, 'If the government enhanced monitoring for poachers, this policy would cause starvation to death' (cited in Yamada 2011: 178).

His proposal was based on an on-the-spot investigation along the Chitose River in 1882 as an official of Sapporo prefecture, which succeeded the administration of the commission (that is, the Hokkaidō Colonial Commission was replaced by Sapporo prefecture). He suggested that what the government should do was first to protect the spawning grounds in the upper reaches of the Chitose River and then allow the Ainu people to catch salmon downstream. However, his superior did not accept his proposal. The government strengthened the monitoring of Ainu poachers and many of them were arrested. The arrest of Shigeru Kayano's father was one 'accomplishment' of such a regulation.

## Restoration of a ritual for salmon in 1982

As time went by, to prevent poaching, the places where salmon are collected for artificial breeding have been relocated from headwater areas to estuaries or streams far downriver. Under this situation, the government could neglect the productivity of the rivers as fisheries and change its rationale for river improvement to the prevention of floods and the supply of irrigation water. Rivers in Hokkaidō were straightened, embanked with concrete and stopped up by erosion-preventing dams. Rivers in urban areas, like the Toyohira River that flows through Sapporo, have become polluted by household drainage containing detergent. Living creatures in Hokkaidō's waterways have disappeared and 'the number of salmon caught in the Toyohira River decreased from 2600 in 1950 to six in 1953' (Yoshizaki 1982: 81–82).

In 1978, the Sapporo citizens' movement 'Come Back Salmon' appeared, combining activities for the improvement of the Toyohira River's environment with the release of salmon fry. They succeeded in finding the first adult salmon returning in 1981 and now the number of salmon coming back has increased to around 2,000 annually.

Figure 5. *Asircepnomi* (the ritual to receive the first salmon of the season) on the riverbanks of the Toyohira River, Sapporo. The leader of the prayer is Tatsujirō Kuzuno.

Source. Photographed by the author, 15 September 1993. Used with the permission of Tatsujirō Kuzuno.

In 1982, after a 100-year interval, the wood carver Shigeo Toyokawa, who was a descendant of one of the Sapporo Ainu villages that had disappeared in the 1880s, in conjunction with Shōji Yūki, an activist for the restitution of Ainu rights, restored the Ainu ritual, *Asircepnomi*, to receive the first salmon of the season on the riverbanks of the Toyohira River (Figure 5).

Toyokawa negotiated with the Hokkaidō prefecture government and succeeded in 1986 in being allowed to catch salmon in the river for this traditional ritual. Following Sapporo, this ritual was restored in Chitose, Asahikawa and Shiraoi, amongst other places, under the name of either *Asircepnomi* or *Kamuycepnomi*.

Though the right to catch salmon has been restricted to ritual events, I appreciate that the restoration of ritual is an advancement towards the restitution of the Indigenous people. I think the Ainu people can demand further Indigenous rights to catch salmon to maintain their lifestyle, in other words, demand for the right to exist, because their ancestors depended on salmon for their survival before the Japanese Government annexed Hokkaidō.

The decision delivered by the Sapporo District Court on the Nibutani Dam Case in 1997 gave support to arguments for the Indigenous right to harvest salmon. The verdict by the chief justice, which insisted that the Ainu people's culture must be respected, recognised the Ainu as an Indigenous people. The Law for the Promotion of Ainu Culture was also enacted in 1997; however, the object of the law was confined to only culture and language. In 2008, both Houses of the Diet adopted a resolution to request official recognition of the Ainu people as an Indigenous people. However, at present there is no obvious activity demanding further Ainu rights to catch salmon except for preliminary discussion in Citizens' Alliance for the Examination of Ainu Policy and the Monbetsu Ainu Association led by Satoshi Hatakeyama.

I deeply regret that the citizens' movement 'Come Back Salmon' did not have the vision to connect their activities with the revival of the Ainu culture concerning salmon. It is also regrettable for me that Shōji Yūki, who had been keen on restitution of the Ainu, died in 1983, the year following the first ritual on the Toyohira River. Shigeo Toyokawa died in 2015.

# References


Katō, Yoshio. 2017. *19 seiki Kōhan no Sapporo, Ishikari no Ainu Minzoku* [Ainu People in Sapporo and Ishikari in the Latter Part of the 19th Century]. Sapporo: Sapporodō Shoten.

Kayano, Shigeru. 1990. *Ainu no Ishibumi* [Monument of the Ainu]. Asahi Bunko, Tokyo: Asahi Shimbun Press.

Kayano, Shigeru. 1994. *Tsuma wa Karimono: Ainu Minzoku no Kokoro, Ima* [A Wife is a Borrowed Possession: Spirit of the Ainu People Today]. Sapporo: Hokkaidō Shimbun Press.

Kosaka, Yōsuke.1994. *Ainu o Ikiru, Bunka o Tsugu: Haha Kina-fuci to Musume Kyōko no Monogatari* [I Will Live as an Ainu to Hand Down Culture: The Story of Kina-fuci and her Daughter Kyōko]. Tokyo: Ōmura Shoten.

Nabesawa, Nepki. 1998. 'Kariba o Tsukasadoru Kami to Okikurmi' [The God Who Controls Hunting Lands and Okikurmi]. In *Kayano Shigeru no Shinwa Shūsei* Vol. 3 [A collection of Ainu myths by Shigeru Kayano], edited by Shigeru Kayano, 74–89: Tokyo: Heibonsha.

Strong, Sarah M. 2011. *Ainu Spirits Singing: The Living World of Chiri Yukie's Ainu Shin'yōshū*. Honolulu: University of Hawai'i Press.

Yamada, Shin'ichi. 2011. *Kindai Hokkaidō to Ainu Minzoku: Shuryō Kisei to Tochi Mondai* [Hokkaidō in the Modern Period and the Ainu People: Regulation of Hunting and the Land Problem]. Sapporo: Hokkaidō University Press.

Yoshizaki, Masakazu. 1982. *Sakeyo, Toyohiragawa o Nobore* [Salmon! Go up the Toyohira River!]. Tokyo: Sōshisha.

Yukie, Chiri. 1978. *Ainu Shin'yōshū* [Ainu Gods' Tales]. Iwanami Bunko, Tokyo: Iwanami Shoten.

# 6

# The Racing of Ainu Hearts: Our Wish for One Salmon River

Shizue Ukaji (translated by Miku Maeda)

My name is Shizue Ukaji.[1] I come from Saitama prefecture, and am 84 years old. I wish to rest peacefully in heaven as an Ainu, but I cannot put my mind at rest, because the situation surrounding Ainu people never gets better. I even think that it is worse than when I was born.

We had once traded across the northern sea, hunted deer in the meadows and hills of Ainu Mosir (the land of the Ainu), picked edible wild plants and captured salmon swimming upstream in the rivers. But in the Edo period (1603–1868), the shogunate system made its presence felt on Ainu Mosir and the Matsumae Domain was set up in its southern part, the Oshima Peninsula. Our ancestors were forced to stop trading over the seas and the area in which they could conduct business was limited. The Ainu economy was seized exclusively for the support of the Matsumae Domain.

A modern state was established in the Meiji period (1868–1912) but what they did in the first place was to rename the land of Yezo as 'Hokkaidō' and govern it as a territory of Japan. Only 1 per cent of Hokkaidō was Wajinchi (the land of Japanese) and rest was Ainu Mosir. In spite of that, the Japanese Government took the land of Yezo by force, asserted

---

1    Shizue Ukaji, 'The racing of Ainu hearts: Our wish for one salmon river', Speech prepared for the International Conference on Policy towards Indigenous Peoples: Lessons to be learned, Sapporo, 2–4 December, 2017.

a principle of terra nullius, and failed to seek the consent of the Ainu. Who can be ignorant of such injustice? Not even one piece of land has yet been given back to Ainu people. Injustice continues.

A scene from my childhood is printed in my memory. When my father got home from work in the mountains, the old Ainu men and women of our neighbourhood would gather at our house. My father treated his Utari, his friends, to liquor and food. Such feasts lasted for days. Men and ladies danced, and I felt their energy was powerful enough to break the floors. It was the same as young people these days being excited with rock music. I saw and found that they were full of joy in being Ainu.

I do not see such scenes anymore. We have lost our Indigenous power. Surely, our culture, such as songs, dances, embroidery and woodcarving are still with us thanks to our ancestors. Many Utari are learning embroidery, woodcarving and Ainu language. I also invented a technique of embroidery called *kofūe*, which creates pictures from cloth that depict Ainu ancient myths. I have had exhibitions throughout Japan and I have received prizes too. But there is no peace in my mind. My Ainu heart is not racing.

They danced by the fireside all night long, but now I see that the tide of hearty joy has gone from us. I feel loneliness in this situation where we cannot have our way of life and our culture, even if we can learn our culture itself. Ainu culture, such as embroidery, woodcarving, songs and dances, was once enmeshed in our life; it could not be separated from it. Our hearts are not racing for this lifeless culture.

Chiri Yukie, the author of *Ainu Shinyōshū* wrote the following:

> Getting over deep snow in the winter forest, in the face of a fit of shivering, hunting bears over mountain ranges / a green wave with cool breeze played over it at the summer ocean, with songs of dear white seagulls, catching fish on a leaf-like boat all day / under the peaceful sunlight in the flower-blossomed spring, a life with birds singing, eternally picking butterburs and wormwoods / an autumn day, a blowing windstorm over pampas grass with ears, no bonfire for salmon fishery, echoing sound of deer for friends in valley, a dream under the round moon (1978: 3).

It might sound extremely idealistic. This kind of life, integrated with nature, was already deep in the past even at the time of my parents. But my father still hunted in the mountains and captured fish, and harvested tangled seaweed from the sea. All of my family was engaged in collecting seaweed and we still had an Ainu life with nature.

Chiri Yukie also wrote the following:

> We have been defeated in the keen competition, but someday, some strong people will appear out of us and we will rise up to compete with the world, as it moves on and on (1978: 4).

It has been approximately a century since she wrote *Ainu Shinyōshū* in 1922. But I still wonder whether 'some strong people' have really appeared amongst us. Perhaps they have appeared once in a while, and then vanished straight away. We have been labelled as Japanese, discarded and sunken deep into their society. We are still struggling to rise to the surface.

Young Ainu Utari are working hard—some of them even have global horizons. However, the structure of Japanese society is just the way it was. Even after a century, we are still not able to see a world in which the injustice toward Ainu people has been rectified, making life as peaceful for Ainu people, as it is for the Japanese.

The Japanese Government eventually recognised the Ainu as the Indigenous people of Japan in 2008. They promised to create a comprehensive Indigenous policy toward Ainu people. But their current policy does not include Indigenous rights. The base of such rights includes rights related to land, resources, occupation and independence. The policy includes none of them. I find it hard to believe that the government takes our issues seriously.

I will not come close to being one of Chiri Yukie's 'strong people'. I am just one of the grass-roots Ainu. I am full of the feeling of wishing to pass a better situation on to young Utari in my remaining lifetime.

My idea is quite simple. I want the government to give us back one river in Hokkaidō. It is very clear that salmon fishing was our main occupation. *Asircepnomi*, the ceremony for welcoming new salmon, is still conducted throughout Hokkaidō every year. But, our right to fish salmon was taken away in the Meiji period. There is no choice but to join a Japanese fishermen's union if Ainu people want to fish for salmon now.

But if just one river of Hokkaidō was given back, we could engage in salmon fishing for and by Ainu people in an Ainu river.

It will not be easy, for sure. Questions such as who manages the river and how, how profits will be distributed, how the river and its resources will be shared and, apart from such economic issues, how we can do all this in an Ainu spirit need to be considered.

But we can start from the process of *ukoitaku* (negotiation, discussion), and address these issues one by one between Ainu. It is difficult for us now to sit down and discuss something. Mutual trust is crucial for communication—to speak your mind, to listen to others, and revise your opinion if necessary. Sadly, we have lost the sense of Utari along with the loss of our community, *kotan*. One salmon river is the first step to retrieving our lost circuit of communication.

We can learn by trial and error. If an attempt goes successfully, it can become a model, and can generate the next one. In this way, we can practise Indigenous Ainu rights step by step. We have to do it by ourselves, with difficulty, not by unilateral agreement. That is the only way to get back the power of Ainu. However, it needs an enormous effort to claim back one river of Hokkaidō since the Japanese Government has adopted the stance of not accepting Indigenous rights. We must explain the fairness of our rights not only to the government but also to the public, by going back to Ainu history. We have been the people who were made smaller—now we need a bigger voice. I would like to ask your help, my Indigenous brothers and sisters in the world. I would like to ask your help to make our voice into the voice of the world. One river can become a breakthrough.

Spring brings me a memory, though we are still in winter. It is a memory of *chitatap* made of the big-scaled redfin fish. *Chitatap* can be translated into English as 'to mince'. Big-scaled redfins used to come to irrigation channels with spawn inside their bodies in the warm spring. We caught them and minced them, and ate them with grated horseradish. It was so tasty. That is Ainu food culture, eating Mother Nature's flavour fresh, with as little processing as possible. Ainu life like that existed until half a century ago.

But schools of big-scaled redfins vanished when people started spraying pesticide on their rice fields. This disappearance of these fish from the irrigation channels due to the forces of modernisation seems to me to overlap with the disappearance of the Ainu's traditional occupation.

We Ainu people must engage in salmon fishing in our own river. Ainu hearts must race in the body of Ainu men. Mine also races as well, just thinking about it. Claiming one of our salmon rivers—it sounds like a small claim compared to having our Indigenous rights acknowledged. But for me, it is the big first step towards inverting national policies towards Ainu people.

I believe that the spirit of the Ainu will be gradually regenerated along with the revival of our life. This is the important point. We have the great legacy of Ainu Shinyō, the Ainu epics of the gods. They are full of Ainu thought and spirit. But now, they are still confined to the world of paper. They have to be brought back as living thought and spirit to our daily life. Ainu culture can finally thrive with that, and my heart will race again.

We Ainu wish for one salmon river. To make this small wish come true, I would like to ask your help, our Indigenous brothers and sisters from around the world. *Iyairaikere* (thank you).

## References

Ukaji, Shizue. 2017. 'The racing of Ainu hearts: Our wish for one salmon river'. Speech prepared for the International Conference on Policy towards Indigenous Peoples: Lessons to be Learned, Sapporo, 2–4 December.

Yukie, Chiri. 1978. *Ainu Shin'yōshū* [Ainu Gods' Tales]. Iwanami Bunko, Tokyo: Iwanami Shoten.

7

# Viessuoje Mujttuo: Saving an Indigenous Language through New Technology

Oscar Sedholm

The Ume Sami language is an Indigenous language that stretches from the Baltic Sea, across Sweden and Norway to the Norwegian Sea. Before colonisation it was one of several dominant languages spoken in northern Scandinavia. Due to colonisation efforts, nationalistic policies and racism, the language has now been decimated to roughly below 50 known native speakers.

Ume Sami has yet to be formally accepted as a 'proper' minority language in Sweden (instead being considered a dialect by some) and it lacks a formalised orthography—that is, formal rules of how to write and spell the language. The process of becoming accepted into both the general Sami community and the nations of Sweden and Norway has been a long process that has only recently started to yield gains.[1]

With fewer than 50 remaining speakers of the language, the situation is dire. Most of these speakers are Elders and fewer remain for each year that passes. The speakers are spread out over an area roughly the size of

---

1    Editors' note: The Ume Sami language was recognised in April 2016 by the Samiskt Parlamentariskt Råd (SPR), a council that consists of representatives from all three national Sami parliaments (Påve 2016).

mainland Britain. Most speakers do not meet other Ume Sami speakers more than once a week, which means that Ume Sami cannot effectively be used as their primary language.

Under these conditions it is tough to not only to organise the Ume Sami community, but also to have new pupils learn the language. Today there is no formal education option to educate Ume Sami teachers. There is also a lack of proper learning materials, with no textbooks, no dictionary and no media produced in Ume Sami. Currently, there are only two Ume Sami videos on the popular video platform YouTube: both are songs produced to teach Ume Sami words.

The Såhkie Umeå Sami Association (based in Umeå, Sweden) together with the Ume Sami language association Álgguogåhtie decided to start a cooperation to try and save the Ume Sami language from extinction. The Swedish state has a few initiatives to help preserve minority languages, but Sami language projects are at this time 'laughably underfinanced', to quote a minority coordinator that works with Ume Sami. To solve the aforementioned problems, the project Viessuoje Mujttuo (*Living Memory* in Ume Sami) was started. Utilising the free online learning platform Memrise, Viessuoje Mujttuo set a goal of gathering words and phrases to be put together into an interactive learning experience, available for free for everyone with an Internet connection. Memrise uses an easily worked system of lessons and memorisation that helps users both learn how to spell words as well as pronounce them (if the creator has added sound). Pictures and video footage can also be added to the lessons for extra flavour.

An initial beginner's lesson of 250 words was recorded and put together by the Såhkie Umeå Sami Association in the spring of 2014, and during that summer Viessuoje Mujttuo was organised by contacting both Álgguogåhtie and Memrise. Whilst the summer was spent applying for funds (Sweden has a rather advanced system of applying for municipal, regional and state funding for NGO and nonprofit projects, instead of charity fundraising), the project itself took flight in late autumn of 2014 with the goal of creating broader digital learning material and arranging a conference with international visitors from Memrise in late 2014.

A goal was set that the new lesson would include roughly 1,000 different words and phrases with the possibility of gradually adding more after the conference. Memrise sent us a general list (in English) of words that were to be used in their new video function for the platform, where short video clips were meant to enhance the learning experience by not only adding something more memorable to look at, but also showing a user of the language in his or her cultural setting. The idea behind these clips is that normal people would easily be able to record them on the fly through their smartphones, wherever they may find themselves, and then easily add them to the platform.

We suffered a number of setbacks due to bad communication when trying to work with the word list. Some of the people we recruited to work with the word list opted out of the project work without informing us, which meant that in the end the word list had to be hastily translated over the course of a week. Optimally, the list would have been gradually translated, grammatical explanations added to different sections, and unsuitable words and phrases replaced by something more useful to the Ume Sami community. The list was translated in the end, but with great stress put on the project group and our contacts.

Our deal with Memrise, beyond the opportunity to work on something very interesting together, would be to attain positive attention to our common work. We kept our operation on a nonprofit basis at all times, and all footage and learning materials produced during our project was to remain the property of the Sami community through our associations, with Creative Commons licence giving Memrise rights to use the material. After the word list had been completed, our visitors from Memrise arrived together with journalist Holly Young from *The Guardian*. We set out on a road trip across the Ume Sami area to both record words and phrases on the spot, as well as to give Holly Young the opportunity to learn about Ume Sami and Sami culture. In the end, we managed to meet around 10–15 Ume Sami speakers, and record a few of them.

Due to the time limit, it was soon obvious that we would not be able to produce the material right there and then. Instead, the week became more of an introduction to the project itself, where we learned more about what was needed to take the project further. Working relations were established between the partners of the project as well as the Ume Sami community. That week culminated in the conference itself, which gathered around 15–20 participants for a day to introduce the project, and realise the opportunities at hand. Afterwards, an article was published in *The Guardian*, which garnered a lot of attention around Christmas 2014 (Young 2014).

We are currently looking for new funds to continue the project, which will mean local recording out in the Ume Sami area for parts of 2015. Hopefully this will mean that both Swedish and English speakers will be able to learn some Ume Sami for free over the internet with sound, video and spelling, by the start of 2016.

## References

Påve, Marja. 2016. 'Umesamiskan godkänns som eget skriftspråk' [The Ume Saami language approved as an official written language]. *SVT Nyheter.* Online: www.svt.se/nyheter/lokalt/vasterbotten/umesamiskan-godkanns-som-eget-skriftsprak (accessed 28 June 2018).

Young, Holly. 2014. 'Reindeer herders, an app and the fight to save a language'. *The Guardian.* Online: www.theguardian.com/education/2014/dec/22/-sp-reindeer-herders-an-app-and-the-fight-to-save-a-language (accessed 28 June 2018).

# 8

# In Search of Virtual Learning Spaces for Sámi Languages

Hanna Outakoski

The sense of self as a meaningful member of a community, and a sense of connection to ancestral lands, cultural traditions, family and relatives are often the core elements of Indigenous meaning-making and identity building processes (Smith 2008; Kuokkanen 2009; McCarty, Nicholas and Wyman 2012). Those with close connections to the culture, and who live in the proximity to Indigenous cultural and linguistic centres are more likely to be able to convey cultural heritage to the next generation. Jin Sook Lee and Eva Oxelson (2006: 455) summarise the importance of knowing and being proficient in a heritage language by saying that for the speakers and learners,

> Losing proficiency in their heritage language is more than just a loss of a linguistic system; it is a separation from their roots, a denial of their ethnic identity, and a dismissal of their potential as a bilingual and bicultural member of society.

Although Lee and Oxelson refer to children and young learners, I believe this to be true of adult heritage language learners as well.

In Sápmi,[1] the land of the Sámi, physical distances between the speakers of a certain Sámi language or a dialect can be so huge that daily face-to-face meetings are often impossible to arrange. The Sámi who live in the periphery of Sápmi, that is, some distance away from the cultural centres, may also have a hard time finding adequate linguistic and cultural arenas that can support and strengthen their Indigenous identity and linguistic connection to the heritage language. The same is even more evident in the case of those Sámi who have, for different reasons, moved out of the traditional settlement areas of their families and kin. For such individuals, the personal connections and occasional visits to the home community may be the only tie to the place of origin. Creation of new local (and often urban) language arenas and the possibility of meeting and interacting with other speakers of Sámi (preferably with the right language or dialect) becomes very important, and sometimes the only way of nurturing Sámi identity. Sámi identity in the real world is thus closely tied to the links that individuals have to certain spaces, locations, skills, language and people.

For language maintenance and development to take place, proximity to other speakers is as important as the closeness to cultural arenas and the connection to the past. For the Sámi, a part of the present language maintenance struggle is related to the fact that fluent speakers of the language often live in 'language pockets' far from learners, in communities where the language is still used in many areas of private and official communication with others. It is among such speakers that I find the most prominent teachers of both language and traditional knowledge. So, not only is the Sámi population getting more scattered and influenced by increased mobility, but the concentration of the language speakers does not (necessarily) follow the trajectories of the learners. Many people must choose between staying in the language community and leaving in search of a living.

High speaker density in a community is positive for language maintenance (e.g. see Grenoble and Whaley 1998: 49 on the case of Māori), while low speaker density, especially in urban areas, tends to be an impeding factor for language maintenance and development. However, among

---

1    Sápmi reaches from the Kola Peninsula in Russia sweeping over the northern municipalities of Finland to the mountain lands of mid-Sweden and mid-Norway. Many Sámi live outside Sápmi, for example, in the Nordic capitals of Helsinki, Stockholm and Oslo. There are several linguistically distinguished Sámi languages of which nine still remain at the time of writing. Some of the smallest varieties are under a serious threat of disappearing and even the largest Sámi language, North Sámi, is estimated as having a maximum of 15,000 speakers left.

others, Claire Bernard et al. (2008) have in their mathematical models shown that the negative impact of low speaker density numbers on the maintenance of viability and resilience of endangered languages can be fought when focused educational and political efforts are directed to strengthening the endangered language. One such effort, as suggested by the author, is the development and advancement of distance education in Sámi languages that utilises all the different aspects, applications and teaching tools of present day online education.

Umeå University, as with many other institutions for higher education worldwide has, since the beginning of the twenty-first century, seen an increase in demand for online courses. As a consequence of the recognition of such a demand, the university has amended and adjusted a great amount of the course offerings to meet students' wishes to study online or at a distance. A mix of different flexible learning solutions is used by various departments to accommodate these new online courses. Sámi courses at Umeå University are no exception. However, while many other subjects can be studied online without great adjustments to the course setup, teaching languages (and especially beginner courses) comes with extra challenges. Simply sharing information and documents via a common learning platform and having a discussion or chat forum on the internet will not be enough when the students are expected to train their communicative skills and to engage in extensive meaning-making processes.

In search of a teaching model that can do all of the above, I have focused on virtual learning environments in which real-time interaction (voice, chat, movements, visual cues) between students and/or with the teacher are made possible. Online courses should, not simply be storage places of information, which students are expected to internalise. A good online language course should give students possibilities for communicative training, as do campus courses. This, in turn, means that one may have to compromise on the flexibility of the course when it comes to synchronicity (virtual meetings and co-working in a virtual environment require planning and predefined schedules) and the number of participants must be manageable. The two main arguments (flexibility and capacity) used for promoting online education in general are thus, in the view of the author, not going to be the strongest arguments for online language teaching in particular. In the case of Sámi online education, the main arguments in favour of online teaching models have to do with accessibility, that is, the fact that they make the education available for a group of learners that are geographically scattered and not in proximity to other heritage language learners. The second argument has to do with the benefits of the relative anonymity of online courses; learners of Sámi often carry with them an emotional load that has discouraged them from speaking and using the language in their private lives.

With the nature of the heterogeneous Sámi language community in mind, virtual learning environments[2] offer the possibility of bringing together learners and speakers of endangered languages that would not be likely to form learner groups otherwise. Further, virtual 3D environments (such as SecondLife or OpenSim) offer the possibility of adjusting and altering the teaching environment to resemble, in as much detail as possible, the settings for natural learning situations. This, in turn, gives the online Sámi language teacher the opportunity to teach speakers and learners of Sámi in a setting that can, in the best case, strengthen the ties to the ancestral place of origin and, at the same time, offer the learner a language learning experience that frees them from potential internal stigmas. Diving into the complexity of language, its syntax, semantics and pragmatic levels in a nontraditional learning environment (as opposed to a traditional class room environment) can also accommodate the needs of learners with different learning styles (for more on learning styles, see Kolb 1984; Dunn 2000).

Hanna Outakoski (2014) offers a detailed description of a pedagogical project that has had as its goal to create a teaching model or solution for online courses in Sámi languages. The challenge has been to find a way to replace, or at least to complement, physical face-to-face meetings by online teaching situations where the same communicative, linguistic and pragmatic learning goals can be met as in the traditional campus courses. The approach presented in Outakoski (2014) is flexible enough to accommodate different takes on online teaching, varying from fully fledged online scenarios to the use of online tools as complementary features to traditional campus courses. The project described in Outakoski (2014) is one of the core approaches to online language education behind the Euroversity Good Practice Framework. This framework was designed by Euroversity, a European Union networking project that aimed at supporting teachers from different disciplines who teach, or were planning to teach in, or with the help of, virtual worlds. Outakoski's approach recognises the

---

2    By virtual learning environments I mean the mix of different online applications, programs, learning platforms, social forums and other learning environments designed for education that for the most part happen online.

potential of 3D virtual environments as new Indigenous learning places, but also identifies challenges having to do with technical, financial and epistemological issues (discussed briefly in Motteram et al. 2014).

3D learning environments can thus aid the teaching of an Indigenous language in many different ways. A concrete example of such a bridging between the language and its learning environment is how we can aid understanding of space and location in a language that morphologically marks direction and spatiality in the language. In the virtual environment, the teacher and the student can interact and engage in meaning-making processes in a way that resembles the same processes in the real world. The spatiality expressed in the language (e.g. by different cases or adpositions) can be trained both in a traditional way working on paradigms and grammar exercises, and through interactive 3D world training where the word forms can be tied to actions, locations and movement. Therefore I argue that virtual environments have a tremendous potential to create a versatile tool kit for teaching an endangered language at a distance to students that otherwise lack access to important language domains and arenas.

# References


Bernard, Claire, Laetitia Chapel, Guillaume Deffuant, Sophie Martin and Maxi San Miguel. 2008. 'Maintaining viability and resilience of endangered languages'. Working paper. European project PATRES. Online: www.patres-project.eu/images/f/ff/viability_languages_v3.pdf (accessed 16 June 2018).

Denzin, Norman K. and Y.S. Lincoln (eds). 2008. *The Landscape of Qualitative Research*. Thousand Oaks, CA: Sage Publications Inc.

Dunn, Rita. 2000. 'Learning styles: Theory, research, and practice'. *Applied Educational Research Journal* 13(1): 3–22.

Euroversity Network. Online: www.euroversity.eu (accessed 19 June 2018).

Grenoble, Lenore A. and Lindsay J. Whaley (eds). 1998. *Endangered Languages: Language Loss and Community Response*. Cambridge: Cambridge University Press. doi.org/10.1017/CBO9781139166959

Grenoble, Lenore A. and Lindsay J. Whaley. 1998. 'Toward a typology of language endangerment'. In *Endangered Languages: Language Loss and Community Response*, edited by Lenore A. Grenoble and Lindsay J. Whaley, 22–54. Cambridge: Cambridge University Press. doi.org/10.1017/CBO978113 9166959.003

Jager, Sake, Linda Bradley, Estelle J Meima and Sylvie Thouësny (eds). 2014. *CALL Design: Principles and Practice*. Dublin: Research-publishing.net.

Jones, Mari C. and Sarah Ogilvie (eds). 2014. *Keeping Languages Alive: Documentation, Pedagogy and Revitalization*. Cambridge: Cambridge University Press.

Kolb, David A. 1984. *Experiential Learning: Experience as the Source of Learning and Development*. Englewood Cliffs, NJ: Prentice-Hall.

Kuokkanen, Rauna. 2009. *Boaris Dego Eana: Eamiálbmogiid Diehtu, Filosofiijat Ja Dutkan* [Old as the Earth: Indigenous Knowledge, Philosophies and Research]. Kárášjohka: ČálliidLágádus.

Lee, Jin Sook and Eva Oxelson. 2006. '"It's not my job": K–12 teacher attitudes toward students' heritage language maintenance'. *Bilingual Research Journal* 30(2) 453–77, doi.org/10.1080/15235882.2006.10162885

McCarty, Teresa L., Sheilah E. Nicholas and Leisy T. Wyman. 2012. 'Re-emplacing place in the "global here and now" – critical ethnographic case studies of Native American language planning and policy'. *International Multilingual Research Journal* 6(1): 50–63, doi.org/10.1080/19313152.201 2.639244

Motteram, Gary, Ton Koenraad, Hanna Outakoski, Kristi Jauregi, Judith Molka-Danielsen and Christel Schneider. 2014. 'The Euroversity Good Practice Framework (EGPF) and its application to minority languages and elder learners'. In *CALL Design: Principles and Practice*, edited by Sake Jager, Linda Bradley, Estelle J Meima and Sylvie Thouësny, 241–47. Dublin: Research-publishing.net, doi.org/10.14705/rpnet.2014.000225.

OpenSimulator. Online: opensimulator.org/wiki/Main_Page (accessed 19 June 2018).

Outakoski, Hanna. 2014. 'Teaching an endangered language in virtual reality'. In *Keeping Languages Alive: Documentation, Pedagogy and Revitalization*, edited by Mari C. Jones and Sarah Ogilvie, 128–39. Cambridge: Cambridge University Press.

Second Life: Your World, Your Imagination. Online: secondlife.com/ (accessed 28 June 2018).

Smith, Linda Tuhiwai. 2008. 'On tricky ground: researching the native in the age of uncertainty'. In *The Landscape of Qualitative Research*, edited by Norman K. Denzin and Y.S. Lincoln, 113–44. Thousand Oaks, CA: Sage Publications Inc.

# 9

## *Tjutju*

Coppélie Cocq

New technologies and digital practices for language acquisition are in a constant state of exploration and development, and these developments are particularly noticeable in many minority and Indigenous communities. Indigenous peoples around the world make use of digital media, and Sámi initiatives make a contribution to the search for new understandings of the internet as a locus for storytelling. Internet technologies do not only provide a wide range of tools for representing oral traditions, but also offer possible empowering strategies and triggers for revitalisation.

This case study focuses on *Tjutju* (Utbildningsradion 2011a), a born-digital multimedial narrative in Lule Sámi. This example illustrates how traditional storytelling emerges in new formats and in contemporary settings. The story of two children looking for their puppy (called *Tjutju*) provides one with the opportunity to travel in a world inhabited by mythological beings from the Sámi storytelling tradition. The website is produced by Driva Produktion and the Swedish Educational Broadcasting Company (Utbildningsradion) and presents the story as a fairy tale. A version in North Sámi, *Cugu*, was first produced in 2010 (Utbildningsradion 2010), and later translated into Lule Sámi to create this version. A South Sámi version, *Tjågkoe*, was published shortly thereafter (Utbildningsradion 2011b).

The story follows a linear structure through different chapters. The role of the storyteller is represented through writer and filmmaker John Erling Utsi, producer Birgitta Lindström and illustrator Maria Beskow. *Tjutju* includes interactive features that the user can choose to follow or skip over. Thus, it contains both narrative elements and interactive exercises that allow one to practise and memorise vocabulary, for instance about recipes for *gáhko* (bread), things to have in your rucksack, about animals, or about the weather. A Swedish translation is provided in a PDF file that can be accessed while navigating through the chapters.

Oral tradition is stressed as a point of reference (Sameradion 2010) in a similar manner as other instances of legends and tales on the internet (Cocq 2013). One narrative motif, for instance, concerns the invisible beings *gadniha*, and the website provides an interactive exercise where the user has to identify items that one should not accept from these beings if one does not want to become trapped in their world. This narrative detail makes a reference to the Sámi legends and traditional knowledge about how one should behave in a situation when encountering these beings.

Cultural knowledge is embedded in storytelling not only by its reference to traditions, but also through a grammar of symbols. Paratextual features, such as visual and aural elements, contribute to establishing a relationship to other narratives. For instance, the use of principles of form from traditional Sámi design, the colours of the traditional costumes and the music (inspired by the *yoik*) create associations with Sámi identity.

*Tjutju* illustrates how the oral and the textual are embedded in the digital, but the written word is still the main means for introducing and framing these stories. The digital format is an additional means that combines audio-visual and interactive features with spoken and written words. Interactivity between the story, the storyteller and the audience is possible to a greater extent than a written and printed text. The participant can make choices and create their own relationship to the narratives. The readers and the audience are not viewed as passive recipients, but rather as participants.

*Tjutju* is one example of Sámi online productions, and one of the few in Lule Sámi. The Sámi have long been invisible minorities in their own countries, and new forms of literature and storytelling in digital media contribute to an increased circulation of information about Sámi traditions, culture and languages that become accessible to a broader audience.

A consequence of the spreading of knowledge, and one of the objectives of the producers of Sámi media, is the affirmation and consolidation of a Sámi identity. A recent report about the situation of the Sámi people underscores the importance of promoting minority languages and of the close relationship between language and identity (Anaya 2011). Different media have a central role in the promotion of languages, and their impact on and significance for the dissemination of words and pedagogical communication is acknowledged. Media are also significant in the preservation and vitality of these languages because they constitute arenas for creativity and renewal. For instance, terminology related to contemporary topics or technology can be shaped and spread through the internet. But in terms of standardisation and modernisation of language, the use of new media for storytelling deserves critical investigation. There are several Sámi languages, and the processes of revitalisation in relation to the redefinition of the Sámi identities need to be taken into account. Even though productions in the Lule Sámi and South Sámi languages have increased to some extent over the past decade, they are still greatly outnumbered by productions in North Sámi. As for the diversity of Sámi languages, North Sámi has become a synonym for Sámi, and other minor Sámi languages remain disregarded. Moreover, the dialectal variations within a specific Sámi language run the risk of being overlooked due to the implicit standardisation of language caused by the centralisation of media production.

Adaptations of storytelling also imply a risk of losing the variety that exists within a strong storytelling tradition. The communicative dimension of storytelling appears secondary in contemporary examples, and it is the entertainment dimension—which has traditionally been only a rhetorical means—that is now the primary focus. In former times, storytelling as a social practice was central in the transmission of social norms and codes within the community. Narratives did not function only to entertain, they also played important roles in education and socialisation. The transcoding that takes place when taking into account a new audience, new technologies, and new premises for consumption patterns affects the form and contents of narratives in many ways.

Although the internet serves as a place for creation and as a meeting place, processes of revitalisation cannot be studied solely online. They are initiated and put into practice offline, and they are triggered by people and are related to many arenas of life. There is a strong connection between what happens online and offline. The internet and digital practices give indications about efforts that should be studied in relation to offline activity in order to further evaluate the effects of digital media on the ongoing processes of cultural and linguistic revitalisation.

# References

Anaya, James. 2011. *Report of the Special Rapporteur on the Rights of Indigenous Peoples. Addendum. The Situation of the Sami people in the Sápmi region of Norway, Sweden and Finland*, 18th session, UN Doc A/HRC/18/35/Add.2. (6 June 2011). Online: www.ohchr.org/Documents/Issues/IPeoples/SR/A-HRC-18-35-Add2_en.pdf (accessed 11 July 2018).

Cocq, Coppélie. 2013. 'From the *Árran* to the internet: Sami storytelling in digital environments'. *Oral Tradition* 28(1): 125–42. Online: journal.oraltradition. org/issues/28i/cocq (accessed 16 June 2018).

Sameradion. 2010. 'Cugu, ny barnradio' [Cugu – a new children's radio program]. *Sameradion & SVT Sápmi*, 12 January. Online: sverigesradio.se/sida/artikel. aspx?programid=2327&artikel=3365060 (accessed 7 December 2014).

Utbildningsradion. 2010. *Cugu*. Online: www.gulldalit.se/cugu (accessed 9 July 2018).

Utbildningsradion. 2011a. *Tjutju*. Online: www.gulldalit.se/tjutju (accessed 9 July 2018).

Utbildningsradion. 2011b. *Tjågkoe*. Online: www.gulldalit.se/tjakoe (accessed 9 July 2018).

# 10

# Establishment of the Ainu Indigenous People's Film Society

Chisato Abe

I established the Ainu Indigenous People's Film Society in October 2014. The Ainu Indigenous People's Film Society is a private group which works to contribute to the creation of a society in which everyone, no matter what their ethnicity, can live happily. This group also promotes awareness of Indigenous peoples—not only their history and culture, but also the problems that they face at present. The group's main activities are holding a monthly film meeting, and we are planning to run an annual film festival. We disseminate information on a website (Ainu senjuminzoku deneisha 2018). I would like to introduce this group in this article, and discuss how it was formed and how it works.

A member of the Sapporo City Council (at that time) tweeted in September of 2014,

> Ainu people as an ethnic group do not exist anymore. And if they did, they would be Ainu-ish Japanese, and should not be called 'Ainu people'.
> I cannot explain to tax-payers why they keep exercising rights and interests.

Such posts should be considered hate speech and hate crimes that conjure prejudice, discrimination and hatred against the Ainu, and are unacceptable. It was a shame that a public official made a comment like this. However, as an Ainu person, this led me to take action and take a step forward.

At that time, I was a second year student in the master's course at Hokkaidō University of Public Policy, studying the future of public policy for Indigenous peoples. Right after the tweet by the member of the council, a few NGOs and scholars from the ethnic majority spoke out against him and wrote articles in both local and national newspapers. I thought this movement by the majority group was very healthy; however, I was not completely satisfied with the self-advocacy movement of both old and young generations of the Ainu. This was a significant motivation for me to establish my group, the Ainu Indigenous People's Film Society.

I thought the first thing to do was to have a place in which people could gather and talk about what Indigenous peoples are. After going to friends and other people with expertise for advice, I decided to have a monthly 'movie meeting', which we named the Ainu Indigenous People's Film Fest (AIPFF). The reason why I chose movies as a keyword for our group was that my aim was to gather people with a variety of interests, not only those who have strong interests in ethnic minorities. Even though more and more Ainu people are learning and practising Ainu culture and are proud of it, not many Ainu people are interested in Indigenous peoples' rights or have knowledge of what 'Indigenous peoples' are (people's or peoples' - both are used in this chapter). I hoped that this meeting would help more people become familiar with Indigenous peoples, and I wanted to think with them about a vision of what a Hokkaidō where Indigenous peoples are living should be.

Most Japanese do not often focus on their or others' ethnicity in their daily lives. So, watching movies relating to 'Indigenous peoples', selected by participants at the meeting, provides a good opportunity to think about this issue. The consciousness of 'ethnicity' or 'peoples' has not been widespread in the Japanese public. For example, not all of those who have family records of Ainu ancestry claim it. They might feel inferiority or shame, but additionally, I can say they also may not understand the concept of 'ethnicity' and 'peoples'. Likewise, the ethnic majority also may not understand these concepts. There is a tendency for Japanese people to neglect to reflect on their negative history in order to move forward. I needed to advance my activities in consideration of this aspect of the nature of Japanese people.

Excluding a single small performance, there are three organisations which plan and provide Ainu events in Sapporo. The first one is the Foundation for Research and Promotion of Ainu Culture. This is a foundation established to promote Ainu culture, so the events often focus on this.

The second is the Center for Ainu and Indigenous Studies at Hokkaidō University. Events conducted by this group are mostly academic. The last one is the Sapporo Ainu Association. This group provides interactive participatory events, but the event venue is often in the suburbs because of the location of its office.

Our event would be able to bring new attention to the younger generation with movies and music—unconventional new tools. We held our first event, the 'Ainu Indigenous Film Festival', on 3 May 2015. The event had three parts: screening a film, discussion and a *tonkori* performance, an Ainu traditional musical instrument.

The film we screened was *The Sapphires*, about a female vocal group of Aboriginal Australians. Since this was the first event for us, I didn't want to make it too serious or to insist heavily on information about Indigenous peoples. Our target audience was the youth who have been less interested in Ainu or ethnic minorities. So, the film was a good choice, with tears and laughter describing human drama, rather than Indigenous peoples in a society.

The part we really could not miss was holding a discussion after the screening. We invited two young Ainu and one woman from an Indigenous Taiwanese tribe to speak. I didn't ask the two Ainu to wear our traditional clothing because I wanted to emphasise, and wanted the audience to realise, that the Ainu everywhere are leading an everyday westernised life, like other people are. The three guests talked about what being Indigenous means to them, and when they felt that they were Ainu/Indigenous Taiwanese. One of the panelists said, 'I am never without the feeling that I am the Ainu. Even when I am sleeping, eating, or drinking, I am Ainu'. I should say that this comment was a new one that gave us a chance to think about what 'ethnicity' is. This is exactly what I had hoped for.

The *tonkori* performance was the climax of this event, and we were very lucky to have the representative Ainu musician of Japan, OKI, perform. The success of this event relied heavily on his performance. We hoped for this to be an opportunity to show the Ainu living in the present, while cherishing their traditional culture.

The event was held in the middle of Sapporo, and I was moved by the fact that the word 'AINU' was shining forth from posters on the busy city streets. The event appeared in the newspaper twice and attracted about 80 people, aged from their late teens to their 40s, which exceeded the target number and age.

Everyone can participate in the events relating to the Ainu that are conducted by the three organisations, mentioned above, for free. So, I can say our event was attractive, even for its cost. Some of the audience answered in our questionnaire that this was the first time they had joined an event related to the Ainu. If it was by emphasising the casualness of the event that made it easier for people who had not cared about ethnicity, Indigenous peoples, or the Ainu before to join in, then there's nothing that could make me happier.

Recently, the Ainu Indigenous People's Film Society started a new 'roots-seeking' program, and began writing blog articles about it. As part of the program, I would go to a city hall with someone who is interested in checking their family background, and we would get a family register and search whether she/he had a family record of Ainu ancestry. I assume many people are not aware of their Ainu-ness or even their roots. The Japanese register system has some problems, which I won't go into here, so this project might be slightly controversial. However, the first person whom I searched with in June of 2015 had a good change of mind. In the end, it transpired that she didn't have any Ainu ancestry. Nevertheless, in the process of exploring her family history, and on finding out that her ancestors had come to Hokkaidō from Akita prefecture about just 70 years ago, she said, 'I am totally new to this island compared to the Ainu. I noticed that this island is the Ainu people's land and they have a right to it'. Whatever measures it takes, it is necessary to get people to think about ethnicity and the history of Ainu Mosir, Hokkaidō. Without understanding the background history, we cannot go forward. I intend to keep thinking about a vision of what a Hokkaidō, where Indigenous peoples are living, should be. Through the Ainu Indigenous People's Film Society, I will continue working until the day when my vision turns into reality.

# Reference

Ainu senjuminzoku deneisha. 2018. Online: ainuindigenouspeoplesfilmfest. blogspot.com/ (accessed 28 June 2018).

# 11

# The Sápmi Awards

Mattias Berglund

The Sápmi Awards is a competition that aims to highlight Sámi culture and traditions that enrich Sápmi. The importance and the unique values in Sámi culture and knowledge in their field are highlighted by the contestants within each category. Members of the public, together with the expert jury, choose the winners. By rewarding skilful Sámi representatives, we create strong role models and attractive ambassadors for Sámi culture. Competition categories vary from year to year, and are decided by the organisers, in consultation with the concept's owner.

The Sápmi Awards was arranged for the first time in 2012. It has since been held twice, in 2013 and 2014. Preparations begin six months before the event, even though the festival for the awards only takes two to three days.

The weekend is filled with seminars, festive activities, and finals, and in the evenings, Sámi artists enter the stage, while tasty food experiences are served. Approximately 1,000 people visit and take part in the evening events. Daytime events are free, so unlike the evening events, when tickets are sold, there is no exact figure regarding how many people visit these. Sámi language is, and should be, a natural part of the arrangements.

In fact, the Sámi language is not one single language – there are several varieties. Language is important both for Sámi identity and for Sámi culture overall. Unfortunately, the use of this language has decreased during the last century. According to the United Nations Educational, Scientific and Cultural Organization (UNESCO), all Sámi languages are classified as threatened. On the Swedish side of Sápmi the situation is critical for the Lule and South Sámi languages.

Therefore we have considered that the language in particular is important for Sápmi Awards. It is important that the languages are visible and in use. I think that not only I, but in fact everyone, has a responsibility to promote this. During the Sápmi Awards, we have had the ambition to make the Sámi language visible and to use it as much as possible. We have deliberately chosen to work with more than one variety. We have, for example:

- sent information to all contestants in several languages, including Swedish, Lule Sámi, North Sámi and English. This meant, for example, that 25 different versions of letters to the nominees, both those who progressed through the competition and those who did not, were sent;
- printed signs and information in Swedish and Sámi varieties (Figure 6);
- used multilingual hosts that speak and understand Swedish, Norwegian, Lule, North and South Sámi;
- allowed and encouraged competitors to submit their materials in their preferred language and variety;
- published news and Facebook posts in Swedish, English and Sámi;
- named all the competition categories in Swedish, English and Lule, North and South Sámi;
- produced several versions of the Sápmi Awards logo in Lule, North and South Sámi;
- encouraged the organisers to use the language in each competition area (Figure 7).

Figure 6. Multilingual signage at the Sápmi Awards.
Source. Photographed by author, Jokkmokk, 2014.

*Sápmi Awards lea bálkkašupmi ja doallu mii ávvuda sámi várrogas eallinoainnu. Sierra surggiin gudnejahttot njunnožat geat olgguldasas jurddašit ođđa vuogi mielde váikko doalahit árbevieru ja ollislaš gova. Sápmi Ášards lea doallu hutkkálaš ja bistevaš ovdáneamis gos don ja olles máilbmi lehpet mielde. Doallu lea geassemánu 12-14 b. 2014 Jåhkåmåhkes.*

Jåhkåmåhkke 2014-04-14

## Ollu lihkku!

**Don leat evttohuvvon dán jagi Sápmi Awardsii. Lea stuorra bálkkašupmi dutnje "Árbevirolaš duojis".**

Sápmi Awards galgá nammadit oassálasti guhte lea gait čeahpimus olles Sámis. Hávskes geassedoalus čalmmustahttá mearkkašumi ja erenoamáš árvvu maid visot doaimmalaččat sámi biepmuin, dujiin, dáidagiin ja maid boazodoalus addet.

Sápmi Awards lea jahkásaš doallu ja čađahuvvo dál goalmmát gearddi. Doallu boahtá ovttastit allaheakkalaš ávvudeami diehtojuohkimiin ja movttiidahttimiin. Go bálkkaša čeahpes sámi ovddasteddjiid de mii ráhkadit sihke buriid ovdagovaid ja bivnnuhis ambasadevrraid sámi kultuvrii ja daid sámi ealáhusaide.

Juryjoavku boahtá válljet **guhtta semifinalisttaid** daid evttohuvvon mat leat ovdanbukton webbasajis www.sapmiawards.se. Das šaddá maŋŋil jienasteapmi finálii. **Golbma finalisttat** válljejuvvojit vuođđuduvvon álbmoga jienaid vuođul ja juryjoavkku jienaid vuođul. Loahpalaš finála lea gehččiid ovddas Jåhkåmåhkes geassemánu 13-14 beaivvi 2014. Dat golbma loahpalaš finalistat iešguđet suorggis bovdehuvvojit Jåhkåmåhkkái loahpalaš finálagilvvuide ja árvvoštallamiidda.

**Vuoitosupmi vuoitái lea 100.000 ruota ruvnnu. Goappeš nuppit ožžot 10.000 ruota ruvnnu goappát!**

### Eavttut

Vai galgá vuoitit Sápmi Awards gáibiduvvo hutkkálašvuohta ja ođđa jurddašanvuogit mat heivehit ja lea gudni sámi árbevierus ja ollislašvuođas. Dasa lassin vuoiti ferte leat buoremus go gáibiduvvo danin go finála mearriduvvo Sápmi Awardsas. Nammadit vuoiti de gávdnojit sihke oppalaš ja erenoamáš gáibádusat.

Evttohasat galget:
- Bargat hutkkálaččat ja ođđa vuogi mielde ovttas ja gutniin sámi árbevieruide ja ollisvuhtii

| Postadress | Telefon | Webbsida | Organisationsnummer |
|---|---|---|---|
| 962 85 JOKKMOKK | 0971-170 00 vx | www.jokkmokk.se | 212000-2676 |
| Besöksadress | Telefax | E-post | Bankgiro |
| Västra Torggatan 11 | 0971-172 01 | kommun@jokkmokk.se | 625-7331 |

Figure 7. Letter of congratulations in North Sámi. It could also be sent in Lule Sámi.

Source. Used with the written permission of the Jokkmokk Municipality.

In addition to, we tried to make the language a natural part of the arrangements. Even when it came to the entertainment, we deliberately chose artists from different language areas. It was important to us that the Sámi language was heard and used in the awards. This is urgent for Sámi speakers, and also for those who have not yet learned their language. With the language being spoken in a natural way, we believe that it is easier for visitors to use the language.

Unfortunately, we have not reached all the ambitious goals that I had wished for. When working with language revitalisation, there is need for a clearly spoken plan, and adequate time, staff, and financial resources are necessary. We had a limited opportunity for this within the project. Even so, I believe we can be happy with the result. We have made the Sámi language visible, incorporated it naturally in the arrangements, and made it possible for the participants to choose their own language. For me, as a project manager, this is crucial.

# 12

# South Saami Children's Choir: A Successful Project, Despite the Obstacles

Åsa Virdi Kroik

Røyrvik is a community situated in the southern part of Saepmie, on the Norwegian side, in Nord-Trøndelag, with Jämtland District in Sweden to its east. The community is inhabited by approximately 500 persons, of which 10–20 per cent are believed to be Saami. From a South Saami perspective, this area is considered to be among the most culturally strong and significant areas, as many Saami have their origin here. Some important and powerful persons in South Saami history also have their origins here. One example of such a person was Ella Holm Bull (1929–2006), a preserver of the Saami language who produced a considerable amount of educational literature and music in South Saami, and was an initiator of, and for a couple of years the principal of, the Saami school Åarjel saemiej skuvle (Hermanstrand 2009: 345). The geographical area of the Røyrvik community was colonised rather late in Norweigan history, with the earliest settlers coming as late as 1806.

Colonisation, and damming and mining in the area from 1950–2000, dramatically changed the daily life of the reindeer-herding Saami people in the Røyrvik area. Reindeer herding became markedly disturbed, for instance, by the damming of Lake Namsvatn, where a whole village was drowned and had to be rebuilt on the new shore higher up (Jürgensen, et al. 2013: 93–94). Among the Saami many lakes are believed to be sacred, and this lake's name, Namsvatn, implies that this might be the case. 'Vatn' is 'water' in Swedish/Norwegian and 'nam' may refer to 'name' in Saami (*nomme* or *nïmme*), possibly associated with the idea that some things are too sacred to speak about or name (see Kroik 2005a). Place names surrounding the lake also indicate that it was sacred (Kroik 2005a). These things are rarely talked about in public among the Saami themselves and can only be studied with difficulty in contemporary South Saami society. Just as with many other Indigenous peoples, Saami are often described as a people of few words (Dahl 1940: 192; Jernsletten 2000: 7; Devy 2006: 55; Svestad 2013: 57). The Saami traditional reindeer-herding economy is vital in today's society and it is the largest local primary economy—an economic power that cannot be neglected by the community leaders.

Because of this and other factors, the conflicts between reindeer herders and settlers that increased during the 1980s were dealt with in a historic theatre project called Bru mellom kulturer [Bridges between cultures]. The project involved an impressive proportion of the total inhabitants of the Røyrvik community, and had a calming effect on the increasingly heated emotional climate in the community (Jürgensen, et al. 2013). There were moments of insight and regret during the work period, which were described by the participants as very powerful.

There have been, and still are, strong ties between the Saami on the Norwegian and Swedish sides. The national border was delineated in 1751 and cleaved a coherent traditional Saami area in two. However, it never completely divided the Saami people, who remained tied to each other by intermarriage, genealogy, culture, economy and a common history (Kroik 2007: 29–30). Still, the Saami have been culturally affected by the nation state and domination culture in each country, something that is obvious, for instance, by their first language, which is often, but not always, that of the national majority.

For three years, I lived and worked in Røyrvik. As a coordinator for local Saami language and culture, I had the challenge of recruiting participants to different language and cultural projects out of the small population of the Saami in the area.

Of all the education I have received in my life, there is one thing I learned that I've had no substantial use for at all, and that is my education in music. For more than two years I learned music theory, spending hours and hours practising scales and etudes on guitar and piano. To my mother's despair, who was convinced that I had no singing voice, I not only practised my singing exercises at home, but I even asked the preacher in my home village if I could sing in the chapel. Anyone who knows how socially unacceptable it is for a Saami in the Nordic countries to make such a request, and thereby state that you think you have a competence worth showing, will understand how motivated I was and how much I must have enjoyed singing and performing. Well, as I said, once my education in music was complete, I never used my skills again in my working life, apart from once turning a page for a pianist holding a concert, while I was working as a verger in a church, as I was the only person who could read notes apart from the pianist.

In my work in Røyrvik, my ambition was that every generation should somehow benefit from the project. Most of the Saami children went to the boarding school in a larger village, Snåsa, 140 kilometres from Røyrvik, a community that promotes itself as being the South Saami capital. These children came to Røyrvik only on weekends and holidays. Luckily for me, there was one Saami family with four girls permanently staying in Røyrvik. And even luckier was that the youngest twins in this family were the same age as my daughter, and the oldest of the four girls just loved singing and performing. When I contacted the family, the oldest girl immediately agreed to participate, singing with me as her accompanist in the chapel at the midsummer festival.

Ankarede is a very important place—particularly for the South Saami. Nobody lives there permanently, but in summertime a café opens there and some huts are rented to tourists. The area is divided in two, with a Saami side where traditional *gåetieh* (Saami buildings) are located and Scandinavian summer houses are raised on the other side for the non-Saami population. All of them are owned privately by individual families. The café is situated opposite the church close to the parking place. It is not known when the first chapel was raised, but the current chapel was built in 1895. The place has been a traditional meeting place at certain times of the year for the Saami reindeer herders, and the chapel was situated there so the Christian church could proselytise the Saami. Today, Saami from everywhere, as well as locals celebrate midsummer there. The oldest of the four sisters, Emma, and I performed in the chapel during the service. Emma gave a great performance, and it was very much appreciated to hear and see Ella Holm Bull's granddaughter singing songs in Saami that Ella had written.

I realised that even if Emma was the most experienced and extroverted, the other girls were also very motivated. So, I started practising with all of them together with my own daughter, Jenny, who was six years old. As the girls lived on my way between home and work, it was easy for me to stop, and have a session, or just talk over a cup of coffee. The girls got along really well and even if we did practise some singing there was a lot of pauses where the youngest girls played with the dog or just had fun. That was also a good time for me to practise with the two eldest girls.

The sessions weren't very well planned from my side, and the girls also had a lot of other things to do, so the two oldest girls gave up after some time. To my surprise, the twins wanted to continue. We gathered some other Saami children from the nearby villages and spent one day practising in the village of Jorm, on the Swedish side, at the local hotel. That day was very joyful, and the children not only played with and teased each other, but we actually did some singing and *joiking*—traditional Saami singing—as well. We also gave a general rehearsal concert for some of the guests. I was very happy that the couple who ran the place let us use their hotel. They also had horses, which were fun for us to meet in the pauses. This was a rehearsal, preparing us for a concert in a retirement home in Røyrvik. The funny thing was that when we came there and sang our songs, the girls' uncle was there, visiting an elderly person. I had, of course, not had time to advertise the concert (my planning skills were, as I said, somewhat insufficient) so it was only by luck that he was there and had the opportunity to listen to the performance. I think his surprise was a happy one. After performing, we felt invigorated, so we gave an improvised bonus concert at the community house (Figure 8).

Even though I loved working with the girls, there were many obstacles. Lack of time was one, and lack of my ability to plan was another. I constantly had a bad conscience for not working with the girls as much as they were worth. I had some complaints about the lack of discipline and, yes, I was not focusing at all on discipline, but on fun. I didn't care if the girls were playing and singing at the same time—I just wanted them to use Saami words and see the Saami language and *joik* as something positive. The performances were only organised to motivate them, and maybe to make other people happy as well. None of us asked to be recorded or broadcast on radio, but rumours spread about our work and resulted in the radio station contacting us and recording us anyway. I don't know if the children learned any Saami at all. Except for the first performance in Ankarede, we did not promote ourselves any more, but people asked us to come and perform. There was definitely a need that we met.

Figure 8. Maria Rustad (left) and Jenny Virdi Kroik wearing traditional South Saami clothes. Tin embroidery is used for decoration on the belt. They are playing outside after the concert.

Source. Photographed by Åsa Virdi Kroik, Röyrvik (Nord tröndelag, Norway), c. June 2010. Used with permission.

What made me most happy was when one of the twins said that before they started, they didn't know the Saami children from the other villages nearby, but after participating in our activities they all knew each other well. They now meet from time to time and they know that they are Saami. Hopefully, they also know some *joik* and songs. I think they do, because when they met in the school at Snåsa a few years later, they were able to perform a *joik* together without any preparation.

## References

Dahl, Georg. 1940. *Två år som Indian i Colombias Urskogar* [Two Years as an Indian in the Virgin Forests of Columbia]. Stockholm: Natur och Kultur.

Devy, Ganesh N. 2006. *A Nomad Called Thief: Reflections of Adivasi Silence.* New Delhi: Orient Blackswan.

Hermanstrand, Håkon. 2009. *Røyrvik – Samene i Østre Namdal* [Røyrvik – The Saami of East Namdal]. Røyrvik: Røyrvik kommune.

Jernsletten, Jorunn. 2000. *Dovlede Jirreden. Kontekstuell Verdimidling i et Sørsamisk Miljø* [With the Past Into the Future. Context-based Value Transmittance in a South Saami Environment]. Tromsø: Universitetet i Tromsø.

Johnsen, Tore and Line M. Skum (eds). 2013. *Erkjenne Fortid – Forme Framtid. Innspill til Krikelig Forsoningsarbeid i Sápmi* [Recognise the Past – Shape the Future]. Stamsund: Orkana forlag.

Jürgensen, Einmo, Ada Svestad, Anne-Bjørg Evensen and Fiskum Berit. 2013. 'Teater som Verktøy i en Forsonende Prosess - Røyrvik Kommune fra 2000 og in i Fremtiden' [Theatre as a Tool in the Process of Reconciliation – Røyrvik Municipality From the Year 2000 and Into the Future]. In *Erkjenne Fortid – Forme Framtid. Innspill til Krikelig Forsoningsarbeid i Sápmi* [Recognise the Past – Shape the Future], edited by Tore Johnsen and Line M. Skum, 93–107. Stamsund: Orkana forlag.

Kroik, Åsa V. 2005a. 'Namsvatn – Heligt Vatten Med Samiskt Namn' [Namsvatn – Sacred Water Named in Saami]. In *Där Renflocken Drar Förbi* [Where the Flock of Reindeer Passes], edited by Åsa V. Kroik, 66–73. Göteborg: Boska – Förningen för bevarande av samisk kultur och folkmedicin.

Kroik Åsa V. (ed.). 2005b. *Där Renflocken Drar Förbi* [Where the Flock of Reindeer Passes]. Göteborg: Boska – Förningen för bevarande av samisk kultur och folkmedicin.

Kroik, Åsa Virdi. 2007. *Hellre Mista Sitt Huvud än Lämna Sin Trumma* [Rather Lose Your Head Than Leave Your Drum]. Hönö : Boska – föreningen för bevarandet av samisk kultur och folkmedicin.

Svestad, Anne-Bjørn E. 2013. *Kulturminnebasert Verdiskaping – En Balansegang Mellom Ulike Intresser* [Valuemaking Based in Cultural Mememories – A Balance Between Differing Interests]. Trondheim: NTNU Norge teknisk-naturvitenskaplige universitet.

# Towards a Respectful Repatriation of Stolen Ainu Ancestral Remains

Yuji Shimizu (translated by Jeff Gayman)

## Introduction

It has been 85 years since Hokkaidō University began desecrating Ainu graves and removing the human remains of our revered ancestors. In 2012, several Ainu descendants decided to take action to achieve the repatriation of their ancestors' remains. Banding together under the slogan, 'Return the Ainu Remains to the Soil of the Ainu Kotan (village)', they brought a suit against Hokkaidō University (see Figure 9).

After a number of hearings, however, it had become plain from the advanced age of the plaintiffs that continuation of the litigation would be extremely difficult. Faced with the agonising decision of whether or not to proceed with the lawsuit, the lawyers for the plaintiffs, together with the citizens' support organisation, the Hokkaidō University Information Research Disclosure Group, eventually agreed to pursue other avenues. As a result, on 25 March 2016 an historic out-of-court settlement was reached between the plaintiffs and Hokkaidō University. With this, the repatriation of Ainu ancestral remains achieved its first legal victory.

Figure 9. Yuji Shimizu and other members of the Kotan Association in a demonstration demanding the return of ancestral remains.

Source. Photographed by freelance journalist Tsuyoshi Hirata, in front of the Sapporo District Court, 26 January 2018. Used with permission.

As a result of the settlement, the matter arose of who should be the recipient of the ancestral remains. In response, Ainu activists rapidly established the Kotan no Kai (Kotan Association). This association was made up of Ainu hailing from Hokkaidō's Hidaka District, and their task was to serve as the legal recipient organisation for the remains. However, this development in turn brought the members face-to-face with the historically unprecedented task of reinterment of the Ainu remains, which was completely uncharted territory for them. In order for the ancestors to return to the beloved soil of their village, the top priority became to find a suitably proper and dignified way of conducting the reception and reburial ceremonies. The members of the Kotan no Kai were thus faced with the daunting challenge of responding creatively, progressively and with appropriate caution.

# The historical background to the collection of Ainu human remains

Starting from the latter decades of the nineteenth century, European and North American scientific researchers from the disciplines of Comparative Anthropology and Physical Anthropology collected, weighed and measured thousands of skulls from ethnic groups around the globe. They were seeking to advance comparative research which would verify racial traits such as personality and intellectual ability, and thereby ultimately shed light on 'human evolution'. At this time, scholars' attention came to focus intensely on the Ainu, who, due to their physical resemblance to Caucasians, were considered to be a possible 'Racial Isolate of the Orient'.

Beginning in the mid-Meiji Era (1868–1908), Japanese researchers joined the bandwagon of those searching for human remains. The Japanese, furtively, and at times blatantly, desecrated Ainu graves and robbed the contents for the purpose of collecting skull specimens. From the 1930s onward, Hokkaidō Imperial University was responsible for collecting more than 1,000 Ainu individuals from over 50 locations in Hokkaidō and neighbouring islands. According to a recent official survey by the Japanese Ministry of Education and Culture, researchers from 12 universities throughout the nation of Japan collected and conducted research on the remains of 1,637 Ainu individuals. These remains are currently housed at their universities.

Incidentally, in what was likely a variation on such research, I have memories from childhood of having my skull measured for survey purposes, and my blood drawn for specimens. In this way, in the process of the modernisation of Japan, the Ainu were put into the position of being mere objects of research. I believe that, presently, the discipline of Cultural Anthropology continues to expand the scale of these one-sided survey and research activities.

# Approaching Hokkaidō University about initiating talks

On the morning of 17 February 2012, Ainu Elders Mr O. and Mrs J. visited the Administrative Headquarters of Hokkaidō University. They sought a personal or informal audience with the University President. However, not only were they denied seeing the head of the university, but they were further confronted unceremoniously outside the front door by burly security guards who the university had hired to prevent their entrance. Despite the fact that these two elderly Ainu had sent an advance letter requesting an interview, the barring of their entrance by physical force continued for five hours in the midst of biting cold and spitting snow. Ultimately, the two Elders' quest ended in the mere submission of another letter again requesting an interview.

Nonetheless, several more months passed with no response or answer. Ultimately, this meant that two Ainu descendants who had approached Hokkaidō University seeking consultation about the repatriation of their ancestors were met with nothing other than silence and a forceful rejection of their requests.

## Litigation towards repatriation

As a result of this unreasonable treatment, the two Ainu filed suit with the Sapporo District Court against Hokkaidō University for the repatriation of their ancestors. Starting from 2012, approximately 10 hearings were conducted, with no progress being made. Then, as the advanced age of the three plaintiffs was beginning to delay the court proceedings, they agreed, in response to urgings from the court, to shift to out-of-court talks, which continued for another twelve months.

On 25 March 2016, a historic and unprecedented out-of-court agreement to repatriate 12 Ainu individuals to their home community was reached, in opposition to all previous repatriation guidelines set out by either the Japanese State or Hokkaidō University. Until that time, under the 'Household System' prescribed by Japanese civil law, only direct descendants of the deceased had had the right to gain possession of the remains of their ancestors or serve as ritual successors. Indigenous policy guidelines likewise had required that all Ainu applying for repatriation must be direct descendants of the deceased. The Sapporo District Court, in issuing a recommendation that the out-of-court settlement be achieved through repatriation to a group which could, 'serve in the Kotan's place', honoured the Ainu tradition of all members comprising a *kotan* that qualified as the proper caretakers of the village's ancestors. The organisation born out of this series of events was the Kotan no Kai.

# Toward a dignified repatriation of Ainu ancestral remains

On 20 December 2015, Kotan no Kai was established as the recipient body for the Ainu ancestral remains. One crucial matter for our group at this juncture was to clarify the original context at stake behind the return of our ancestors. In other words, through discussing the issues and learning about and verifying the historical facts of the process leading up to the return of our forebears, we were able to come to a consensus amongst ourselves that possession in the first place by scholars and researchers of our ancestors' remains was nothing other than 'theft for the sake of gathering specimens'. What follows are the points we mutually agreed should serve as the principles guiding the activities of our group as the receiving organisation for the ancestral remains:

1. We will seek an earnest and ethically motivated apology from Hokkaidō University (the Japanese State) and scholars/researchers.
2. We, as Ainu, will receive the ancestors according to our own will, and will engage in all earnestness according to Ainu custom in ceremonies for the appeasement of their souls.
3. We will proactively disseminate information about our activities both domestically and internationally; the weighty historical significance of the repatriation mandates that this knowledge be shared.

The above are not only mere promises that we made amongst ourselves, but rather a commitment to broadcasting and seeking support for our philosophy both domestically and internationally.

Concretely speaking, we were able to achieve the repatriation of the remains of 12 individuals, which we welcomed back to the village over the course of three days of ceremonies. Day one included *Kamuynomi* (a prayer ceremony to the Kamuy, Ainu spirits) to honour the return of the ancestors to their home village, after their hurriedly having been transferred over several hours by car from the Hokkaidō University Ossuary to the Kineusu Cemetery in Urakawa Town. On day two the ceremony included *Kamuynomi* to appease the spirits of the ancestors for having suffered detainment for 85 years in an unhospitable environment. On day three we held the reburial (*Kamuynomi*) ceremony and *Icarpa* (ancestral remembrance ceremony) to pray that the souls of the ancestors might rest in eternal peace.

# In conclusion

The reburial of our ancestors' remains finished without undue occurrences. Questions had plagued our minds as to the proper way for Ainu to perform a 'reburial', without causing offence to the spirits of our ancestors. After all, it was the very first time in history that such a task had been performed. We proceeded with enactment of the rituals without ever having received any certain confirmation that what we planned to do was in no way offensive to our ancestors. Nonetheless, our efforts were constantly driven by a progressive, creative *esprit*, and the genius of innovation. And we made a point of always maintaining a calm and reverent attitude and proceeding with sanctity, despite our anxiety. Today, I know from the peace of my dreams since the reburial that we succeeded in faithfully carrying out our duty and achieving a noteworthy reburial of the ancestors' remains.

However, the majority of the 1,637 ancestors still remain housed at Hokkaidō University and 11 other universities. Already the process of reconciliation is further clouded by a project designed to transfer Ainu ancestral remains from these universities to a shared charnel facility to be constructed inside of the National AINU Museum and Park scheduled to open in Shiraoi in 2020. This agenda is political, which must be halted at all costs (see Figure 10).

Figure 10. Yuji Shimizu at a press conference in the Sapporo Bar Association Hall.

Source. Photographed by freelance journalist Tsuyoshi Hirata, 26 January 2018. Used with permission.

# Part Two: Practices of Efflorescence

# Introduction: Practices of Efflorescence

Gerald Roche

Whilst the broad, contextual developments discussed in Part One of this book have enabled and supported Indigenous efflorescence, it is important to acknowledge that what has actually brought it about are the tireless efforts of Indigenous peoples themselves. Indigenous efflorescence has been driven not only by structural change, but also by the hope, tenacity and effort of Indigenous people. The individuals bringing about Indigenous efflorescence come from all walks of life: nurses, farmers, teachers, artists, journalists, chefs, lawyers, activists, livestock herders, academics, politicians and others. What they all share is a common desire to see their languages and cultures flourish again, a conviction that this is possible, and a dedication to making it happen.

In the context of continuing structures of colonisation, and the continuing impacts of colonial trauma, it is important to acknowledge how much work goes in to doing even simple acts of Indigenous efflorescence. Indigenous scholars have begun giving theoretical attention to the embodied and quotidian politics of resurgence, of *being* Indigenous, of 'thinking, speaking and acting with the conscious intent of regenerating one's indigeneity' (Alfred and Corntassel 2005: 614). This is often based in an acknowledgement of the 'cunning' of liberal multiculturalism (Povinelli 2002) as a 'shape-shifting' form of colonialism that seeks, through practices of recognition, the continued subjugation of Indigenous peoples (Coulthard 2013). What we therefore see emerging are approaches centred in the *refusal* of the liberal multicultural state and its practices of recognition (Simpson 2014), and a commitment to personal sovereignty.

This requires continuous work by Indigenous people, to 'diagnose, interrogate and eviscerate the insidious nature of conquest, empire, and imperial thought in every aspect of our lives' (Simpson 2011: 18).

The psychologically invasive nature of colonisation, the ways in which it transforms the subjectivities of colonised peoples (Fanon 2004, 2008; Memmi 1990) make this a difficult task. It is therefore common to find numerous emotional and psychological tensions running through revitalisation work. A common experience is thus what Camilla Rindstedt and Karin Aronsson (2002) call the 'revitalization paradox'— the stated desire to work for the revitalisation of language and culture, but accompanied by a certain indecision or paralysis that makes action impossible. Nora Dauenhauer and Richard Dauenhauer (1998), in exploring language revitalisation, describe this as being the result of the 'mixed messages' that people receive—positive attitudes and ideologies about the language, on the one hand, but also deeply felt emotions of shame and anxiety about learning the language, as well as negative attitudes towards the language and its utility on the other. Rather than being failures to achieve 'ideological clarification' (Fishman 1991) about what the community *really* wants, the persistence of such tensions are more fruitfully viewed as the legacy of ongoing colonialism and expressions of intergenerational trauma.

All of the contributions in this section deal, in various ways, with the presence of ongoing colonialism and the ways it impacts on individual efforts to reclaim language, identity and culture, and to *be* Indigenous. We have organised contributions in this section according to two themes: subjectivities and quotidian practices. The first contribution on the theme of subjectivities, from Leena Huss and Sigrid Stånberg, looks at the strong affective contradictions present in language revitalisation: the ways in which an Indigenous language can be experienced simultaneously as a burden and a joy, for example. They see such tensions as the legacy of prior assimilationist policies and the way in which the stigmatisation of certain languages has been intergenerationally transmitted. Ryoko Tahara's contribution on 'Ainu Women in the Past and Now', meanwhile, reminds us that neither the impacts nor the legacy of colonialism are distributed evenly amongst all Indigenous people, even within the same population. She describes how Ainu women have suffered from 'double discrimination', oppressed both by Japanese colonialism and patriarchy, and how this makes their contemporary predicament radically different from that of Ainu men.

The next contribution on the theme of efflorescence subjectivities, by Nobuko Tsuda, begins with a startling account of the author trying to remove her body hair, as 'hairiness' was taken as a sign of being not only Ainu, but also primitive and backwards. From this beginning, in a shame-driven attempt at identity erasure, the author describes her journey to being the first Ainu woman to be awarded a PhD, with a study of Ainu traditional clothing. Following Tsuda's chapter, Mana Shinoda's contribution tells a similar story of erasure and pride, rejecting the assumption that 'real' Ainu no longer exist, that their culture lives only in the past, and that they have no place in the present, let alone the future. She chronicles a variety of ways in which Ainu culture is changing and developing.

The final two contributions on efflorescence subjectivities once again remind us of the diversity of experiences of Indigenous efflorescence, this time by looking across the lifespan. In 'A Quest for What We Ainu Are,' 83-year-old Shizue Ukaji looks back on her life of activism and forward towards the afterlife when she will join her elder sister, parents and ancestors. In the following contribution, we hear the youthful voice of a young Sami female, describing her trip to a mountaintop, as part of a project aiming to help young Sami reconnect to the land and the traditional knowledge associated with it. Whereas Shizue Ukaji's account is replete with memories from a long and eventful life, Jenny Virdi Kroik's story presents vibrant but fragmented memories of the mountaintop experience. Together, these two accounts encourage us to consider the experience of engaging in efflorescence over a life span, and what that might feel like.

The following set of contributions, on the theme of quotidian practices of efflorescence, demonstrate how even simple, 'banal' actions are saturated with the legacy of historical process, and conditioned by systems and structures of ongoing domination and manifestations of power asymmetries. Kanako Uzawa looks at the predicament of Ainu living in Tokyo, and the practices of gathering, sharing food, and making art that they employ to create a sense of community. In doing so, she calls for a rethinking of how indigeneity exists away from, but not disconnected from, the land, through 'everyday acts of resurgence'.

The next two contributions examine the intersection between Indigenous efflorescence and commerce, one with a brief look at Saami coffee culture, and the other describing a North American business that makes and sells traditional Sami dwellings. Chris Kolbu and Anne Wuolab's chapter on coffee serves as a reminder of the complex historical threads that run through something as simple as a cup of coffee, whilst the contribution by Chris Pesklo shows the intricate considerations that go into balancing economic success with efforts to curtail cultural appropriation.

Finally, a contribution from Saami dancer Nils-Jonas Persson discusses *sydisdans*—a new traditional dance in Sapmi that draws attention, once again, to the creative, generative nature of Indigenous efflorescence, and the complex links between past, present and future that this entails.

# References


Alfred, Taiaiake and Jeff Corntassel. 2005. 'Being Indigenous: Resurgences against contemporary colonialism'. *Government and Opposition* 40(4): 597–614. doi.org/10.1111/j.1477-7053.2005.00166.x

Coulthard, Glen. 2013. *Red Skins, White Masks: Rejecting the Colonial Politics of Recognition*. Minneapolis and London: University of Minnesota Press.

Dauenhauer, Nora Marks and Richard Dauenhauer. 1998. 'Technical, emotional, and ideological issues in reversing language shift: Examples from Southeast Alaska'. In *Endangered Languages: Language Loss and Community Response*, edited by Lenore Grenoble and Lindsay Whaley, 57–98. Cambridge: Cambridge University Press. doi.org/10.1017/CBO9781139166959.004

Fanon, Frantz (trans. Richard Philcox). 2004 [1963]. *The Wretched of the Earth*. New York: Grove Press.

Fanon, Frantz (trans. Richard Philcox). 2008 [1952]. *Black Skin, White Masks*. New York: Grove Press.

Fishman, Joshua. 1991. *Reversing Language Shift: Theoretical and Empirical Foundations of Assistance to Threatened Languages*. Clevedon: Multilingual Matters.

Memmi, Albert (trans. Howard Greenfeld). 1990 [1960]. *The Colonizer and the Colonized*. London: Earthscan Publications.

Povinelli, Elizabeth. 2002. *The Cunning of Recognition: Indigenous Alterities and the Making of Australian Multiculturalism*. Durham: Duke University Press. doi.org/10.1215/9780822383673

Rindstedt, Camilla and Karin Aronsson. 2002. 'Growing up monolingual in a bilingual community: The Quichua revitalization paradox'. *Language in Society* 31(5): 721–42. doi.org/10.1017/S0047404502315033

Simpson, Audra. 2014. *Mohawk Interruptus: Political Life Across the Borders of Settler States.* Durham and London: Duke University Press. doi.org/10.1215/9780822376781

Simpson, Leanne. 2011. *Dancing on Our Turtle's Back: Stories of Nishnaabeg Re-Creation, Resurgence and a New Emergence.* Winnipeg: Arbeiter Ring Publishing.

# 14

# The Yoke and the Candy Bowl: Beliefs and Emotions in South Sami Revitalisation

Leena Huss and Sigrid Stångberg

## Background

While Sweden has a rather long history of promoting language maintenance among immigrant populations, it was not until the year 2000 that a national minority and minority language policy was launched to protect minority languages and cultures that have a long historical presence in Sweden. The new policy was a result of the Swedish ratification the same year of two Council of Europe conventions: the European Charter for Regional or Minority Languages (ECRML) and the Framework Convention for the Protection of National Minorities (FCNM). According to this policy, the five national minority languages of Sweden—Meänkieli (formerly called Tornedalian Finnish), Romani, Sami, Sweden Finnish and Yiddish—were to be protected and promoted on societal as well as individual levels, and three of them—Meänkieli, Sami (including North, Lule and South Sami) and Sweden Finnish—had their own administrative areas designated, consisting of seven municipalities in the northernmost parts of Sweden. In these areas, their speakers had the right to communicate with municipal authorities in their own languages.

They also had the right to childcare and care of the elderly 'wholly or partly' in the minority language (Swedish Parliament SFS 1999:1175; SFS 1999:1176).

During the following years, evaluations and criticism on the part of the Council of Europe, minority organisations, and various Swedish authorities showed that the implementation of the national minority policy was seriously lacking, and in 2010, a reformed minority policy was launched (Proposition 2008/2009). This was the year when the first traditional South Sami municipalities were included in the Sami administrative area—a fact that altered the official status of South Sami considerably and gave new opportunities to the South Sami to learn, use and develop their language. A Sami Language Centre divided into two locations within the traditional South Sami area was established the same year. The main task of the Language Centre was to develop and spread innovative revitalisation methods not only for South Sami but for all three Sami languages in Sweden, and already after its first six years of existence it could be regarded as one of the most successful ways of counteracting language endangerment in the country (Huss 2017).

In the following, some findings from a sociolinguistic study concerning the role of the reformed minority policy in South Sami revitalisation are discussed. First, the aims and the material used in the study are described briefly, followed by a description of the site of the study and its special characteristics. After that, the study participants' perceptions of the role of the minority policy reform in Sami language revitalisation are taken up. Last, the presence and impact of thoughts and emotions concerning the ongoing revitalisation process is discussed, the question of ideological clarification is addressed and some suggestions are given to strengthen the ongoing revitalisation among the South Sami in Sweden.

## The study: Revitalisation against all odds?

The present paper discusses some of the findings from a recently finished study titled *Revitalization Against all Odds? South Sami in Sweden*.[1] The aim of the project was to study the situation of the South Sami language and culture before and after the year 2000, when the national minority policy

---

1    The project was financed by Riksbankens Jubileumsfond (The Swedish Foundation for Humanities and Social Sciences) 2009–13.

first came into force in Sweden, and to investigate whether the new policy, including the minority policy reform of 2010, has impacted on the situation of South Sami in terms of linguistic and cultural revitalisation.

From the beginning, the project strove not only to highlight and analyse statistical and other objective data, but also the subjective thoughts and feelings of people somehow involved in South Sami revitalisation. During 2010, interviews were done with South Sami families, cultural workers and representatives for South Sami organisations. In 2011, questionnaires were distributed and answered by over 60 teachers and parents of school children studying South Sami in the municipal schools in Vilhelmina and Storuman or attending the Sami school in Tärnaby, Storuman. Around 50 school children also answered a questionnaire the same year.

This chapter presents a discussion of the questionnaire and interview findings, looking at salient themes that emerged in this process, without focusing on the quantification of outcomes.[2] Because we do not analyse patterns by age and gender, further details of the speaker population are not provided or identified throughout the article. However, as the local context of language and history are pertinent to the study, we proceed with a description of these in the next section.

## Storuman and Vilhelmina, the sites of the present study

Two of the traditional South Sami municipalities added to the Sami administrative area in 2010 were Storuman and Vilhelmina. They are part of the southern Lappland county that is 250 kilometres in length and bordered by Norway in the west. There are around 6,000 inhabitants in Storuman and 7,000 in Vilhelmina, and approximately 10 per cent of them are of Sami origin.[3]

Reindeer herding is an important livelihood for those Sami who are members of the *samebyar* (economic reindeer-herding associations), but in Storuman there are also reindeer-herding Sami who are excluded from the local *sameby*. For them and for many other inhabitants, combinations

---

2    See Appendix 1 for a summary of the interview and questionnaire tools used in this study.

3    Personal communication with Sigrid Stångberg. The percentage of Sami is a rough estimation, as registers of ethnic and linguistic populations are officially forbidden in Sweden.

of livelihoods such as hunting, fishing, handicraft and small-scale farming are important. Especially in winter, tourism and other livelihoods connected to it provide work for many.

Both in Storuman and Vilhelmina, reindeer herding as well as other Sami livelihoods have been impacted on by former state measures, such as the relocation of people and water regulations. In the 1920s and 1930s, the state relocated reindeer herders from the northermost parts of Sweden to the southern part of the reindeer-herding area, and many of them landed in Storuman and Vilhelmina. In terms of language, this relocation resulted in all three Sami languages being spoken in the area. The reason given for the relocations was that the Norwegian and Finnish borders were closed for reindeer from Sweden, which led to a lack of grazing land in the North. In that context, the state categorised the Sami population in the South Sami area into two groups: those who were included as members in the officially recognised *sameby*, and those who were left outside. The latter was the case of the local South Sami in Storuman and Vilhelmina.

In the 1950s and 1960s, extensive hydro projects in Storuman and Vilhelmina led to the submersion of large areas of reindeer grazing lands and villages. Part of Storuman was heavily affected, as three villages were flooded and 250 Sami had to move elsewhere. Part of the local Sami history in the form of buildings, places of sacrifice, and artefacts were lost in the process.

Mining prospecting is another issue which has caused concern among the local Sami in Storuman and Vilhelmina. During the last decade, mining companies have shown increased interest in the area and an active resistance movement against mining has emerged among the Sami (Persson 2015).

The history of the Sami language in Storuman and Vilhelmina, as in all Sweden, includes a long period of forced assimilation policies, most efficiently carried out by schools, where the speaking of the Sami language was forbidden. This was also the case of the special Nomad Schools, boarding schools with a shortened education, established for the children of reindeer herders. Today, these schools are not boarding schools anymore and they are called Sami Schools. Nowadays, they are open to all Sami children, and one of their most important tasks is to teach the children Sami language and culture. The former Nomad School and present Sami School in Tärnaby, Storuman, is the only such school in the traditional

South Sami area in Sweden. Sigrid Stångberg, the second author of this chapter, was a pupil in the school when it still was a segregated Nomad School where the Sami language was forbidden (Stångberg 2015). Decades later, she was a teacher, and still later, the principal of the same school. She has been, and still is, a very central person in the South Sami revitalisation movement in the area. Over several years, she organised and ran joint language immersion camps for South Sami school children from Sweden and Norway that became very popular. She has also organised language immersion camps for adults, and, in 2014, she initiated a weekly drop-in language activity organised by the local Sami organisation in cooperation with the local Christian congregation and the Sami Language Centre. Since 2015, she also runs a small-scale individual South Sami language revitalisation project for adults, applying the Ulpan language learning method created in Israel.

## Strengthened legal minority rights and the South Sami revitalisation

One of the key questions in the present study was the possible impact of the national minority policy on South Sami revitalisation. The results show that the participants generally perceive the national minority policy (2000, reformed in 2010) as a guarantee for language maintenance without which the South Sami language would very soon have been lost. One parent writes that without the new policy, '[W]e would continue to be deprived of our Sami identity and culture' (female 3, Storuman, 2010). Another parent comments:

> The Sami have risen [in status] and they have been recognised as a people. I think [without the policy] we would have been assimilated into the majority population and there would only have been a few families left who would have had the strength to maintain the language (female 1, Storuman, 2010).

A third writes:

> Of course the languages would be more concealed [without policy]. It takes time for languages to be accepted by the 'greater society'. When the languages become part of everyday life also for 'non-Sami', the situation of the whole Sami people is strengthened! (male 3, Storuman, 2010).

Several participants mention that new financial resources and new possibilities to learn and use the Sami language have emerged, but many also comment on the lack of implementation of the minority policy.

Many respondents thus clearly see the minority policy as a prerequisite of revitalisation on the individual level. The very fact that there is a minority and minority language law which gives special rights to Sami speakers is felt to have given a new legitimacy to language revitalisation efforts. Parents and teachers appear conscious of their legal rights and in some cases are prepared to act when the authorities are not fulfilling their obligations. There are several examples from the Sami media of parents who protest against the municipality's failure to fulfil its obligation to provide Sami-medium preschool education. Other examples of initiatives during the past 10 years triggered by the minority policy reform are community-based, government-funded revitalisation projects among parent networks and adult Sami, some of which were presented above. The local revitalisation movement has been supported by the fact that one of the two offices of the Sami Language Centre, serving all Sami languages, was opened in Tärnaby, Storuman, in 2010. This has greatly enhanced the visibility and use of South Sami as well as the other Sami languages in the region.

## South Sami revitalisation and Fishman's GIDS scale

In Joshua Fishman's famous GIDS (Graded Intergenerational Disruption Scale) (Fishman 1991), minority language transmission from parents to children is identified as the most important factor in reversing language shift from majority to minority languages. The role of school instruction is also deemed important, although not as important as language transmission within the family. Moreover, the most efficient school support for the minority language, according to Fishman, is given by a school controlled by the community where the language is used as a medium of instruction. In the light of all this, the situation of South Sami is weak: Sami is rarely spoken in families and the kind of support the municipal schools or the Tärnaby Sami School offer the children is limited to lessons on Sami as a subject, while the rest of the school instruction is in Swedish. Neither the municipal schools nor the Sami School are community controlled. The Sami Schools have their own school board with a majority of members who are Sami, but they are state owned and part of the Swedish public school system.

Although Sami is a subject and not a medium of instruction in the municipal schools and the Tärnaby Sami School, the national minority policy reform has had beneficial effects, not least for South Sami pupils. In the municipal schools, two requirements for getting mother tongue tuition in the national minority languages were eased: the required minimum number of pupils in mother tongue classes was taken down to one pupil in the municipality, and the requirement of daily use of the language at home was dropped altogether. On 1 July 2015, the requirement that the pupils have at least some basic competence in Sami when starting was also dropped.

Several parents in our study commented on the fact that the National Minorities and Minority Languages Act (Swedish Parliament SFS 2009:724) from 2010 gave their children the right to preschool activities 'wholly or partly' in the minority language, which was a great step forward. However, some of them were worried about the nonexistence of strong bilingual or Sami-medium instruction models in the schools when their preschool children would advance to primary school. They feared that the good results from the preschool were at risk of fading because of that.

The minority language legislation has also impacted on other factors relevant for the GIDS scale, which would seem to strengthen the situation of South Sami beyond attained diglossia (Fishman 1991). Sami speakers nationwide now have the right to use their Sami languages in written form with authorities like the Ombudsmen of the Swedish Parliament, the Chancellor of Justice, the Swedish Social Insurance Agency, the Tax Agency and the Equality Ombudsman. In the Sami administrative area, contacts with the municipalities can take place in South Sami both orally and in writing. In childcare and care of the elderly in these municipalities, it is possible to use South Sami as the working language, and the municipalities are expected to actively recruit Sami-speaking staff. Even outside the Sami administrative area, municipalities are supposed to offer elder care in Sami if there are personnel available with Sami language competence, and there, too, municipalities are to ensure that such personnel are available, if needed. All municipalities in Sweden, not only those belonging to the Sami administrative area, are also supposed to offer South Sami language tuition in the school if parents ask for it, and, as mentioned above, the requirements for getting such tuition have been lowered for the Sami and other national minority groups. There are also signs that more people than before enrol in courses in South Sami at various levels, up to university level. Nevertheless, as the Council of Europe monitoring reports, other evaluations and minority media reports show, there are continuous implementation difficulties especially in relation to school education in minority languages including South Sami.

## Emotions and beliefs in the context of language revitalisation

While the official policy vis-à-vis the Sami and their languages has changed considerably and the South Sami revitalisation movement seems to have gained momentum in society, the interviews conducted in the study reveal the lingering, intergenerational legacy of colonially imposed traumas on the individual level. Negative and mixed emotions seem to cause problems even among the most dedicated language revitalists.

Linguist Aneta Pavlenko writes in her monograph about emotions and multilingualism:

> As linguistic human beings, we get emotional about what languages we should and should not be using, when and how particular languages should be used, what values should be assigned to them, and what constitutes proper usage and linguistic purity (2005: 195).

Even though Pavlenko is not referring explicitly to language revitalisation, her comments are very much applicable in this context. Pavlenko's examples are often taken from immigrant and refugee contexts and, most often, the emotional value of the first language, be it negatively or positively perceived, is emphasised. However, Pavlenko also shows that strong emotional investment in a second language is possible in certain circumstances. What, then, about emotions and language revitalisation? What is the impact of thoughts, beliefs and emotions in the context where an individual wants to reclaim a language he or she never acquired or used before? Or when the language has been used around the person, resulting in some receptive but very few if any productive language skills? Or, when the language has virtually been beaten out of a child?

The traumas inflicted on Sami children in the former Nomad Schools or other schools and resulting in native language loss are not directly comparable to Pavlenko's examples of Holocaust survivors' rejection of their native German language in diaspora. Nevertheless, we could claim that many of the children in boarding schools, as well as many other Indigenous children in the world in similar circumstances were, like Pavlenko's German-speakers, 'scared out of language maintenance and internalized the feelings of fear, shame, and embarrassment linked to the language' (Pavlenko 2005: 205). The strong negative experiences of being threatened and punished for using their language as children affected them later in life when the opportunity to reclaim their Indigenous language came and was even desired within the community.

Nora Dauenhauer and Richard Dauenhauer (1998) write about a Tlingit-speaker in Alaska, a former pupil in a residential school where only English was allowed, who could taste the soap in his mouth whenever he tried to use his Indigenous language. Similar difficulties have been found among adult Sami who have tried to relearn and use their lost language. Previous forced assimilation policies and negative school experiences strongly affected generations of Sami speakers in Scandinavia. Jane Juuso, a cognitive therapist from Norway and herself a North Sami, has created a method based on Cognitive Behavioural Therapy to overcome the emotional consequences of such policies. She observed that numerous non-Sami taking part in Sami courses quickly learnt the basics of the language and started using it productively, while those with Sami origin seemed to have great difficulties in learning and using Sami in spite of having heard and sometimes even having used the language earlier in life. For these learners, using the words of Pavlenko, 'historically shaped emotional memories' (2005: 208) seemed to play a role in the learning process. Juuso concluded that the negative language-related experiences among many Sami caused emotional blocks that hindered them from advancing in their studies in spite of a strong desire to take back the language. Her book was recently translated into Swedish and South Sami, and the method was tested and found useful by the Sami Language Centre in Sweden (2013). It has also been translated into English and is today used by the First Peoples' Cultural Council, British Columbia, Canada (Juuso 2015).

In Storuman and Vilhelmina, the heritage of former assimilation policies is felt by many Sami. Taking back a language used in the childhood home but negatively valued by the majority society is challenging because it presupposes a personal revalorisation of a stigmatised identity. Moreover, even in a new situation where the state explicitly encourages minority language maintenance, the choice to learn and use the minority language is not always appreciated by the surrounding society, and negative reactions are possible.

One interviewee in the present study is filled with mixed feelings in a situation where he is speaking South Sami with his children in the presence of his own father. In his childhood home, only Swedish was spoken, and the interviewee is unsure of how much Sami his father actually knows.

> My father is sitting beside and listening, or, he asks what did the reindeer earmark look like and I'm supposed to describe [using the Sami words for earmarks]. It feels awkward somehow. Because he might know what I'm saying, but anyway, I don't think he … Why should I use a language that he does not … that I think he might not know. But maybe he knows the language, I don't know. Maybe he knows those terms. But I feel uncomfortable. It is artificial somehow (father 2, Storuman, 2010).

Another frequently mentioned feeling is linguistic insecurity. One interviewee feels intimidated by perceived negative attitudes on the part of native speakers regarding his less-than-native competence in South Sami. Justified or not, these perceived attitudes make it harder for the interviewee to increase his use of Sami.

> I don't know what it is but it is like a block one has. And that is weird. It shouldn't be like that … It might be that you know that maybe … the attitude I have understood for instance he has, well, if you can't speak Sami you shouldn't do it. Maybe it is something like that which is in the way (father 1, Storuman, 2010).

A strong personal commitment is called for when the use of the language is questioned within one's own family or the surrounding community. But even then, the trajectory of every individual, with all its twists and turns, makes the personal language revitalisation process dynamic and difficult to steer. One interviewee comments:

> The language issue is like everything else in life—it comes and goes like the waves. It certainly depends on which part of your life you are in at present, so you'll want to try to keep the language alive, but let's say like it is now and like it has been the last ten years, it has been a bit difficult to keep the language going. Because you have just been working like a madman to keep the wolves from the door, so to say (father 2, Storuman, 2010).

He recalls memories from his school years, and a gradually growing interest in the South Sami language, then years filled with work and establishing a family, with little time left for language work. And even then, he recalls the joy of experiencing his children's interest in the language, and a nagging bad conscience about not doing enough himself.

Another interviewee describes the language issue as an arduous task, or a yoke, but at the same time something that simply must be done. He says:

> [I]n general, there is a much stronger Sami consciousness and knowledge than before. People also show interest in their background and they are proud of their cultural heritage and so on. But the language, that is something that has been neglected in this region. So it is our responsibility to take it back. It is our task. But it is a bit onerous (father 1, Storuman, 2010).

The last two interviews show clearly that these fathers are fully aware of the endangered situation of South Sami and the historical background to it. They are also convinced that they have a personal responsibility for language maintenance. Both of them have made efforts to speak South Sami in their own families.

Using Sami is by no means common among all the families taking part in the research project. The questionnaire study shows that in only a very few of the families was South Sami used by one or several family members, and the percentage of fathers using Sami at home was even lower than that of the mothers. 'Using Sami' could also mean that Sami was used occasionally, or very rarely. Several parents commented that they sometimes made efforts to speak Sami at home, without revealing how successful these efforts could be. Several parents also described their efforts to learn Sami themselves. A father wrote: 'I'm learning Sami and teaching it to my children, and I'm pretty good at it right now. But the rest of my family only know a couple of phrases and some words' (male 2, Storuman, 2010).

Irrespective of the language or languages used in the family, all these parents had chosen Sami mother-tongue tuition for their children, thus signalling that they wanted their children to learn Sami. The parents seemed to have faith in the school system in restoring South Sami in Storuman and Vilhelmina, in spite of the largely interrupted intergenerational transmission of Sami in the family. Some parents commented that the new minority policy was important for the survival of South Sami because it had made it easier to get mother-tongue support in South Sami in preschool and school, although this did not seem to have any stronger impact on the language choices made within the families. As many as a third of the 50 school children involved in the study reported that they only used Sami during mother-tongue lessons at school.

The main reason for not using Sami in the family seems obvious among the parents in Storuman and Vilhelmina. Many of them had not spoken Sami in their childhood homes. Their grandparents were the generation who had still heard and used Sami in their daily lives. One interviewee talked about her own grandfather who learnt Sami as a child but whom she never met herself because he died before the interviewee was born. Being of Sami origin was not taken up in the family, and the interviewee tells about the sadness and a feeling of loss it has caused her.

> I don't think I was ever conscious about having Sami roots. It did not come up until I met [my husband] … now both grandmother and grandfather are gone and my mum, I would say, would never say that she is a Sami. She would not do that. So it is like, you feel like, well it is so very sad. You feel that you have lost so much, but I and [my husband] say that we feel like we are now taking something back, yes, but you feel like that (mother 2, Storuman, 2010).

The feeling that the time has come to take back the Sami language and identity is strong in this interview, and the sadness expressed at first, later on turns to very positive feelings of joy and happiness about finally being able to access something valuable and extremely pleasurable:

> You see, the Sami language is like a bowl of candy that you really long to plunge your hand into and grab whatever you want, like all of it, until the bowl is empty. That is how I would describe it. That is the relation you have to the language. There is an unbelievable longing for it, to be able to grab it (mother 2, Storuman, 2010).

A mixture of negative and extremely positively feelings is also present in the interview of a teenager. She never experienced the forced assimilation policy of the past, and she has had the opportunity to study South Sami at school. Her own family encourages her to use Sami. However, negative or questioning attitudes from the surrounding society play a role for her, too. She says:

> I feel embarrassed, like, when I'm at school with Swedish friends and they
> don't know Sami and they just think it is weird and they don't understand
> anything. Then it is tough to speak [Sami] and it is quite embarrassing
> (daughter 2, Storuman, 2010).

Later on in the interview, she describes her language skills in a very positive
way, proud of her multilingualism:

> Well, my language, you could say it is like a power. Like a superpower,
> to be able to speak, like, several languages and, like, this superpower is so
> special! (ibid.).

While the participants generally perceive that the interest in the South
Sami language is rising among adults, many express a fear and a belief
that children and young people might not be as interested. For youths,
Swedish and international youth culture and the English language are
supposed to be more interesting than their Sami heritage.

However, unexpectedly positive attitudes and feelings vis-à-vis the Sami
language were found in the answers of the special questionnaire from
50 school children in Storuman and Vilhelmina. Only around a tenth
of them stated that they used Sami every day and none of them felt that
they spoke Sami fluently or could use Sami in many different situations.
Around 60 per cent also considered that Sami was a difficult language.
Nevertheless, the South Sami language appears to arouse very positive
associations in many of them. About 80 per cent stated that they found
it pleasurable ('nice', 'good', 'cool' etc.) to speak Sami. About half of
them mentioned that when they spoke Sami they felt 'like a Sami', 'more
like a Sami', like a 'Sami who knows his/her language' or 'like myself',
'like a member of the family'.

A rather unexpected result was also that as many as 95 per cent of
the children stated that South Sami was a 'useful' language—a result
somewhat different from their parents and teachers who emphasised
the identity function of Sami over the expected usefulness on the labour
market (see below).

When asked which languages they wish they could speak in the future,
over 70 per cent of the children wished that, among other languages,
they would be able to 'speak Sami', 'speak fluent Sami', or 'more Sami',
and around as many commented that South Sami felt 'close' to them, as
opposed to 'distant'. One 14-year-old girl wrote:

> I think that all Sami children should learn to speak and write Sami so that the language will not die out. I want to be able to speak Sami with others like they did in old times. I feel that learning Sami is an obvious thing to me. To be a Sami is something most people can't experience. I am going to teach my children Sami. When I hear somebody speak Sami with me I feel safe—at home (Storuman, 2010).

# Ideological clarification in South Sami revitalisation

Fishman pointed to the importance of a prior ideological clarification in language-shift reversal (Fishman 1991). He argued that for revitalisation efforts to be successful, it was necessary for the speakers of minority languages to reflect on the causes of the situation at hand. Why was the language threatened? What was the history behind it? What could be done to improve the situation? And most importantly, what were the community members themselves prepared to do about the situation?

The crucial role of prior ideological clarification has also been emphasised by Dauenhauer and Dauenhauer (1998) and Paul Kroskrity (2009). Dauenhauer and Dauenhauer attribute failures of revitalisation efforts among Alaskan native communities to the lack of prior ideological clarification. These communities openly showed a strong wish to take back their languages, and efforts were made to give adults and children more opportunities than before to learn and use their languages. When the methods proved unsuccessful, it was perceived that something in the technical aspect was missing, and efforts were taken to produce new materials, find new teachers or establish a new alphabet, just to see, later on, that even these efforts failed to produce new speakers (Dauenhauer and Dauenhauer 1998: 62). The authors point out that in spite of an openly declared willingness to take back the language, there is a general unwillingness among community members to be involved in the process themselves, which is a prerequisite of a successful language revitalisation. Instead, there was a tendency to expect that somebody else would do the job for them (Dauenhauer and Dauenhauer 1998: 63).

Kroskrity defines what he calls 'language ideological clarification' in the following way:

> Language ideological clarification is the process of identifying issues of language ideological contestation within a heritage language community, including both beliefs and feelings that are indigenous to that community and those introduced by outsiders (such as linguists and government officials), that can negatively impact community efforts to successfully engage in language maintenance and renewal (2009: 73).

Kroskrity states that identifying and raising awareness about linguistic issues could ideally lead to discourses between community members, or between community members and outsiders, with differing opinions, so that these discourses would lead to clarification or 'foster a tolerable level of disagreement that would not inhibit language renewal activities' (2009: 73).

When looking at the interview and questionnaire data from Storuman and Vilhelmina, we can find several similarities with the Alaskan situation described by Dauenhauer and Dauenhauer (1998). While the Sami in general see the need of intergenerational language transmission, only a minority of the parents use Sami at home and most often in these cases it seems to be used rather irregularly. Most parents seem to believe, as in the Southeast Alaskan situation that Dauenhauer and Dauenhauer (1998) have described, that somebody else, or the educational system, will take care of the language, for example, when they are enthusiastic about the teaching of Sami at school but do not speak the language with their children at home.

However, the interviews and questionnaires also show that there is a strong historical consciousness among parents and teachers of the reasons for the present threatened situation of Sami. Many answers also reflect a conscious personally taken stance on the question. As shown above, some of the interviewees express clearly that it is the task of their generation to take back the language, although they find it personally demanding.

Language is seen by many as a core value (Smolicz 1992) in Sami identity and slightly over half (52 per cent) of the study participants claim that Sami culture would disappear if the language was lost. Even among many of those who claim the opposite (41 per cent), language loss is seen as something very negative in the Sami context. Although it would not threaten the total survival of the culture, the participants comment that the loss of the language 'would reduce Sami culture to an empty shell', 'the culture would not really be the same', the culture would lose its strength', or it 'would only become a sales product'. Others comment, 'You are Sami in your soul and your heart, but language is important for yourself', and 'Strong efforts would be needed in other fields'.

The perceived high value of language in Sami identity was also reflected in the answers to a task to sort in descending order of relevance five suggested components of Sami identity ('Sami livelihoods', 'Sami food and clothing', 'Sami ways of thinking', 'Sami language', 'Something else; what?'). In 44 cases, language was chosen as the most, or second-most important component. The results for the rest of the suggested components were 34 (ways of thinking), 22 (food and clothing) and 16 (livelihoods) respectively.[4]

The importance of language in the minds of the participants was equally shown in the answers to questions concerning the teaching of Sami at school. The parents could choose between three alternatives:

> The Sami language is important for my child:
> a.  as part of Sami identity;
> b.  as a merit on the labour market;
> c.  for other reasons; what reasons?

In the last case, the participants were expected to suggest other motives. The teachers in turn were similarly asked which motivation (a, b or c) they thought was most important for their pupils. Sami identity as the only alternative was chosen by over a half (64 per cent) of all parents and teachers, and Sami identity combined with merit on the labour market was chosen by a quarter (25 per cent), resulting in a total of 92 per cent of the respondents mentioning identity in their answers.

In the light of these answers, another finding appears paradoxical. When asked if one could claim Sami identity without knowing a word of Sami or just a couple of words and phrases, a great majority (92 per cent) answered that one could do that without knowing a single word. One interpretation of such a result could be that there is a widespread understanding of the historical past and the assimilation policies which forced many Sami to stop speaking their original language and transmitting it to their children. This view was also confirmed in some comments and interviews. Given

---

4    The result for 'Sami livelihoods' can perhaps be partly explained by the exclusion of South Sami reindeer herders from the local *sameby* (see above).

the widely acknowledged importance of accepting all interested and committed people into revitalisation efforts, regardless of their capacity to use the language, these results can be interpreted as creating a very favourable environment for language revitalisation efforts. The next step is to find ways for various groups, from fluent speakers to beginners without any previous knowledge, to get suitable possibilities to advance in their individual language reclamation efforts.

## Summary and discussion

The participants in the study were recruited with the help of a small number of people familiar with the situation of the South Sami in Storuman and Vilhelmina. Participation was voluntary, which can mean that the sample included proportionally more of those who are favourable to South Sami revitalisation than those who are not. Even given this bias towards recruiting participants who are involved in and enthusiastic about language revitalisation, our data still shows that there are considerable challenges involved with language revitalisation.

That said, the results also show that many people feel that there is a positive development regarding the possibilities of strengthening South Sami language and culture development in society. The new minority policy from 2000 and its reform 10 years later are seen to have made South Sami more visible and more useful on the labour market. New possibilities have emerged to learn and use South Sami, and parents and teachers feel that there is more official support for their language and culture than ever before. There are also new work opportunities for those with a competence in the Sami languages in the municipalities of the Sami administrative area and the cultural sector. There are better opportunities to get support for South Sami in preschool and school, and other kinds of language instruction is also available. It is also possible for anyone to use South Sami locally and in certain official contexts nationwide. The new value of South Sami is reflected in the answers of parents, teachers and the school children participating in the study.

While the study participants generally perceive the national minority policy as a guarantee without which the South Sami language would very soon have been lost, many of them point out that the implementation of the minority policy is lacking, which can slow down a positive development that would otherwise have been possible. Nevertheless, the legal improvements, municipal efforts to highlight the Sami languages and cultures, and other measures are felt to have given new legitimacy to revitalisation efforts.

Many participants also feel that the new minority policy gives them compensation for past history and oppressive policies which deprived the Sami people of their language and stigmatised their culture and identity. A growing minority-political consciousness among the South Sami has also led to individual protests in the media when municipalities have failed to fulfil their obligations. Such protests hardly ever reached the media before the minority policy reform.

Signs of an ideological clarification in the form of a consciousness of the causes of the present endangered situation of South Sami and the need to act can be found in the data.

In spite of the fact that a majority of the participants view language as a core value in the South Sami identity, a great majority of them also, somewhat surprisingly, state that Sami language competence is no precondition for being Sami. The South Sami seem to accept the fact that many among them have lost or never learnt Sami because of former forced assimilation policies, while, because of that, the need for revitalisation is considered acute. Some take a personal responsibility for South Sami language and the culture, which sometimes can be heavy to bear. Many others again put their hope in the school system that they wish will give their children the language their parents and grandparents were denied. The present school support for Sami in Storuman and Vilhelmina is nevertheless very weak in terms of the Fishman GIDS scale.

All in all, the interviews and questionnaire comments show that former forced assimilation policies continue to cause problems for many individuals and families. In spite of a strong dedication to South Sami reclamation, individual parents have difficulty learning and using the language that was previously lost or suppressed. The task is to overcome one's own family history, and to revalorise a language and an identity that have been heavily stigmatised over a long time. Some results reflect ambivalent feelings and doubts on the personal level between a will to further revitalisation, on the one side, and an uncertainty about the wisdom or the feasibility of it on the other. However, taking part in language revitalisation is not only perceived as a burden, or a yoke, but also as part of a healing process and of 'righting old wrongs', two goals far beyond a mere language shift reversal. Such goals are likely to give strength and determination in a situation of seemingly overwhelming odds.

Finally, what could then be done to improve the prospects of South Sami language revitalisation in Storuman and Vilhelmina? The weaknesses of Sami language support within the school system make the role of the family and community all the more important in this context. The present cross-border South Sami language immersion camps for school children should be bolstered to compensate for the insufficient support from the school and to give the South Sami children from Sweden and Norway opportunities to meet each other. Many among the adult South Sami generation are in an acute need of opportunities to (re)learn Sami in ways that are compatible with demands of work and family life. Parent-network activities and family language programs, already in place in some Sami contexts in Sweden, would be helpful. The work of the Sami Language Centre, especially as regards applied Master-Apprentice programs (see for instance Hinton 2013 [2001]) and ways to tackle the emotional issues involved in revitalisation efforts (see above), should be continued and strengthened in the South Sami context. There is also an acute need for political work to upgrade the Swedish ratification of the ECRML to include primary and secondary school education so that strong models of bilingual and minority language medium education will become possible and accessible for South Sami children in Sweden. The insufficient support on the part of the education system is a serious impediment to the reclamation of South Sami as well as the other Sami languages in Sweden.

# Appendix 1. Summary of interviews and questionnaires

## Interviews

### 11 persons

No formal interview guide was provided; the interviewees could talk freely but the interviewers checked that the following issues were covered: language choice in childhood, during school years, and in the present family, as well as recounting of a possible incident/experience which had a special impact on language choice.

## Questionnaires

### 62 adults (parents and teachers)

The questionnaire for adults contained 25 questions, some of them different depending on whether the respondent was a teacher or a parent. The main themes were:

- Language background: language choice/s in the family; use of Sami media, etc.;
- Self-identity;
- Thoughts about Sami identity;
- The role of language in Sami culture;
- The role of the national minority policy in South Sami revitalisation;
- Further efforts needed for revitalisation to continue?

### 50 school children

The questionnaire for school children contained 22 questions, most of which involved choosing between different alternatives or filling in missing words. The questions focused on: What language/s do you speak? / when? / with whom?

- What do you think of Swedish, Sami, English/other languages?
    - near/distant; easy/difficult; useful/of no use, etc.
- How do you feel when you speak Swedish, Sami, English or other languages?
    - 'When I speak Sami, I feel…' / 'When I speak Swedish, I feel…', etc.
- Which languages do you wish to know when you are a grown-up?

# References


Dauenhauer, Nora Marks and Richard Dauenhauer. 1998. 'Technical, emotional, and ideological issues in reversing language shift: Examples from Southeast Alaska'. In *Endangered Languages: Language Loss and Community Response*, edited by Lenore A. Grenoble and Lindsay J Whaley, 57–98. Cambridge: Cambridge University Press. doi.org/10.1017/CBO9781139166959.004

European Charter for Regional or Minority Languages (ECRML). Online: www.coe.int/t/dg4/education/minlang/ (accessed 16 June 2018).

Fishman, Joshua A. 1991. *Reversing Language Shift: Theoretical and Empirical Foundations of Assistance to Threatened Languages*. Clevedon: Multilingual Matters.

Framework Convention for the Protection of National Minorities (FCNM). Online: www.coe.int/en/web/minorities/home (accessed 16 June 2018).

Hinton, Leanne. 2013 [2001]. 'The Master-Apprentice Language Learning Program'. In *The Green Book of Language Revitalization in Practice*, 3rd ed., edited by Leanne Hinton and Kenneth L. Hale, 217–26. Leiden: Brill.

Huss, Leena. 2017. 'Utvärdering av Samiskt språkcentrum. I Nästa steg? Förslag för en stärkt minoritetspolitik. Delbetänkande av Utredningen om en stärkt minoritetspolitik' [Evaluation of the Sami Language Centre. In: The Next Step? Proposal for a Strengthened Minority Policy. Partial Commission Report, The Inquiry about a Strengthened Minority Policy]. *Bilaga* 2, s. 319–482. SOU 2017: 60. Stockholm: Ministry of Culture.

Juuso, Jane. 2013. *Jag tar tillbaka mitt språk = Mov gïelem bååstede vaaltam* [I will take back my language]. Translation into South Sami, Ellen Bull Jonasen; translation into Swedish, Semantix and Sylvia Sparrock. Kiruna: Sametinget.

Juuso, Jane. 2015. *I am Taking My Language Back* [translation into English, of *Jag tar tillbaka mitt språk – Mov gïelem bååstede vaaltam*]. Brentwood Bay, BC: First Peoples' Cultural Council.

Kroskrity, Paul V. 2009. 'Language renewal as sites of language ideological struggle. The need for "ideological clarification"'. In *Indigenous Language Revitalization: Encouragement, Guidance & Lessons Learned*, edited by Jon Reyhner and Louise Lockard, 71–83. Flagstaff AZ: Northern Arizona University.

Pavlenko, Aneta. 2005. *Emotions and Multilingualism*. Cambridge: Cambridge University Press.

Persson, Marie. 2015. 'About the Rönnbäck Nickel Mining Project in Ume River, Tärnaby, Sápmi, Sweden'. A letter submitted by the organisation Stop Rönnbäck Nickel Mining Project in Ume River, Tärnaby, to the United Nations Special Rapporteur on the Rights of Indigenous Peoples Ms. Victoria Tauli-Corpuz prior to the 2015 August visit to Rönnbäck, Sápmi and Sweden.

Proposition (Government Bill) 2008/2009:158. Från erkännande till egenmakt – regeringens strategi för de nationella minoriteterna (From recognition to empowerment – Government strategy for the national minorities). Online: www.regeringen.se/rattsdokument/proposition/2009/03/prop.-200809158/ (accessed 16 June 2018).

Smolicz, Jerzy J. 1992. 'Minority languages as core values of ethnic cultures. A study of maintenance and erosion of Polish, Welsh, and Chinese languages in Australia'. In *Maintenance and Loss of Minority Languages*, edited by Willem Fase, Koen Jaspaert and Sjaak Kroon, 277–305. Philadelphia: J. Benjamins. doi.org/10.1075/sibil.1.19smo

Stångberg, Sigrid. 2015. 'Minnen från nomadskolan i Dearna, Tärnaby' [Memories from the Nomad School in Dearna, Tärnaby]. In *'När jag var åtta år lämnade jag mitt hem och jag har ännu inte kommit tillbaka': Minnesbilder från samernas skoltid* ['When I was eight years old I left my home and I have not come back yet': Recollections from the school time of the Sami], edited by Kaisa Huuva and Ellacarin Blind, 168–76. Stockholm: Verbum.

Swedish Parliament. *Lag om rätt att använda samiska hos förvaltningsmyndigheter och domstolar* [Law on the right to use Sami with administrative authorities and in courts], SFS 1999:1175, 3 December 1999. Online: www.notisum.se/rnp/sls/lag/19991175.htm (accessed 30 August 2018).

Swedish Parliament. *Lag om rätt att använda finska och meänkieli hos förvaltningsmyndigheter och domstolar* [Law on the right to use Finnish and Meänkieli with administrative authorities and in courts], SFS 1999:1176, 3 December 1999. Online: www.notisum.se/rnp/sls/lag/19991176.htm (accessed 30 August 2018).

Swedish Parliament. *Lag om nationella minoriteter och minoritetsspråk* [Law on national minorities and minority languages], SFS 2009:724, 10 June 2009. Online: www.riksdagen.se/sv/Dokument-Lagar/Lagar/Svenskforfattnings samling/Lag-2009724-om-nationella-m_sfs-2009-724/ (accessed 30 August 2018).

15

# Ainu Women in the Past and Now

Ryoko Tahara (translated by Hiroshi Maruyama)

## Introduction

Since the Meiji Restoration, we, the Ainu, have been dispossessed of our land, language and customs, for approximately 140 years, by Japan's invasion of Ainu land and subsequent assimilationist policies. Even now, the Ainu are subordinate to the majority Japanese in terms of education, economy and living standards, as a result of structural discrimination against the Ainu. In particular, Ainu women have found themselves subject to severe discrimination. Discrimination and suppression have led them into poverty, taken away their opportunities for education, impeded the development of their economic activities and hurt their pride as humans. These effects have been passed down through the generations. Infringement of human rights is mainly attributed to discrimination on the grounds of gender, ethnicity and so on. Gender and ethnic minority status combine to create special problems, that we Ainu women have come to recognise as double discrimination through our own learning activities. After becoming aware of our double discrimination we, the Ainu women, for the first time conducted a survey concerning the actual conditions of Ainu women. I will describe first, what discrimination Ainu women have experienced in the past and now, and second, what activities we have carried out in relation to the double discrimination we experience as minority women.

# Ainu women in the past and now

In general, the settlers and immigrants involved in the invasion and development of Indigenous peoples' land were mostly men. Indigenous women, therefore, have been targeted for men's sexual desires. The 1789 war of Menashi-Kunashir[1] was directly triggered by the fact that two Ainu died unnaturally after eating their meals at a *banya* or workshop and lodging for fishermen. Against the backdrop of the war, the Ainu were forced to work for fisheries under daily threats and violence, and Ainu women were explicitly exposed to sexual violence by the Japanese merchants who ran the fisheries.[2]

The most brutal treatment of Ainu women was that they were kept as mistresses by Japanese bosses and immigrants, regardless of whether they were married or unmarried. If they resisted, their husbands were sometimes abused or even killed by the Japanese involved. After being raped by Japanese bosses, some Ainu women committed suicide by consuming a poisonous plant named *torikabuto*.[3] A significant number of Japanese who kept Ainu women as their mistresses forced them to procure abortions if they became pregnant. Worse still, some Ainu women were infected with syphilis or smallpox by Japanese men. If such infections became known to the Japanese abuser, the Ainu woman was abandoned and left to her fate without even a bowl of rice or medicine. After death, her body was left to decay on a mountain in a make-shift shelter made from Japanese butterburs (*petasites japonicus*).

This situation, of Japanese looking down upon the Ainu and treating Ainu women as mistresses, lasted for several centuries. For example, some Japanese men, who had left their wives and children on the main island of Japan and worked as migrant workers in Hokkaidō, lived together with Ainu women there. After a year or so, those Japanese men would return to their homes, leaving the Ainu women and new-born babies of mixed parentage behind. When leaving Hokkaidō, they often made the Ainu women believe that they were going to look for a job or that they wanted

---

1    In May 1789, the Ainu rose up in rebellion against the cruel Japanese treatment of the Ainu. Events took place on the Shiretoko Peninsula in northeastern Hokkaidō. Seventy-one Ainu persons died at the hands of the Japanese. The Matsumae domain, which was endorsed by the Tokugawa Shogunate as the Lord of Hokkaidō, immediately suppressed the rebellion in cooperation with some Ainu leaders. Thirty-seven Ainu were charged with rebellion and beheaded.

2    Throughout this article, 'Japanese' implies ethnically Japanese.

3    *Torikabuto* is a poisonous plant and usually used as poison for hunting by the Ainu.

to obtain their parents' consent to marry them. Such despicable behaviour by Japanese men against Ainu women came to an end just a few decades ago. Many Ainu women suffered from this sort of deception. However, other Ainu women intended to marry Japanese men so they would have half-Japanese and half-Ainu children. Their desire was that their children would not inherit the physical characteristics of the Ainu, so they would avoid discrimination.

Inferior living standards, destitution and the ideology of male dominance implanted by the Japanese all prevented Ainu women from gaining adequate education. As a result, there are still illiterate Ainu women. In our own survey of Ainu women for the UN (described below), nearly 30 per cent of the surveyed Ainu women found it difficult to read the Japanese language, and a third of them wrote Japanese characters with difficulty. They have no choice but to engage in physical labour or restaurant work; both of which provide unstable employment and pay low wages.

Cases in which Ainu women are refused marriage or close relationships with Japanese men because of their ethnicity are sometimes reported. These women attempt to hide their Ainu identity, disparage their parentage and suffer from mental agony. They also tend to choose underprivileged men for their husbands. These men sometimes inflict violence on them as a way of giving vent to their everyday frustrations. It is not uncommon for such couples to be unable to afford tuition and other expenses for their children's schooling. Thus the children too are caught in a vicious cycle of reproducing destitution.

## The idea of double discrimination in our hands

As soon as we Ainu women started to understand that the term 'double discrimination' is applicable to the situations we face, we have been motivated to organise a campaign for the restoration of Ainu women's rights. The term 'double discrimination' encouraged us to entertain hopes that we could emancipate ourselves from discrimination. We began examining the idea and the structure of double discrimination by attending study meetings. We confirmed the situation facing us and talked with each other about our bitter experiences of discrimination. In tears, one

Ainu woman, for the first time, laid bare her true feelings and experiences of discrimination. She did not want to let those experiences be known to others and to make her family feel sad by knowing about them. Those who feel ashamed are the Ainu women who were discriminated against, not the Japanese who discriminated against them. It is absurd, but a reality. Through attending just a few study meetings, we drastically changed our minds. In other words, we came to have the courage to see ourselves as we are by learning about the idea of double discrimination.

We brought the actual conditions of minority women, including Ainu women, to light through the above-mentioned survey. Further, we worked to improve our living conditions and to eliminate the discrimination against us. We wanted to help the authorities take measures and prepare regulations. Then, we turned our attention to the International Convention on the Elimination of All Forms of Discrimination against Women. From 30 June to 18 July 2003, the Committee on the Elimination of Discrimination against Women (CEDAW) held its 29th session to examine the country reports of state parties, including the fourth and fifth periodic reports of Japan, at the United Nations Headquarters in New York. We submitted our report on the actual conditions of Ainu women to CEDAW before the session. Also, we had an opportunity to attend the session. Additionally, we carried out lobbying and briefing for persons concerned.

In August 2003, the report on the 29th session came from the CEDAW. According to the report, the committee expressed concern on two points. One was the lack of information in the reports about the situation of minority women in Japan. Another was the multiple forms of discrimination and marginalisation that these groups of women may face with respect to education, employment, health, social welfare and exposure to violence, including within their own communities (CEDAW 2003: 135). Based on these concerns, the committee recommended the Government of Japan provide,

> in its next report, comprehensive information, including disaggregated data, on the situation of minority women in Japan, especially with regard to their educational, employment and health status and exposure to violence (CEDAW 2003: 135–36).

Thus, the sufferings and difficulties that Ainu women have faced for centuries finally came to light for the first time in history. We were convinced that we could change our fate if we could eradicate our resignation to discrimination.

From October 2004 to February 2005, we carried out a survey on the actual conditions of Ainu women for the first time in history. The motivation for the survey was that we wanted to know more about ourselves. Involvement in the survey gave the participants, including me, self-confidence. Those participants, who had once taken no notice of discrimination and human rights, gained the ability to see what constitutes double discrimination. The survey and associated activities functioned as therapies to heal our wounded pride, and encourage us to have hope for the future.

Before coming to recognise double discrimination, we, Ainu women, had difficulties in wording the variety of challenges faced by us. We cleared up these difficulties by learning and taking actions on our own. I would like to continue activities of this sort to raise questions faced by Ainu women. Also, I hope Ainu women, who worked with me on the survey, will be actively involved in a variety of fields to end discrimination. Further, I was impressed by the fact that an illiterate Ainu woman was pleased to be able to read a signboard with 'TOYOTA' written in Roman letters on the street, after learning Roman letters along with the Ainu language. It is not easy for Ainu women, who have had no chance to learn Japanese grammar and Roman letters, to learn the Ainu language. Japan's colonisation of Ainu land is still punishing Ainu women. Learning culture, however, sometimes makes these marginalised persons confident in their identity as Ainu. Recognition of double discrimination and learning Ainu culture go hand in hand with each other for the decolonisation of Ainu women.

# References

Ainu Association of Hokkaidō (Sapporo Branch). 2007. Research Project for Double Discrimination against Minority Women, including Ainu Women, *Ukopararui*. Sapporo.

Committee on the Elimination of Discrimination against Women (CEDAW). 2003. Report of the Committee on the Elimination of Discrimination against Women, General Assembly, Official records, Fifth-eighth session, Supplement No. 38 (A/58/38). Online: tbinternet.ohchr.org/_layouts/treaty bodyexternal/Download.aspx?symbolno=A%2f58%2f38(SUPP)&Lang=en (accessed 15 July 2018).

# 16

# Heading towards the Restoration and Transmission of Ainu Culture

Nobuko Tsuda (translated by Hiroshi Maruyama)

When attaining puberty, I tried to hide that I was an Ainu by removing the hair on my hands and feet—'hairiness' is a feature said to be representative of the Ainu. I often heard negative ideas about the Ainu: the Ainu language has no written form; the Ainu have no sense of propriety; the Ainu are inferior to the ethnic Japanese. I am of mixed Japanese and Ainu background, but I had been troubled by my blood relationship with the Ainu for a long time. One day, I realised that the Ainu have inhabited this land, which is called Hokkaidō at present, since time immemorial, and that our ancestors handed down their wisdom for living in harsh winters, for example, how to make their houses, instruments of everyday life and clothing. This realisation connected me later with my job at the Hokkaidō Center for Ainu People. The Ainu Association of Hokkaidō is entrusted with the management of the centre by the Hokkaidō Government, and provides information on the history and culture of Ainu people for visitors. Before describing how I have revitalised Ainu embroidery (see Figure 11), I want to record some memories of my family.

My paternal grandfather, named Ekashimatkk, was born in 1876 and died in 1958. When I was four or five years old, he talked to me about how to catch and eat *sirkap* (swordfish). Also, he talked to me about *rakko* (sea otter) hunting in the sea. While listening to his stories while he sat cross-legged, I felt like I was riding waves whenever he shook his body. When I was seven years old, my sister died at the age of three. My grandmother cried in front of the memorial tablet while leaning her body many times in many directions. Her tearful voice had a sad tune and that lasted a long time. I realised at a later date that it was an Ainu manner to mourn the deceased. In my childhood, I was curious to see tattoos around the mouth and on the arms of my grandmother.

My father was born in 1923 and died in 1988. My parents had only Japanese names, while my grandparents had Ainu names. My father often accompanied his father to the neighbouring mountains to hunt weasels, foxes and raccoon dogs in winter. At the same time, he often cast a net to catch fish in the neighbouring river. I later saw him making shapely Ainu folk utensils, including *inaw* (ritual wooden shaving stick), *ikupasuy* (a prayer stick) and *heperay* (a ritual arrow). My memory of Ainu knitted goods was traced back to my childhood. I had the experience of seeing my aunt, who lived in my neighbourhood, knitting cotton into an *emusat* (a cord from which a sword is hung over the shoulder) like a magician.

When I was older than 40 years, I felt impelled to learn about Ainu culture. I appealed to museums and persons who were working on the transmission of Ainu culture to be taught. Those persons included Urakawa Tare in Urakawa, Sirasawa Nabe in Chitose, Sasamura Toyo in Chitose, Sugimura Kyoko in Asahikawa, Nakamoto Mutsu in Chitose and Toyama Saki in Anecha. They revered almost all natural resources for food and instruments of everyday life, considering them as gods, and had knowledge and techniques that enabled them to live in harmony with nature. They taught me not only craftsmanship, but also Ainu ways of thinking and Ainu perceptions of spirituality. I learned from them a principal rule that handicrafts tell us the state of culture when they are produced. In addition, Ainu clothing and miscellaneous goods, which were made by Ainu women with pious prayers, are considered to have strengthened Ainu people's sense of belonging and to have connected Ainu people with each other.

In 1994, at the age of nearly 50 years and having finished raising my children, I started my career as curator of the Hokkaidō Center for Ainu People. I provided people who intend to learn about Ainu culture with a program of craftsmanship. In the course for making *pon saranip* (a small knitted basket), participants made a sack from string. In the course for knitting *tar* (a rope used to carry loads on the shoulders), participants learnt the basic technique of Ainu embroidery such as how to knit, twist and plait thread. Participants knitted a rush mat from cattails in the course for making a *chitarpe* (a rush mat), and they made a small sack or a covering for the back of the hand and wrist in the guide to Ainu embroidery course. These courses were taught on the seventh floor of a building. Unfortunately, the participants could not learn about the materials for these courses, where they were collected, and how they were processed. In order to hand Ainu traditions of craftsmanship down on to the next generation, we need to intentionally learn and become proficient at Ainu perceptions of spirituality and techniques through experience.

One day, I saw a *tar* or packing rope made by Ainu among the excavated items in the Bibi 8 remains from 270 or 300 years ago, in Chitose. My research into *tar* demonstrates that it is made of herringbone patterns and that the technique traditionally used to interweave the *tar* is not seen today. Also, I found a sack for flints in the Museum of the Department of Agriculture of Hokkaidō University. It was made from cattails and had more complex herringbone patterns than the *tar*. No Ainu women knew how to make this pattern, so I restored the complex herringbone patterns on my own. I was successful in knitting *emusat* in addition to *tar* by analysing the *emusat* that had been collected by the above-mentioned museum. Further, I was able to restore the technique to create a pair of shoes from salmon skin by referring to a video archive that shows Kato Katsuyo making shoes from salmon skin in Teshikaga in 1988. Based on these experiences, I would like to say that it is important to digitally record cultural activities for the transmission of traditional techniques from generation to generation.

Figure 11. This *ruunpe* (a traditional Ainu dress) was modelled on a work exhibited in the Hokkaidō Museum. Artist Nobuko Tsuda.

Source. Photographed by the artist's husband, Hiroaki Tsuda, summer 2006.

In Japan, tens of thousands of Ainu items are kept in museums. However, they tend to lack fundamental information (provenance), including when, where and by whom those items were made or used. In contrast, Ainu items in foreign countries, especially in the West, have such information recorded and this helps researchers understand the characteristics of Ainu culture in specific areas and periods. I hope the progress of research on Ainu items made in the West will encourage us to organise information on Ainu items in Japan. In May 1999, I had a chance to see Ainu items held by the University of Pennsylvania Museum of Archaeology and Anthropology in Philadelphia, and by the Smithsonian in Washington DC. At the University of Pennsylvania Museum, I saw Ainu items, including embroidery, from Usu and Shiraoi in Hokkaidō, and exchanged opinions about threads, ways of knitting and Ainu patterns with the curator. I realised again how important such exchange is for the full-fledged revitalisation of Ainu culture. In the Smithsonian, the Ainu items, as well as items from Okinawa, were classified by area and period, and preserved in a repository in which climate conditions were controlled. Additionally, each of the Ainu items, which were labelled, could be accessed through the internet.

In December 1998, I called Ainu women, who were involved in the transmission of Ainu culture, to organise the Association of Ainu Women for the Transmission of Ainu Culture, commonly known as *Karip*. The association aims to improve our skill through involvement in the restoration of traditional works, to learn how to make Ainu embroidery from records or direct interviews with elderly memory keepers, and to strengthen connections between the members across the area. The first project of the association was to knit the rush mat, *saranip* and *emusat*, using traditional techniques, and to hold a workshop on *upopo* and *mukkuri* for the 1999 special exhibition of the Ainu in the Smithsonian. On display were a variety of Ainu folk utensils made from the Jomon Period (13,000–300 BC) to the Meiji Era (AD 1868–1912), a *chise* or Ainu traditional house built by Nomoto Masahiro, carvings by Sunazawa Bikki, and so on. Unfortunately, there were not many modern Ainu works using traditional techniques on display. Overall, I was proud of the Ainu cultural items from the northern part of Japan, which attracted many visitors to the Smithsonian.

Many researchers came to the Hokkaidō Center for Ainu People. When I was nearly 60 years old, a Japanese anthropologist gave me the opportunity of taking a master's degree at his university. Afterwards, another Japanese anthropologist encouraged me to become the first female Ainu PhD holder. In September 2014, I finally got my PhD at the age of 69, from the Graduate University for Advanced Studies in Hayama, Japan. My doctoral dissertation focuses on Ainu clothing. There were earlier studies on Ainu clothing before I wrote my dissertation (Tsuda 2014). However, those were carried out by male researchers, and were confined to the areal classification of Ainu clothing. Based on close examination of Ainu clothing collected by museums inside and outside of Japan, as well as my practical knowledge of knitting Ainu clothing I made the following findings. First, in the eighteenth century, cotton, which came to Hokkaidō from China, replaced animal skins and bark as the material from which Ainu clothing was made. Cotton was easy to process and knit, and inspired Ainu women to make a big difference to the culture of Ainu clothing. Second, earlier studies mostly showed that Ainu patterns came from China, but I concluded that Ainu patterns represent the bonds of a sacred place to avert evil, while those in China are borrowed from trees and birds. I will continue doing research on Ainu clothing and hand down information on how to view Ainu collections in museums to younger generations of the Ainu.

## Reference

Tsuda, Nobuko, 2014. 'Ainu i bunka no kenkyu' [A study of Ainu clothing culture], PhD dissertation. Hayama: Graduate University for Advanced Studies.

# 17

# Living a Modern Life in Hokkaidō as a Young Ainu Dancer

Mana Shinoda (translated by Hiroshi Maruyama)

I live in an Ainu village in Hokkaidō where a number of Ainu people once made their living by hunting, fishing and trading. I was born in 1987 to a Japanese mother and an Ainu father; my mother raised me as an ethnic Japanese. As time passed, I came to identify the Ainu-ness in my blood. Today, I spend time learning about Ainu traditional embroidery and manual work and make a living by performing Ainu traditional dance at the Ainu theatre 'Ikor' at Akan Lake in Kushiro. I have met some people who say that Ainu culture is dying, or who utter that there may not be any Ainu. They have the following assumptions: Ainu culture is a relic of the past; Ainu live in traditional houses and wear their traditional clothes and speak the Ainu language. Are those assumptions right?

## Is Ainu culture dying?

### Transmitting Ainu clothes to the next generation

Ainu clothes are made from different types of materials. They were once made from grass fibres, animal skins, fish skin and bark. In the Edo period, some of them were made from cotton, which came to the Ainu through trading with the Japanese. These cotton clothes were embroidered by women for generations to avert demons. They were used for clothing called *ruunpe* and *chinjiri* (see Figure 12). There are different Ainu embroidery patterns in each Ainu community. At present, we Ainu wear Western clothes on a daily basis as do the Japanese and we wear Ainu clothes for rituals and cultural gatherings. Thus, Ainu clothes have been transformed by Japan's colonisation of Hokkaidō and the assimilationist policy, but we Ainu did not lose our identity as Ainu people. We Ainu women have succeeded in transmitting the technique of making Ainu clothes and doing embroidery from mother to child at home and from other Ainu women, who have devoted themselves to preserving Ainu culture, in each community (see also Tsuda, Chapter 16).

Figure 12. Mana Shinoda in a traditional Ainu dress, *ruunpe*, playing the *mukkuri* (Jews' harp).

Source. Photographed by Ryo Yonezawa at the Shiraoi office of the Foundation for Ainu People's Culture, 4 September 2018. Used with permission.

## Transmitting Ainu food to the next generation

The Ainu once sustained their livelihood by hunting, gathering and fishing. They lived in the neighbourhood of a river, where salmon went upstream to spawn, and they farmed in some areas. The main crops of the Ainu included cereals such as Japanese millet, foxtail millet and soba, which were harvested by the slash-and-burn method. In Hokkaidō and the northernmost part of Honshu where they settled down, soil was fertile and food resources were abundant. Also, they survived the harsh winters by developing techniques to preserve deer meat, salmon and edible wild plants. In regard to today's diet, there seem to be no more than a few differences between what the Ainu and the Japanese eat. Nevertheless, our Ainu community sees that elderly women take a lead in cooking traditional food and making *tonoto*, or raw sake, for rituals. They teach their juniors these recipes and techniques while singing traditional songs all together. This spring, I was taught how to make *potcheimo*, dumplings made from potatoes that fermented in winter, by a *fuchi*, or female elder. It takes time for us to make or cook any Ainu cuisine, which is closely associated with nature. Whenever going into the mountains to harvest edible wild plants in early spring, we say our prayers to the gods of the mountains for sharing the blessings of nature with the gods. The most well-known Ainu ritual for harvest is *Asircepnomi*, which is performed when salmon begin going upstream in a river. This ritual helps us to hand down our concept that we are part of nature and that we have to take wildlife in gratitude. This should be kept in mind among us.

## Transmitting Ainu architecture to the next generation

We Ainu call our residence *chise*. The traditional residence of the Ainu is a plain dwelling that was shifted from a pit dwelling in the thirteenth century. Also, it was made from local trees and plants, and thus differed in structure to some extent from area to area. Many researchers write that the Ainu set up windows in the east side of their residence as the east is sacred for the Ainu, but this is not universally true. Such residences were seen only in Nibutani. However, without exception, any *chise* has an *apeoi* or a sunken fireplace in the centre. In Ainu society, there is a custom of keeping a fire in the sunken fireplace throughout a year. The Ainu have valued fire as a god named Apefuchi kamui, meaning fire in elderly woman form, more highly than other gods in relation to life. Fire is considered to essentially support the lives of the Ainu who traditionally lived in the cold districts, including Hokkaidō, Sakhalin and the Kuril Islands. Since the Ainu do not directly address their gods, Apefuchi kamui is thought to mediate between the Ainu and the gods. That is why Ainu rituals begin with asking Apefuchi kamui to listen to Ainu's prayers and to convey them to other gods. This Ainu traditional belief convinces me that the Ainu originally had no notion of male superiority. Unfortunately, the assimilationist policy toward the Ainu under Japan's colonisation of

Hokkaidō prohibited the Ainu from building traditional *chise*. As a result, no Ainu live in traditional *chise* today. Nevertheless, rituals in relation to residence, including *Chise koenomi*—the ceremony of purifying a building site—and *Chise inomi*—the ceremony to celebrate the building of a new house—have been passed down unbroken from generation to generation.

## Taking a first step beyond the profession as a performer of Ainu traditional dance

In February 2015, the Association of Ainu Youth was established by the Ainu themselves as the first nationwide Ainu organisation, following the example of the Finnish Sami Youth Organisation. The association aims to promote Ainu culture and international exchange programs with other Indigenous peoples. Since the outset, as a board member, I have been involved in making arrangements to carry out a movie event and a seminar on the history of the Ainu. In April 2015, I had the opportunity to address a session of the United Nations Permanent Forum on Indigenous Issues, and I also made a presentation on the status quo of the Ainu at a meeting with Victoria Tauli-Corpuz, the special rapporteur on the rights of Indigenous peoples. The theme of the session was 'Human Rights: The implementation of the UN Declaration on the Rights of Indigenous Peoples'. Below is the text of my address.

Thank you, Chairperson. *Irankarapute* (Hello)

My name is Mana Shinoda. I am Ainu, an Indigenous people in Japan.

I perform Ainu songs and dances handed down from our ancestors with a traditional Ainu dress, *ruunpe*, at Japan's only traditional Ainu dance theater every day. Fortunately, this is my job. Why did I just say 'fortunately'? Because it is not usual nowadays that the Ainu engage in transmission and protection of our own culture for a living in Japan. Most Ainu people have ordinary jobs like other Japanese. Some of them live and work without ever telling their identity as Ainu. One of the reasons why some Ainu hide their identity must be reflected by negative speech against Ainu. Last year, a Japanese politician said, 'The Ainu people do not exist anymore'. Another politician also said, 'It is doubtful that the Ainu are indigenous'. These statements are obviously hate speech and violate our right not to be subjected to forced assimilation under Article 8 of UNDRIP [United Nations Declaration on the Rights of Indigenous Peoples]. The Japanese Government has an obligation to take effective measures to combat such prejudice and eliminate discrimination under Article 15 of UNDRIP and other human rights treaties. However, the Japanese Government has not taken such measures. Moreover, a description of the Ainu history was recently revised from 'the Government dispossessed the lands of the Ainu people' to 'the Government gave the lands to the Ainu people' in the process of the textbook examination of the Ministry of Education. The new description introduces a discriminatory law, the Hokkaidō Former Aborigines Protection Act, in a positive context, which leads to misconceptions. This revision clearly violates our right to transmit our histories under Article 13 of UNDRIP. Histories of indigenous peoples shall be appropriately reflected in education under Article 15 of UNDRIP and other human rights treaties.

Recommendation: The Japanese Government should immediately take measures against hate speech and conduct education in which children can learn the histories of indigenous peoples properly. *Iyairaikere* (Thank you).

The session spared a long time for discussions on Indigenous women who have suffered from double discrimination. What interested me was a speech made by an elderly woman from an Indigenous people in Russia. She said that half of the leaders of Indigenous peoples in Russia are women and that customs of excluding women are not worth cultural transmission. Unfortunately, Russia seems to be an exception in terms of women's leading role in Indigenous peoples. In the case of the Ainu, women disproportionally bear a burden in domestic work and child rearing, in addition to embroidering and performing traditional songs and dances. It must be affected by some bad practices from Japanese society. In order to make a breakthrough in the situation, I hope the Japanese Government and municipalities will provide an appropriate environment for those Ainu women who intend to be involved in activities for cultural transmission and the improvement of their status. It is good not only for Ainu women but also for Japanese women. Further, those who addressed me in the headquarters of the United Nations in New York were non-Japanese, not Japanese. I came to know that we Ainu should make efforts to encourage the dissemination of the existence of ourselves among Japanese people. Also, I recognised again how important it is to deepen communications with other Indigenous peoples via international conferences and the internet. Academic research does not deal with all aspects of Ainu culture. The Ainu themselves, therefore, should strive to transmit our material and spiritual assets to future generations. Ainu culture is not dying. It is always changing, and extending to new genres of music and art.

# Reference

*United Nations Declaration on the Rights of Indigenous Peoples*, GA Res 61/295, UN GAOR, 61st sess, 107th plen mtg, Sup No 49, UN Doc A/RES/61/295 (13 September 2007).

# 18

# A Quest for What We Ainu Are[1]

Shizue Ukaji (translated by Hiroshi Maruyama)

I am 83 years old. Lately, I have been thinking that I will see my elder sister, parents and ancestors again in the world to come in the not very distant future (see Figure 13).

I came to Tokyo and married an ethnic Japanese. Turning 38 years old, I contributed an essay 'Ainu People, Let's Join Hands with Each Other' to the Asahi Shimbun Press. This essay is said to have triggered an Ainu movement for human rights in the metropolitan area of Japan. At first, I did not intend to inaugurate a political movement. I was just thinking that I want to die as an Ainu; in order to do so, I want to have gatherings with my brethren in Tokyo; I want to confirm myself as an Ainu by sharing joy, sorrow and sufferings with them. I have some Ainu blood in my veins. Spurred by the Ainu blood, I called out to my brethren to join hands with each other.

---

1    This contribution was originally a speech made by Shizue Ukaji to the third meeting of the Citizens' Alliance for the Examination of Ainu Policy, held at Hokkaidō University in Sapporo on 19 November, 2016. The original title of the speech in Japanese was '*Ainu narumono wo sagashimotomete*'.

Figure 13. Shizue Ukaji, Ainu embroidery expert.

Source. Photographed by Hiroshi Maruyama, Sapporo Pirka Kotan, 1 December 2017. Used with permission.

At the age of 63, I started learning Ainu embroidery. After seeing an exhibition, it occurred to me that Ainu tales can be expressed by doing Ainu embroidery on Japanese clothes. Afterwards, I had the idea of using Ainu *yukar* (epics) for the expression of my image of a blakiston's fish owl—thus combining Ainu embroidery and Japanese clothes. In 2007, my illustrated tale named 'A Blakiston's Fish Owl and Salmon' saw the light of day. I call my pieces created by the combination of Ainu embroidery and

Japanese clothes 'old cloth pictures'. In Ainu *yukar*, a variety of gods teach us what to do. In other words, Ainu *yukar* give us stories as to how we should behave as humans and how we should be connected to all things in nature. I found out that the spirit of the Ainu people is in Ainu *yukar*.

Under Japan's long colonial rule and its assimilationist policy towards them, our ancestors were losing the proud spirit of the Ainu. In my childhood, however, I saw fathers and mothers at their gatherings saying their prayers and eating, drinking, singing and dancing full of joy all night. At those moments, they could confirm their identity as Ainu. But now, these celebrations have become a thing of the past.

How many chances to feel happy do we Ainu have in our daily life? Happiness does not come from external sources. Instead, our own feelings about being Ainu make us happy. However exploited we have been throughout the modern and postmodern eras, we have an embryo of Ainu in our bodies, insofar as we are related to Ainu by blood. It is Ainu *yukar* that develops the embryo, I believe. I have heard that Ainu *yukar* were shortlisted for the Nobel Prize in Literature. Thankfully, our ancestors transmitted such a nice treasure to us. My only wish is to reclaim the spirit of we Ainu people by means of *yukar*. Reading *yukar* and talking to each other in the Ainu language must be the best literary education for Ainu. I wish we had such a place to gather and share.

In October 2017, I had an opportunity to make a speech at a festival hosted by Chasi-an-kar, which is an association of urban Ainu. The aim of the association is to build space for the gathering of Ainu. In the Greater Tokyo Area there is no public space for Ainu, unlike in Hokkaidō. We have to tackle this problem. There is, however, the Centre for Ainu Culture in the heart of Tokyo. It was built originally for the Tokyo office of the Foundation for Research and Promotion of Ainu Culture. This foundation was designated by the authorities concerned to be the sole corporation in the nation with authority to carry out the services provided by the so-called Ainu Promotion Act of 1997. We Ainu want to create our own spaces in which to gather through our own efforts.

After my speech at the above-mentioned festival, Mr Nishihara, who had been involved in the conservation of gorillas, talked about the Pygmies, an Indigenous people in the Republic of the Congo. The Pygmies have maintained a hunter-gatherer culture in the forest. They share natural resources in the forest with gorillas. Nowadays, 'civilised' humans encroach on those forests to the extent that gorillas and other wild animals are on the verge of extinction. After hearing Mr Nishihara's paper, I read a book about the Pygmies. I was attracted by a story of collecting honey in this book. When honey bees actively fly around in the forest, the Pygmies go out to look for beehives. The beehive that is found belongs to the person who found it, but honey collected from the beehive goes to others. Sharing what they hunt and gather with each other leads to peace-building in their community. After reading the book, I felt like finding the world described by Ainu *yukar* in the existing livelihood of the Pygmies. I realised that I have to translate the nature, Kamuy, and equality of people seen in Ainu *yukar* into practice. Today, war and violence are prevailing across the globe. Those who are entitled to call for equality and peace are Indigenous peoples, because we Indigenous peoples have the spirit of avoiding war and violence.

Japan is not far from the prevalence of war and violence in the world. Maintaining the norm of peace in Japanese society requires a restoration of the spirit of the Ainu people. The restoration should be conducted by Ainu themselves. If we Ainu continue to suffer from poverty, we can't afford the time to read *yukar* and to mingle with other Ainu. The Japanese Government has a responsibility for making it possible for the Ainu to make their living as Indigenous people.

The Council is for Ainu Policy Promotion, which was set up in December 2009, is based on the Report of the Advisory Council for Future Ainu Policy (July 2009). The council hosted by the Chief Cabinet Secretary, and has been discussing future Ainu policy for more than six years now. As yet, no final proposal has been announced. Nonetheless, public facilities for the Symbolic Space for Ethnic Harmony are being built as a fait accompli. Mr Kan, the Chief Cabinet Secretary, has pledged to complete these public facilities by the 2020 Olympic Games in Tokyo, to show to the international community Japan's effort to treat the Ainu respectfully as Indigenous people. I have never experienced throughout my life the Japanese Government treating us Ainu well. We Ainu can't understand why the Japanese Government believes that the completion of those public facilities will bring us happiness.

If the Japanese Government wants to use the term 'ethnic harmony' in order to build the above-mentioned public facilities, it is requested that the government make a formal apology to us Ainu for the historic injustices imposed on us. When those public facilities are inaugurated, we Ainu, in response, shall perform traditional rituals such as *Kamuynomi* and *Icarpa*. An apology from the government could heal the wounds of the Ainu that were caused by the colonisation of Ainu Mosir, or Hokkaidō. If the apology comes, it would be the first step towards reconciliation between Japan and the Ainu.

Finally, I will read my poem, which was composed at the moment when the earthquake and the subsequent great tsunami hit the northern part of mainland Japan on 11 March 2011. It was a spontaneous poem as an Ainu.

# Our land: A contribution to the Great East Japan Earthquake

Did you feel heaviness?
Did you feel a pain?
We should have noticed and paid attention more deeply
to an unusual change in your condition.
We should have had a means to perceive
that a burden and pain lay on you.
A large number of people were washed away by the waves
and returned to land with your burden and pain.
We survivors perceive the pain
and pray to the gods with respect for the dead.

Lastly, I am grateful to Professor Yoshida, Professor Maruyama and others concerned with the Citizens' Alliance for the Examination of Ainu Policy, for giving me an opportunity to make a speech here. I am also hopeful that this citizens' alliance will attract support from many ethnic Japanese and the Ainu policy will proceed in accordance with Ainu people's right to self-determination.

19

# A Trip to the Mountaintop

Jenny Virdi Kroik

## Introduction by Åsa Virdi Kroik

My daughter wrote this story. When she was about six years old, she participated in a revitalisation project that I was the coordinator for while working in Nord-Trøndelag on the Norwegian side of south Saepmie. It was one of several revitalisation projects I coordinated between 2008 and 2010. We worked with language and culture revitalisation in different ways, and this project was designated for the children from six–10 years old, but it also became a project for the fathers/men as I was the only woman to participate. I think that the reason for this specific project's attraction for the men was that they felt comfortable with the mountain environment and the activities we performed. Two of them were full-time reindeer herders and the others were familiar with reindeer herding. The project was very successful and several participants, adults and children, asked for it to be repeated many years later. After the first year's success, we did the camp again at the same dates in August. We had fantastic luck with the weather in both years and it's difficult to differentiate the two camps from each other in my memory. As my family and I later moved from the area and I took another job, I did not have time to coordinate any more camps, but it's not impossible that we will do it again another summer.

# A trip to the mountaintop

Hi, my name is Jenny and I'm going to tell you about the time we went to Sijliesjaevrie.

One year, maybe it was 2010 or 2011, or maybe even as late as 2012 (though probably not), we were living in a big red house in north Sweden, and my mom arranged this trip to a mountain close to us. We got tents and reindeer skins and basically everything we needed. We lived next to a football field (that no one ever used, just so you know) and we had a pilot for the helicopter, which landed on the football field, and which was supposed to take us to Sijliesjaevrie and bring us back. I was with my two cousins, their dad and their dog, as well as my parents. So we took everything—bags and other things—to the field where the helicopter would come. We put everything in the helicopter and flew up. While we were up there, the pilot took us on a small tour around the village that we lived in and told us about everything.

Figure 14. Jenny Virdi Kroik (right) and Ristin Kristoffersson during a trip to the mountaintop.

Source. Photographed by Åsa Virdi Kroik, Sijliesjaevrie, August 2010.

When we got up to the mountaintop, my two *laevie* (relatives), Ella and Ristin, and I inspected the area. There wasn't much there, only a few bushes and there was a very small river further down from our tents that we'd set up. It was windy and sunny. It was a good big area with small trees that were about our height, and we found a bush that had branches that were a little thick. We started cutting some pieces and making passages through the bush. We were planning on making a small tree house or 'bush house' and there was no need for a roof since it was a bush (Figure 14).

So, we worked for maybe 30 minutes, till we helped my parents and my cousins' father set up tents, and then started to eat. After that, I guess we kept working. We spent two days there, but I really don't remember everything. Anyway, here are some moments that I remember very clearly:

1. I might be totally wrong about the bush tree thing (but we did work with it so don't be confused) but I think we played around and recorded ourselves with my new video camera that I had gotten once the tents were up. I remember we'd only play around and I'd be the one talking.

2. The first night that we were there, Ella, Ristin and I decided to sleep together in one tent. It started out well, but then someone moved to the other tent, then another one, then one came back, then the *other* came back, and so on.

3. My relatives' dog, Kejio (I think that was her name), amused herself by chasing small animals.

4. Oh! And when we were going to leave, I put my knife on a rock next to our bush house and it disappeared. How? I don't know. But given that it was windy, it might have just blown away.

On our way home we could choose to walk, ride the helicopter, or ride horses. Ristin and I rode horses, meanwhile my dad, Ella, and her dad, along with Kejio took the helicopter. It was a fun experience.

Sorry, but that's all I remember.

20

# Everyday Acts of Resurgence and Diasporic Indigeneity among the Ainu of Tokyo

Kanako Uzawa

## Introduction

'To stand on the same platform as *Wajin*, we need an education.' These words were spoken to me by Tadashi Kaizawa, who fought for Ainu rights as an activist, farmer, writer and one of the leaders of the Nibutani Ainu community in Hokkaidō. He was not only my grandfather, but also an educator who taught us important values in life. Sadly, he was not able to receive the education he wished for, so his determination to provide a good education for his children led all three of them to pursue a university education. Later, his youngest daughter, my mother, became a school teacher in Tokyo, and married my *Wajin* father. During my teenage years, I understood how important it was for me to receive a higher education in order to become an independent Ainu woman. Through my difficult years in a strict Japanese education system, I always thought of my grandfather, and held on to all my living memories of nature, the smell of the forest and the vivid life of the Nibutani community where I spent all the school holidays with my family. Even though I did not live permanently in Nibutani, I felt it was my home, and considered it so. Tokyo gave me a feeling of disconnection from Ainu culture—that was until I encountered the Tokyo Ainu community.

This article is a reflection on stories from my youth, when I became aware of what it means to be Ainu in Tokyo, and how my experiences of living in both Nibutani and Tokyo affect my daily life as an urban Indigenous person. From the outset, I would like to thank all members of the Ainu Association of Rera[1] in Tokyo who accepted me for who I am and supported me in pursuit of my own path as an urban Ainu. All the experiences I have shared with the Ainu community in Tokyo made me realise how important it is to document and share our life stories and events as urban Ainu, for the further development of Indigenous studies. I perceive this to be my Indigenous pathway, where I can contribute my Ainu perspective for both academic audiences and Indigenous communities of the world.

In this article I use the term *Wajin* to refer to the ethnic Japanese or non-Ainu, to clarify the point that having Japanese citizenship does not define our ethnicity. Ainu today have the same lifestyle as other Japanese citizens, both in cities and rural areas. They have Japanese as a mother tongue and are enrolled in Japanese public schools. Many Ainu migrate to cities for better employment opportunities, and sometimes to escape from discrimination. Given these similarities, the issues identifying how many Ainu there are in Japan, and how many of them live in cities, are complex, partly because Japan does not collect data on ethnicity in the national census. However, a number of surveys help to fill this gap.

According to the Advisory Council for Future Ainu Policy (2009: 16), the Hokkaidō prefectural government has conducted a survey of the Ainu population of Hokkaido almost every seven years since 1972. The aim of the survey has been to have a better understanding of the living and educational conditions of Ainu in Hokkaidō (Advisory Council for Future Ainu Policy 2009: 16).[2] In terms of Ainu living outside of Hokkaidō, the most recent *Ainu Living Conditions outside of Hokkaidō Survey* was conducted nationwide in 2011 by the Japanese central government (Council for Ainu Policy Promotion Working Group 2011). There have been two other surveys on Ainu people living outside of Hokkaidō —in 1974 and 1988 (Watson 2014a: 69)—though these surveys, by the Tokyo Metropolitan Government, focused only on the Tokyo metropolitan area. According to the latest report from the *Hokkaidō Ainu Living Conditions*

---

1    *Rera* means wind in Ainu.

2    The 2009 report states that the *Hokkaidō Ainu Living Conditions Survey* was also conducted by the Hokkaidō University Center for Ainu and Indigenous Studies in 2008 (Advisory Council for Future Ainu Policy 2009: 16).

*Survey* in 2017, the Ainu population in Hokkaidō consisted of 13,118 individuals in 5,571 households across 63 municipalities (Department of Hokkaidō Environment and Lifestyle 2017: 3). Ainu in Tokyo suggest there could be as many as 10,000 living in and around the capital region (Watson 2014a: 69). Although a significantly high number, Ainu use this figure to compensate for undercounting in existing statistics from metropolitan government surveys, which reported a population of 679 in 1974, and 2,699 in 1988 (Watson 2014a: 69).

This article looks at the city as a site for cultural resurgence and revitalisation amongst the Ainu in the final decades of the twentieth century. In writing of these phenomena I position myself as an Ainu researcher and include my own experiences as a member of the Tokyo Ainu community. I refer to those who live around the greater Tokyo and Kantō region as 'Tokyo Ainu'.

Many Indigenous people now define urban space as home. A report by the United Nations Department of Economic and Social Affairs (2014: 2) projects that 66 per cent of the world's population will be living in urban areas by 2050. If one considers the situation of Indigenous people in this overwhelmingly urban future, it may no longer be feasible to define us solely as remaining in our rural ancestral homelands. In urban contexts, social spaces such as schools, community centres, exhibition halls and public institutions may symbolise Indigenous culture and become transformative spaces that provide opportunities for expressing and developing Indigenous culture.

For some, a focus on Indigenous people in cities may seem inappropriate. City people who identify as Indigenous might be perceived as 'out of place' in the urban context. Yet Indigenous migration to cities has become more common in recent years. In this article, I investigate the disparity between modern Indigenous lifestyles and stereotypes of Indigenous people that are fixed in place. I explain how this disparity deeply affects the identity formation of Indigenous people in urban settings. Mark Watson (2014b) uses the term 'diasporic indigeneity' to suggest that Indigenous people often remake their identities in cities through processes of reterritorialisation, bringing lived relationships with ancestral homelands and community members into urban contexts. In considering these issues, I offer a detailed case study of one particular cultural organisation in Tokyo and explore how, within a diasporic context, self-fashioning operates within urban Ainu life.

The analysis for this article is based on auto-ethnography. I reflect upon my own life experiences both in Tokyo, and in the rural Ainu community of Nibutani, in Hokkaidō. Paul Whitinui (2014: 458) argues that an individual's ability to explore, discover and narrate oneself as an Indigenous person is significant, and that such narrations help articulate some of the reasons why Indigenous worlds are culturally and politically different. In my case, positioning myself as an Ainu researcher and using auto-ethnography helps me to locate myself within academia and assists me in the ongoing process of negotiating how my culture should be presented to the academy and to society. In addition, auto-ethnography allows me to recognise and reconnect my past to the present and to the future by enabling me to share my experiences and knowledge as an Indigenous person who is trying to position herself in the world. What I share in this article is not Ainu traditional knowledge, but rather my memories, daily acts and experiences that have taught me to reconnect myself to Ainu culture. This is my interpretation of diasporic indigeneity and everyday acts of resurgence. By focusing on these aspects of Ainu life, I hope to provide a more current interpretation of Ainu culture, history and politics.

There are three main sections in this chapter. In the first, the enforced resettlement of Ainu from Hokkaidō to the Tokyo region and our involvement in international Indigenous politics are explored. In the second section I describe historical events leading up to the resurgence of Ainu cultural identity in the late-twentieth century. In this section, the analytical concept of 'diasporic indigeneity' comes to life through an examination of the literature. The concept of 'everyday acts of resurgence' (Corntassel 2012) is also discussed, in the context of the Tokyo Ainu community. This is followed in the third section by a more detailed enquiry of the recent historical emergence of Ainu cultural organisations in Tokyo, which, I argue, has led to the development of 'diasporic indigeneity' as an accepted form of cultural identity amongst the Ainu. In my conclusion I briefly speculate on a possible future for Ainu cultural identity.

# Tokyo Ainu: Indigenous people in a Japanese city

Watson (2014a: 76) traces the origins of the Tokyo Ainu community to the early 1950s, when Ainu migration to cities became more common. As stated above, an estimated population of Kantō-region Ainu was about 10,000 people in 2014. According to the *Ainu Living Conditions outside of Hokkaidō Survey* in 2011, which had 210 respondents, 50 per cent answered that they had moved away from Hokkaidō to find work, and 11.4 per cent stated that their relocation was because of discrimination (Council for Ainu Policy Promotion Working Group 2011: 27).

For most of my childhood I was raised around Tokyo. I always had a feeling of loneliness and isolation because I was not able to share who I was and where my family came from. I was often seeking a safer place to rest my mind. At the age of 20, two significant events changed my life. The first was the start of my involvement in international Indigenous politics, which I discuss below. The second was that I was introduced to Tokyo's 'Ainu hub'—an Ainu restaurant in the city. This became a place where I could feel 'at home' or in a 'resting place'. It also became my cultural place of learning. By becoming more involved with the Ainu community in Tokyo, I also began to take a more active role in international Indigenous politics. Spending time with Tokyo Ainu opened my eyes and made me realise how much some of them suffered financially and sometimes psychologically. But, at the same time, I also saw how they generously welcomed new members into their community, as well as people who were interested in Ainu culture. What was most striking about my encounter with Tokyo Ainu was to learn that they still passed on and learnt Ainu culture, even though many of them had kept their Ainu identity private for many years. This raised many questions within me, and helped me to become who I am now.

It is generally known within the Tokyo Ainu community that we Ainu have migrated from Hokkaidō to cities more or less out of necessity, to pursue better employment or educational opportunities, or to escape from severe discrimination in Hokkaidō. Ainu have faced many challenges in establishing ourselves in Tokyo. Migration to Tokyo might entail a person securing a job and financial security for their family, but that does not necessarily mean they earn a high income. Through my experiences with Tokyo Ainu, I have observed that the social gap between most Ainu and

*Wajin* in Tokyo is more noticeable than between *Wajin*, especially in the older generation. Identity is a sensitive topic, both at home and in public. These sensitivities around identity, and the social distance between Ainu and *Wajin* in Tokyo emerge from the Japanese state's assimilationist past and continued refusal to recognise the Ainu people as Indigenous.

In 1899, the Hokkaidō Former Aborigines Protection Act was enacted by the Japanese Government. Its aim was to assimilate Ainu into modern Japanese imperial subjects by eliminating Ainu language, values and customs (Siddle 1996: 70). In 1997, this law was replaced by the Ainu Cultural Promotion Act (CPA), which many Ainu were dissatisfied with, as it was limited only to the promotion of Ainu culture and language, and did not include recognition of our status as Indigenous people. In September 2007, when the government of Japan voted 'yes' to the United Nations Declaration on the Rights of Indigenous Peoples (UNDRIP), it still continued to refuse recognition for the Ainu as an Indigenous people of Japan according to the standards of international law. On 6 June the following year there was a major political shift within Indigenous politics in Japan. Both houses of the Japanese Diet passed a resolution calling for the recognition of the Ainu as an Indigenous people of Japan. Despite this, the government has still not, at the time of writing, included recognition of Ainu rights as an Indigenous people of Japan.

The Ainu political movement to redress this situation goes beyond the nation. Since the 1980s, Ainu organisations have been active in international Indigenous conferences such as those held by the United Nations.[3] Tokyo Ainu organisations have also played a role in international Indigenous politics, aiming to present the situations and struggles of Tokyo Ainu, especially because the general public in Japan seems to know very little about the Ainu in Tokyo, and assume that Ainu reside only in Hokkaidō. This limited understanding of Tokyo Ainu could be part of the reason why there have been so few government surveys on Ainu living outside of Hokkaidō. However, as I am Tokyo Ainu myself, I know that there is a Tokyo Ainu population, and that there is an Ainu community in Tokyo.

---

3    The first time an Ainu organisation participated at a United Nations conference was in 1987. The organisation was the Ainu Association of Hokkaidō, the most politically involved and largest Ainu organisation in Japan (Ainu Association of Hokkaidō 2018).

My involvement in international Indigenous politics started in 2001 when I participated in the 19th session of the UN Working Group on Indigenous Populations in Geneva, Switzerland (Ainu Association of Rera 2001) where I presented the Nibutani Dam case as a community member. This was my first attendance at a UN meeting. To be able to present at the UN, other Ainu friends in Tokyo and I were encouraged and trained by Japanese experts specialising in international law and politics. I was about 20 years old at the time. We met frequently for study groups at a café and at the Ainu Culture Center in Tokyo.[4] As I was quite young and inexperienced and did not know anything about international Indigenous politics, this study was overwhelming. In the beginning, all those UN systems, terms and international laws seemed so far away from my reality that I did not grasp what I was doing. Slowly but surely, I began to understand how I might be able to contribute this knowledge to my Ainu community. This encouraged me to take an active role in international Indigenous politics later on.

On 21 May 2007, some members of the Ainu Resource Centre and I presented a joint statement together with the Shimin Gaikou Centre—a Japanese NGO and long-term supporter of the Ainu political movement—at the 6th session of the United Nations Permanent Forum on Indigenous Issues in New York (Ainu Resource Centre and Shimin Gaikou Centre 2007).[5] This was only a year before the Japanese Government adopted the Resolution on Recognition of Ainu as Indigenous People on 6 June 2008 (Advisory Council for Future Ainu Policy 2009: 1). The item of the day was urban Indigenous peoples and migration. The statement (Ainu Resource Centre and Shimin Gaikou Centre 2007) described the situation for Tokyo Ainu living in the large and densely populated Kantō region, explaining how they had begun to organise themselves, and discussed how different Ainu organisations started to appear. As of 2007, there were four active Ainu associations in the Kantō region, who worked collectively under the name of Ainu Utari Renrakukai (Ainu Companions Liaison Group) when shared political agendas were in need of further discussion with the Tokyo Metropolitan Government. On this occasion,

---

4    The Ainu Culture Center is run by The Foundation for Research and Promotion of Ainu Culture, see www.frpac.or.jp/web/english/details/history-of-the-foundations-establishment.html (accessed 8 August 2018).

5    6th session of the United Nations Permanent Forum on Indigenous Issues, *Special Theme: Territories, Lands and Natural Resources*, 14–25 May 2007.

four of the requests to the Tokyo Government raised by those associations since 1970s were presented (Ainu Resource Centre and Shimin Gaikou Centre 2007: 1–2). They were:

1. to create a place where Ainu could gather and transmit culture such as an Ainu community centre;
2. to set up social welfare support for Ainu;
3. to have an Ainu social counsellor;
4. to conduct a survey on Ainu social and economic conditions in order to have a comprehensive understanding of the Ainu.

Furthermore, the *Ainu Living Conditions outside of Hokkaidō Survey* in 2011 shows three major needs raised by survey participants in response to what needs to be done to increase participation in and practise of Ainu culture and traditions:

1. to establish a place where we can learn;
2. to be informed about any Ainu related activities;
3. to be able to feel more relaxed about our financial situation (Council for Ainu Policy Promotion Working Group 2011: 24).

This survey indicates that Tokyo Ainu could benefit from having a common place. This would ideally be run by the Ainu ourselves with Ainu participation in all aspects of its development. The Ainu Culture Center in Tokyo provides space for activities, but participation is limited because it is managed by the state.

Another challenge that Tokyo Ainu face is that we have to take any available jobs to make a living. Often such jobs require so much time and physical effort that it is nearly impossible to engage in any Ainu cultural activities in the evening or on weekends. I remember wondering, 'How can we learn and develop our culture freely when our day jobs limit our capacity both psychologically and physically?' Tokyo Ainu are in a great need of a place and space where everybody is welcomed to participate in Ainu activities, and such a place should be run on our terms. As discussed below, the Ainu restaurant, Rera Cise (now closed), previously provided such possibilities, but the existence of such an institution is tied to its financial success, and such an institution therefore does not provide a sustainable alternative such as a nonprofit self-driven organisation.

In 1974, 33 years before the UN statement by the Tokyo Ainu group, a similar demand for a community centre was made by Tokyo Ainu. Watson describes that Ainu activist Shizue Ukaji and other members of the Tokyo Utari Association conducted the first survey on Tokyo Ainu, officially entitled *Survey of the Socio-economic Conditions of Ainu Residents in Tokyo between 1974–1975* (Watson 2014b: 73). It was funded by the Tokyo Metropolitan Government (Watson 2014b: 73–74). He states that this survey had three purposes:

1. to determine the size of the Ainu population in the capital region;
2. to clarify the problems Ainu faced with a focus on employment, income, culture, education, marriage, and housing;
3. to use these findings to acquire special financial measures and support from the Tokyo Government in order to establish a *seikatsukan* (community center) for Ainu in the city (ibid.).

It is therefore worth noting that the Tokyo Ainu had been demanding exactly the same things for 33 years.

Overall, it is obvious that the Ainu are in need of a periodical nationwide survey to obtain further understanding of Ainu in general in Japan. In order to gain an overview of the social and economic conditions of the Ainu in Japan, the survey should include Ainu living outside Hokkaidō. Tokyo Ainu are in need of a more autonomous institution, like a community centre, where we can be in charge. If the Japanese Government met this fundamental need, it would imply that they recognise Tokyo Ainu's existence as an Indigenous people with collective rights to self-determination in an urban context. The community centre could be used as a place where we as Tokyo Ainu could share our life experiences and challenges in the process of the further development and restoration of our culture. Here, the most important factor that needs to be supported by the government is the recognition that we as Indigenous people are empowered to manage our projects and set our own agendas. Such a community centre in Tokyo would have a similar role as the *kotan* (in the Ainu language), which means a village, or place where people live, and where we gather for various activities to share experiences. I perceive this urban *kotan* as our diaspora. In the next section, I discuss an interpretation of diasporic indigeneity and 'resurgence of Indigenous culture' from my Tokyo Ainu perspective.

# Diasporic indigeneity and everyday acts of resurgence

As I spent most of my youth in Tokyo, the concept of 'diaspora' is something that is familiar and relevant to my environment and the people I relate to. For example, migrating to cities to seek better employment or commuting from Hokkaidō to Tokyo is considered part of the Ainu urban lifestyle in both Hokkaidō and Tokyo. Our memories of our food, language and culture, and even experiences with family and friends, travel with us wherever we go, and eventually become part of our identities.

So then, what do Tokyo Ainu carry with us in Tokyo? In my experience, we live just like *Wajin* in Tokyo—wearing modern clothing, eating Japanese food, and so on. Our life is very much integrated into modern Japanese society. The difference is how and when we practise Ainu culture in Tokyo, and how we carry ourselves as Ainu individuals.

First, we still carry our Ainu food culture with us, especially whenever we are able to get hold of ingredients from Hokkaidō. Unfortunately, from Tokyo we cannot easily go to the mountains to harvest the ingredients we need to make Ainu food, or collect bark from trees to make the Ainu traditional robe called *attus*. All those materials and ingredients are only available in Hokkaidō.

Second, our way of being Ainu needs to be initiated individually. Since we live like *Wajin* in Tokyo, our consciousness and way of understanding the world is what distinguishes Ainu from non-Ainu persons. Thus, Tokyo Ainu need to be creative about how they use urban space in order to hold traditional ceremonies for special occasions, such as a marriage, or how they will conduct a ceremony for the opening of a new restaurant. Nevertheless, the Ainu Culture Center is used daily by Tokyo Ainu for various activities, like song and dance lessons or for doing embroidery. So, in a way, we still share many cultural practices, just like Hokkaidō Ainu, by using urban space and place to practise and revitalise Ainu culture.

Interpretations of space and place differ in various parts of the world. David Gegeo from the Indigenous groups of Kwara'ae and Lau in the Solomon Islands introduces a more flexible way of understanding such concepts based on his Indigenous background. Gegeo writes:

> Space (*kula ni tua*, literally, 'place situated in dwell[ing]': that is, place not of one's existential being but rather of temporary or even long-term staying) refers to a space that is not of one's identity or origin. Space has to do with the *location* where a Kwara'ae person may be at any given time as necessitated by contemporary conditions (such as going to an urban area to get a job to meet basic needs or going overseas in pursuit of an education) (2001: 494).

This approach to 'space' provides a new possibility for us as Indigenous migrants to reroot or relocate ourselves in a new place and environment. What matters is how you position and relate yourself within the environment around you. I share Gegeo's point of view that one can identify with one's place of origin while residing beyond the borders of that place.

Indigenous identities are flexible and changing and reflect, instead of resist, a borderless world. I use and interpret the terminology of Indigenous identity from my Ainu background. For me, Indigenous identity means a way of being myself, the Ainu way—*Aynupuri* in the Ainu language. Each person has his or her own Ainu way of being, and each person explores his or her world on his or her own terms. Following Gegeo's suggestions concerning how Indigenous people make our own places and spaces in the world, I suggest that we need to work towards a framework where we as Indigenous people can decide our own identities and our position in society without these being externally assigned. In case this extended approach to special relations and Indigenous identity sounds unclear, I will introduce the concept of 'diasporic indigeneity' to support this idea.

Our borderless, urban, westernised contemporary world somehow gives us an impression of living in one big machine with advanced technology, shared customs and sense of being. This entails our rapid mobility and dislocation from our homeland to places where a mainstream culture dominates other cultures. In Tokyo, Ainu culture is not readily visible to the general public. Because of our integration into Japanese society, we are almost invisible. However, our consciousness and identity still remain within us. The term 'diasporic' is therefore a useful term to situate our environment and lived experiences as urban Ainu.

Mark Watson, who has worked with Tokyo Ainu for many years, explains the major motivation he had for writing his book *Japan's Ainu Minority in Tokyo*, stating:

> This book has been the opportunity to think about how the inherent complexities of Ainu sociality in and around Tokyo intersect with the more general discussion of urban indigeneity as a focus for research at an international level. Diaspora, for example, is a mainstream theoretical concept that contrary to popular opinion is being used by scholars in a variety of ways to describe and better understand the lived experiences of indigenous people outside of traditional lands (2014b: 147).

I very much share his motivation to look into the complexities of Tokyo Ainu sociality, and believe that many of the challenges Tokyo Ainu face in our daily lives are shared by other urban Indigenous people across the globe. The term 'diaspora' has given me a new direction from which to reflect upon our lived experiences as part of an urban Indigenous community. The term 'diaspora' in the context of our borderless urban world is suggestive of Indigenous mobility and the unique characteristics of urban Indigenous conditions, and contains implications for Indigenous understandings of space and place. Living diasporically has become a necessity for many Indigenous people so we can survive and maintain our culture and identity. This new perspective also underlines the importance of urban Indigenous studies in illustrating and explaining the complexity of urban migration for urban Indigenous communities. It also sheds light on the new cultural formation of Indigenous people in cities, something that I have experienced in my youth in Tokyo.

Another example of how this concept has come to life, besides my own experience, is given by Andrea Avaria Saavedra (2005). Saavedra describes how new Indigenous mobilities transform native understandings of space and place. In drawing on a case study of urban Mapuche migration in Chile, Saavedra states:

> How do we all live here together, arriving from different places, and with distinct indigenous cultures still intact, within the larger Mapuche whole? Evidence for this new shared identity—with all its social, symbolic and cultural implications—can be found in Mapuche practices, individual experiences, new forms of communication, self-reference and self-description. All of these illustrate how the very meaning of being Mapuche can change within the context of an urban and often hostile environment (2005: 54).

How I interpret Saavedra's analysis of shared identity is that one can still find a shared Indigenous identity through one's experiences, new forms of communication, self-reference and self-description. This supports Watson's (2014b) analysis, presented earlier, about the term 'diasporic indigeneity', which posits that Indigenous people remake their identities in cities through processes of reterrititorialisation, bringing lived relationships with ancestral homelands and community members into the urban context.

This perspective of 'diasporic indigeneity' goes beyond the influential working definition of 'Indigenous' in José R. Martinez Cobo's important *Study of the Problem of Discrimination against Indigenous Populations* (1987), which emphasises connection with ancestral territories. Although there are no fixed definitions of the concept of 'Indigenous people' within the United Nations' system, Cobo's working definition is internationally recognised and is still widely used. Here, I present two factors relating to the traditional land of Indigenous people summarised by the Secretariat of the Permanent Forum on Indigenous Issues. These two factors specify that: ancestral lands are occupied, or at least of part of them; and that there is shared common ancestry with the original inhabitants of these lands (Secretariat of the Permanent Forum on Indigenous Issues 2004: 2). Cobo's report, which focuses more on ancestral land, highlights how significant social, economic and political changes occurred in Indigenous communities from the 1980s to the present.

In 2018, defining Indigenous people is now even more complex and politicised, and must take into account an ever-expanding variety of political, cultural and economic conditions in various countries around the world. This working definition was provided for practical purposes, but as stated by Saavedra (2005), Indigenous people have come to a point, through globalisation and modernisation, where we are urged to incorporate social relations that extend beyond geographical boundaries. This means that we should examine Indigenous mobility and Indigenous social and cultural expressions on our own terms, which may bring new understandings of the ontological status of Indigenous people.

One may wonder, then, what kind of experiences, new forms of communication, self-reference and self-description from the shared Indigenous identity might be relevant, especially in cities? Jeff Corntassel (2012) in his article, 'Re-envisioning resurgence: Indigenous pathways to decolonisation and sustainable self-determination', discusses the concept of Indigenous resurgence, which I find useful in thinking about how Indigenous people construct diasporic indigeneity away from their ancestral homelands. Corntassel explains Indigenous resurgence as people having the bravery and imagination to visualise life beyond the state. He explains:

> If one thinks of peoplehood as the interlocking features of language, homeland, ceremonial cycle, and sacred living histories, a disruption to any one of these practices threatens all aspects of everyday life. The complex spiritual, political and social relationships that hold peoplehood together are continuously renewed. These daily acts of renewal, whether through prayer, speaking your language, honouring your ancestors, etc., are the foundation of resurgence (2012: 89).

I share his view and interpretation of 'resurgence', which acknowledges that the various interlocking features of indigeneity are always in flux. Daily acts constitute the foundation of resurgence, and are the substantive content of shared indigeneity based on new forms of communication, self-reference and self-description. Corntassel also emphasises that, within a context of decolonisation practice, it is important to accept daily conditions, and engage oneself with place-based cultural practices (2012: 89). Although I agree with Corntassel in this regard, I think it is important to modulate this place-based emphasis in order to take into account the experience of urban Indigenous people, and look at how acts of resurgence create greater possibilities of new Indigenous pathways in cities. The concept of 'resurgence' can thus be contrasted with Cobo's working definition of indigeneity. Furthermore, if one combines Gegeo's view on the ontological status of Indigenous people, Watson's interpretation of diasporic indigeneities and Corntassel's view on 'everyday acts of resurgence', an important point is clarified—that a person's geographical location does not limit the possibilities of pursuing and developing Indigenous identity and culture.

In the next section, I introduce a detailed case study of the recent historical emergence of Ainu cultural organisations in Tokyo, as an auto-ethnographic story which touches upon my previous discussion of 'space and place' in relation to an expression of Indigenous identity, diasporic indigeneity and the resurgence of Indigenous culture.

# Rera Cise (the 'House of Wind') in Tokyo

How one's identity and culture are expressed in society depends on one's relationship to the environment and to other people. To be able to express one's identity and culture, several factors are needed. I roughly categorise these into:

1. people, place and space;
2. food and material objects;
3. rights to decide one's own identities and position in society without them being externally assigned.

As we are collective beings, the connection and association we have with other people, and even material objects, strengthen and determine our motivation and meaning in life regardless of our origins. As discussed earlier, Indigenous people are often forced to move to areas other than our homeland to seek work or education. We often need to adapt ourselves and to associate with others to be able to express our identities and culture in new settings. The concept of everyday acts of resurgence confirms the importance of such acts to the maintenance of identity in an urban setting. To share such a connection and association with others and other things requires us to have a certain place and space where we can exercise our daily routines, rituals and associated activities. As explained earlier, the place and space cannot be traditional land when it comes to an urban Indigenous context. What matters is how we make the most of the place and space available. This is often the reality for urban Indigenous people, where we have no choice other than to make our own present and future in cities. This is what I discussed above as diasporic indigeneity. Lastly, it is most important that we as Indigenous people should have the right to express our culture freely and to define what 'Indigenous culture' is for ourselves, regardless of our geographical location and without external interference. I would now like to bring in my own experiences as a Tokyo Ainu woman to illustrate these concepts.

I identify as Indigenous, mixed Japanese–Ainu. I am a typical urban Ainu, insofar as I did not have the possibility of learning the Ainu language and culture fully, either in school or at home. Thus, my personal learning arena for Ainu culture and the place where I could have a feeling of 'belonging' as part of the Ainu people were spaces, like the Rera Cise restaurant in Tokyo, where I was able to meet other Ainu, including Ainu Elders.

I was 20 years old when I was introduced to the Ainu restaurant called Rera Cise, and the Ainu Association of Rera, which was an Ainu cultural association established in 1983. Its membership was made up of all Ainu members who worked in or were involved with the Ainu restaurant and other Tokyo Ainu activities. Established in 1994, Rera Cise was the first Ainu restaurant in Tokyo. It was built after a successful national fundraising campaign. Both Japanese and Ainu supporters were involved in the process, which made it possible for Tokyo Ainu to have a place to bring Ainu food culture to Tokyo.

Rera Cise, which literally means 'House of Wind' in the Ainu language, opened in a basement suite in Waseda, Tokyo, opposite Waseda University (Nishi-Waseda campus). It was located in a typical university campus area where many college students passed by every day. The Rera Cise sign was so small that customers could easily miss it. The small entrance to the restaurant may have looked a little mysterious, as there was a long and narrow, dimly lit stairway down to the restaurant. However, when you entered the restaurant, there was, suddenly, quite a different atmosphere.

Ainu music, wooden furniture and *cikoro-inaw* (Ainu ritual wood-shaving stick)—after having been used for the house ceremony—decorated the corners of the ceilings for the protection of the space. The restaurant space was quite small, about 50 square metres, with a tiny kitchen only big enough for two people to work together. Despite the location and limited space in the restaurant, many students and teachers came for a cheap, quick, healthy and fulfilling lunch and dinner. Half of the customers were activists and supporters of Rera Cise; the other half were those who had read or heard rumours about the restaurant, and wanted to taste exotic Ainu food. The menu was based on the memories of the Ainu Elders who worked at the restaurant. Some dishes were traditional Ainu food and some were modern food created after the Meiji period (1868–1912). For example, salmon, which was one of the most important staple foods for Ainu, was a much-used ingredient in the menu. A chopped mixture of the salmon head and milt were used to make pickles—*citatap* in the Ainu language—with roasted seaweed and salt. The head and bones were used as basic bouillon for vegetable soup, which takes two days to make. Salmon eggs were used to make a rice bowl dish called *cipor don*—rice bowl with salmon eggs (a modern food). The fillet was used for making grilled fish with salt. The fillet was also served as *ru-i-be*—a form of frozen sashimi—and it was also dried out with the skin on and served as a snack with beer or sake.

Ainu practise animism, which is a belief that nonhuman entities (plants, animals and other objects) around human beings possess spiritual essences. Ainu have various names for animals and nature, which are sometimes referred to as Kamuy; the closest term we might use is 'gods', but not in the same sense as the Christian God. Salmon is called Kamuy-cep in the Ainu language and is considered one of the most important of the fish species. An aspect of Ainu philosophy concerning food culture is that Ainu are appreciative of all food they receive from nature. Our use of all parts of the salmon reflects this philosophy. Nature and human beings are equal, and therefore, Ainu live in a sustainable way by sharing all food received by nature, and by leaving some food behind when they have finished hunting for other animals in the mountains.

The Rera Cise restaurant provided space and place for urban Ainu and for those who had an interest in Ainu food and culture, and wanted to share and experience them. It was also a bridge between Elders and youth, where we could transmit our knowledge through various activities. The Ainu Association of Rera, the organisation that ran the restaurant, also had political aims, such as the dissemination and promotion of Ainu culture, and of disseminating political messages, by performing dances and songs at public events, schools and concerts.

I became involved in the Tokyo Ainu community through the Ainu Association of Rera and Rera Cise. I was immediately welcomed and considered to be a member of the Tokyo Ainu community. One reason could be that my grandfather was an Ainu leader and activist who everybody knew. Emotionally speaking, I became very passionate about learning Ainu dances and songs and I appreciated the fact that we could have our own style, voice and expression. As a child, I had been trained very strictly to sing in a Japanese choir where everybody had to be perfectly in tune. In comparison to that experience, the Ainu performance group associated with the Ainu Association of Rera encouraged a much freer style of dancing, to the extent that they looked upon what I thought of as mistakes as expressions of my being a 'knower'—someone who (almost) knew how to dance. On one occasion, the training I received from the Ainu Association of Rera led me to perform as part of a music concert in Ebisu, Tokyo, with professional Indigenous musicians from Japan and Australia (the band from Australia was called Waak Waak Jungi). The most inspiring part of their performance was their mixing of traditional Ainu and contemporary music with the didjeridu, a traditional Australian Aboriginal instrument. The deep, strong sound of the didjeridu created a very smooth harmony with the soft and sensitive sounds of the Ainu traditional instrument *tonkori*, played by the world's most prominent *tonkori* musician, Oki Kano.

My part involved five minutes of Ainu traditional dancing before the main concert, and I also performed in the chorus together with other female Ainu performers. We rehearsed for several hours, and I was very nervous, especially knowing that the audience had paid a lot of money to attend the concert. There were about 100 people in the audience. The performance took place in the basement of a tall concrete building. I heard the audience whispering to each other before the concert and I became more and more nervous.

Our group dance opened the show. I made a big mistake with my part in the performance. The dance is called *fu-ta-re-cui*, and expresses the movement of pine trees shaken by a strong wind, so you bend your whole head and upper body to the front and back to express this movement. It is a quite an intense dance and we were all supposed to do the dance movements simultaneously, but I made a mistake by doing it completely opposite to the other performers. I was not able to focus after that. When the show was over, I ran to my dear friend, Takumi Ikabe, a senior Ainu sculptor, with my eyes filled with tears. I said, 'Did you see that I made a big mistake in the group dance!? I feel so ashamed and sad'. He replied, 'Yes, I saw it, but Kanako, that is you. Your mistake is part of you and part of your quality—nothing to be ashamed of'. I was saved by his words. This was unexpected and it surprised me that I was still accepted even with my mistakes. Probably none of my *Wajin* friends would have said such a thing to me. This perception of accepting whoever you are, with or without mistakes, made me realise how my values were deeply influenced by the *Wajin* way of thinking, which is that everybody is expected to perform and behave the same as others, without exception. All the pressure and stress I carried with me immediately seemed to evaporate. This sense of being different appealed to me, and not just because it forgave mistakes. I could see that it accepted creativity. This perception of how to look at, interpret, and be in the world made me feel more confident about myself and gave me a chance to think deeply about who I would like to become.

Up until the time I joined the Ainu Association of Rera in Tokyo, Ainu culture had only existed for me in my memories from Hokkaidō, where I spent my childhood with my grandparents. It brought back memories of my struggles to distinguish between two completely different cultures—

Ainu and Japanese—and I even wondered why I should think and behave differently depending on where I was. I still remember myself as a small child being puzzled by my dual life. Whenever I returned to Tokyo, I acted as a *Wajin* girl who never talked about Ainu culture. It was not conscious, but, as a child, I quickly realised that no one would understand what I was referring to if I spoke about the Ainu. This continued until I encountered the Tokyo Ainu community. Until then, I would never have imagined that I could find such an Ainu community in the middle of Tokyo. Such a space and social sphere eventually became my emotional home where there is a feeling of 'belonging' and 'home' in my heart.

A dynamic urban space provides different possibilities. It fills an economic need, and it attracts many Indigenous peoples, especially Indigenous youth. It is a space where we can experiment with our future and our possibilities. The anonymous part of city life somehow gives us the freedom to be who we are and who we want to become. Urban life can even provide the flexibility and possibility of having complex identities, and allow us to negotiate those identities and find ways to express ourselves that are most comfortable for us. I agree with Watson's description of how Tokyo has become a new geographical place since the 1960s (2014b: 70). For the Tokyo Ainu, it represents the possibility of reflecting upon one's sense of self, despite all the hardships related to our living and negotiating the political conditions in Tokyo.

My Ainu identity in my early 20s was confirmed and strengthened by associating with other Ainu friends and in social spaces such as Rera Cise in Tokyo, without being in my so-called 'homeland'. Such social spaces became something that symbolised my Ainu culture and became a transformative space for me. They helped me to identify myself as an Indigenous person. The curiosity that grew created many opportunities for me to visit and study overseas. Such overseas experiences, together with the collective recognition from others, have triggered my Indigenous identity and made me proud to be an Ainu. The experiences I have had due to my involvement with Rera Cise support the argument that one's geographical location does not necessarily determine one's identity and culture. Rather, it is through relationships to people and places that experiences are constructed through food culture, language, rituals and ceremonies. These are everyday acts of resurgence in diasporic indigeneity.

Finally, when we consider what cities can offer Indigenous people in terms of practical solutions, or agonise over what urban Indigenous people can do to improve our situations, it is critically important that Indigenous people are included in all decision-making by legitimising their participation in all related matters. This could support Indigenous people to decide our own identity and our position in society without this being externally assigned. I would like to introduce Gerald Taiaiake Alfred's suggestion of five measurements or guidelines to fulfil Indigenous regeneration for both individuals and communities:

1. The restoration of Indigenous presence on the land and the revitalisation of land-based practices;

2. An increased reliance on traditional diets among Indigenous people;

3. The transmission of Indigenous culture, spiritual teachings and knowledge of the land between Elders and youth;

4. The strengthening of familial activities and re-emergence of Indigenous cultural and social institutions as governing authorities within First Nations; and,

5. Short-term and long-term initiatives and improvements in sustainable land-based economies as the primary economies of reserve based First Nations communities and as supplemental economies for urban Indigenous communities (2009: 56).

I would argue that measurements 2 to 5 are quite suitable for Tokyo Ainu. All of these points manifest the idea that it is of critical importance for us, as Indigenous people, to have our own place and space to regenerate a flow of Indigenous cultural development, especially through a bridge between Elders and youth, regardless of geographic location. For Indigenous people, to eat a traditional diet brings back all the memories and food habits, and the communication that takes place during the process of making food. Eating traditional food constitutes an 'everyday act of resurgence'. To transmit Indigenous culture, spiritual teachings and knowledge of the land between Elders and youth is obviously important. However, what could be added here from an urban perspective is to teach Indigenous youth about alternative ways of expressing one's identity beyond geographical boundaries, and also to provide strategies for relating to the land or homeland without actually being on the land or in the homeland. Strengthening familiar activities and the reemergence of Indigenous cultural and social institutions as governing authorities could, of course, raise more awareness among Indigenous people and could reinforce their shared identity. This approach could particularly strengthen the Tokyo Ainu community for two reasons:

1. focusing on collective activities could be more effective since we are prone to organising ourselves and thinking collectively;
2. paying more attention to the reemergence of Indigenous cultural and social institutions could reaffirm that we are as important as political and economic institutions.

Short-term and long-term initiatives and improvements in sustainable land-based economies for providing supplemental economies for urban Indigenous communities could also be relevant in many ways.

A place like Rera Cise was capable of supporting most of the elements mentioned above. It was the place where a traditional diet was revitalised, where Ainu culture, language and spirituality were transmitted across generations, and most importantly, it was a cultural and social institution which was independently run by the Ainu. The role of the cultural and social institution of course helped to inform political activities as well. It led to the translation of political messages that were conveyed to Japanese society—voicing our claims as well as describing future possibilities. Rera Cise became the place for everybody to gather together with youth and Elders, to eat Ainu food, to discuss the future and to share Ainu culture. It was definitely a central Ainu organisation in Tokyo from 1994 to 2009. A small urban space like Rera Cise can thus be a foundation for resurgence, where it produces Indigenous knowledge through food, music, art and interactions between Elders and youth. It creates a 'home' where it is possible to feel free to express one's sense of being with both Indigenous and non-Indigenous people.

## Conclusion

I consider myself a Tokyo Ainu, yet I fully acknowledge my complex identity as someone who grew up in Japanese society just like any other *Wajin*. What I consider 'home' is where I have an emotional attachment and through which some of my 'being as Ainu' was formed. For example, Nibutani Village, one of the Ainu sacred places of Hokkaidō, where I spent all my school holidays with my grandparents and cousins, is 'home', as is that particular time and place in Tokyo when I became Ainu with the Ainu community there. But, what does this tell us about how resurgence is intertwined with urban Indigenous life? My memories and experiences are embedded in my body, which influences my daily actions and behaviour, wherever I am. I cannot deny the fact that I am part of the huge machinery of globalisation, and that globalisation has given me so many opportunities to explore the world. All these years of living abroad and in cities has raised a question of how I can position myself and find my own Indigenous pathway as an Ainu person, regardless of geographical location and without being actually at 'home'. It is true that all the memories are embedded in my body, but these memories need to be performed and activated to be able to be part of my real life. What has been helpful for me to reconnect myself to the Ainu culture is to play *mukkuri* (the Ainu traditional mouth harp), which can be played alone, and anywhere in the world. Singing Ainu songs, which I learned from my time in Tokyo, also helps me to reconnect myself to Ainu culture. However, what seems to be most important for me is to be able to share my daily stories and struggles with Ainu friends who accept who I am.

I consider my experiences with the Tokyo Ainu community to consist of many 'everyday acts of resurgence' in a framework of diasporic indigeneity. What we did within the community was to reconnect ourselves with memories from Hokkaidō through food, music, ceremony and even our own consciousness. We revitalised and strengthened our culture and consciousness by securing our urban space and place, without actually being in our 'homeland'. Rera Cise was a good example of such a space and place. It was unique in Tokyo. It fostered our minds to be creative and think critically, and enabled us to explore Ainu culture together. The door of Rera Cise was always open to *Wajin* or anyone who was interested in Ainu culture. Having such an Ainu-driven urban *kotan* (community) provided opportunities for the revitalisation of Ainu culture in urban space. Furthermore, it provided an opportunity for both Ainu and non-Ainu persons to share and discover Ainu culture and, in the process, even to discover themselves. As we are faced with increasing numbers of Indigenous people migrating to cities in the future, such urban *kotan* could offer a way to reestablish a better foundation for a more inclusive social model.

# Acknowledgements

Numbers of experienced scholars and friends from all over the world supported and encouraged me to write this article. First, I wish to thank Tetuhito Oono, who helped me with the Ainu language and Ainu tradition. From Arctic Norway, my supervisors, Torill Nyseth and Torjer Andreas Olsen, as well as Helen Verran from Australia, helped me to conceptualise my life stories in academic discussions. Hiroshi Maruyama from Japan and Gerald Roche, as well as Åsa Virdi Kroik, as editors of the article also followed and supported me throughout the process. Mark Watson from Canada, who is my long-term friend, encouraged me to write about the urban Ainu by introducing me to various related theories and discussions. The Sami scholar from the United States, Troy Storfjell, supported me in the last phase of writing the article by providing comments and perspectives of Indigenous studies from North America.

# References

Advisory Council for Future Ainu Policy. 2009. *Final Report*. Online: www. kantei.go.jp/jp/singi/ainu/dai10/siryou1_en.pdf (accessed 11 July 2018).

Ainu Association of Hokkaidō. 2018. *Ainu Historical Events*. Online: www.ainu-assn.or.jp/english/history.html (accessed 11 July 2018).

Ainu Association of Rera. 2001. *Statement by the Ainu Association of Rera Nineteenth Session of the UN Working Group on Indigenous Populations 23–27 July 2001*, Geneva. Online: www.geocities.jp/indigenousnet/200119thWGIP statementE.pdf (accessed 2 August 2018).

Ainu minzoku o senjū minzoku to suru koto o motomeru ketsugi [Resolution on Recognition of Ainu as Indigenous People], No. 169th Diet Session, House of Representatives (6 June 2008) and House of Councillors (6 June 2008).

Ainu Resource Centre and Shimin Gaikou Centre. 2007. *Situation and Issues of Ainu in the Kanto Region*. Online: cendoc.docip.org/collect/cendocdo/index/ assoc/HASH3862/845fd5a8.dir/PF07ainu211.pdf (accessed 12 July 2018).

Alfred, Gerald Taiaiake. 2009. 'Colonialism and state dependency'. *International Journal of Indigenous Health* 5(2): 42–60. Online: ashbrookclassroom. pbworks.com/w/file/fetch/61011895/Colonialism%20and%20State%20 Dependency.pdf (accessed 14 July 2018).

Cobo, José R. Martinez. 1987. *Study of the Problem of Discrimination against Indigenous Populations*. E/CN.4/Sub.2/1986/7 Add. 4. United Nations. Online: undocs.org/en/E/CN.4/Sub.2/1986/7/Add.4 (accessed 24 July 2018).

Corntassel, Jeff. 2012. 'Re-envisioning resurgence: Indigenous pathways to decolonization and sustainable self-determination'. *Decolonization: Indigeneity, Education & Society* 1(1): 86–101. Online: jps.library.utoronto.ca/index.php/des/article/view/18627 (accessed 14 July 2018).

Council for Ainu Policy Promotion Working Group on the Ainu Living Conditions outside of Hokkaidō Survey. 2011. *The Report of the Working Group on the Ainu Living Conditions outside of Hokkaidō Survey.* Online: www.kantei.go.jp/jp/singi/ainusuishin/dai3/siryou3_3.pdf (accessed 11 July 2018).

Department of Hokkaidō Environment and Lifestyle. 2017. *The Report of Hokkaidō Ainu Living Conditions Survey.* Online: www.pref.hokkaido.lg.jp/ks/ass/H29_ainu_living_conditions_survey.pdf (accessed 12 August 2018).

Gegeo, David Welchman. 2001. 'Cultural Rupture and Indigeneity: The Challenge of (Re)visioning "Place" in the Pacific'. *The Contemporary Pacific* 13(2): 491–507. doi.org/10.1353/cp.2001.0052

Hokkaidō Former Natives Protection Act, promulgated (北海道旧土人保護法公布) by the Meiji Government, 2 March 1899 (Meiji 32).

*Promotion of the Ainu Culture and for the Dissemination and Advocacy for the Traditions of the Ainu and the Ainu Culture* (Law No. 52, 14 May 1997; Amendment: Law No. 160, 22 December 1999).

Saavedra, Avaria Andrea. 2005. 'Mobile identity: The Mapuche of Santiago, Chile'. In *Indigenous Diasporas and Dislocations,* edited by Graham Harvey and Charles D. Thompson Jr, 53–60. London: Routledge.

Secretariat of the Permanent Forum on Indigenous Issues. 2004. *The Concept of Indigenous Peoples*. PFII/2004/WS.1/3. United Nations. Online: www.un.org/esa/socdev/unpfii/documents/workshop_data_background.doc (accessed 14 July 2018).

Siddle, Richard. 1996. 'Former natives'. In *Race, Resistance and the Ainu of Japan,* 51–75. London: Routledge.

The Foundation for Research and Promotion of Ainu Culture. 2018. *History of the Foundation's Establishment*. Online: www.frpac.or.jp/web/english/details/history-of-the-foundations-establishment.html (accessed 8 August 2018).

*United Nations Declaration on the Rights of Indigenous Peoples*, GA Res 61/295, UN GAOR, 61st sess, 107th plen mtg, Sup No 49, UN Doc A/RES/61/295 (13 September 2007).

United Nations Department of Economic and Social Affairs. 2014. *World Urbanization Prospects: The 2014 Revision*. ST/ESASER.A/352, New York: United Nations. Online: esa.un.org/unpd/wup/publications/files/wup2014-highlights.pdf (accessed 12 July 2018).

Watson, Mark. 2014a. 'Tokyo Ainu and the urban Indigenous experience'. In *Beyond Ainu Studies: Changing Academic and Public Perspectives*, edited by Mark J. Hudson, Ann-Elise Lewallen and Mark K. Watson, 69–85. University of Hawai'i Press.

Watson, Mark. 2014b. *Japan's Ainu Minority in Tokyo: Diasporic Indigeneity and Urban Politics*. London and New York: Routledge. doi.org/10.4324/9781315815435

Whitinui, Paul. 2014. 'Indigenous autoethnography: Exploring, engaging, and experiencing "self" as a Native method of inquiry'. *Journal of Contemporary Ethnography* 43(4): 456–87. doi.org/10.1177/0891241613508148

# 21

# Saami Coffee Culture

Chris Kolbu and Anne Wuolab

I grew up with Saami coffee culture.[1] It was always around me; at home, while visiting relatives, in the mountains, by the reindeer enclosure. It's a natural part of my life. I only condense it down to its essential parts and present it for people unfamiliar with it, through coffee, stories and settings.

Saami coffee culture wasn't as conceptually clear to me when I started my café in Lycksele in 2011. Even though I had support from the Indigee Indigenous Entrepreneurship program, I still found it difficult to start the business at first. But later, while I was in my café, I noticed how different people would sit and drink their coffee. Saami customers stood apart with their slow, ceremonial way of interacting with the coffee and with each other. Since then, I've studied our cultural history and spoken with many people, young and old, to better understand the essence of Saami coffee culture. I've learned that, wherever it occurs, Saami coffee culture is basically the same.

The Saami started drinking coffee in the late nineteenth century, shortly after it had become pervasive in the southern parts of the Scandinavian countries. Although coffee probably came to the Saami from the south,

---

1    This text has been edited from an interview with Anne Wuolab by Chris Kolbu on the Nordic Coffee Culture Blog, and republished here with their permission. The original text can be found on the Nordic Coffee Culture Blog. The text begins with a short introduction from Chris, and then switches to a first-person narrative from Anne, based on an interview with Chris.

we have developed a different culture around making and drinking coffee. Coffee was initially used as a complement to reindeer broth, but it soon became viewed as a drink in its own right. Serving it with cow's or goat's milk, as well as coffee cheese and dried reindeer meat is still normal to this day.

Saami will normally know when they are being served coffee, and act accordingly. If they are asked to help out, they will. Not being offered a coffee is tantamount to being given the cold shoulder. However, such things rarely occur, as people seldom wish to cause someone else to lose face in front of others. The coffee is prepared according to the preferences of the host.

Now, I arrange coffee experiences that are based in Saami coffee culture. I might arrange anywhere between four and 10 such events throughout the year, though winter and spring are the busiest times for me. During these events, I talk about how the Saami prepare and drink coffee, while people are served coffee prepared in the traditional manner, with coffee cheese and dried reindeer meat. I put on these events outdoors with a fire, and indoors, in cafés or other settings. I've also organised them as coffee breaks at conferences and business meetings. My customers are both Saami and non-Saami.

Coffee ceremonies are quiet affairs. We use the same coffee beans as everyone else, and we do not prepare them in any special way. The coffee is immersion brewed, and served with cheese and dried reindeer meat. We usually have someone serve the coffee to people—they need to prepare or pour it themselves. To better understand what goes on, it is helpful to imagine a Japanese tea ceremony. It is important that the proper amount of time is taken while drinking coffee, to better create a contemplative and intimate mood. To me, Saami coffee culture is the polar opposite of a short, two-sip espresso or a takeaway coffee. People take their time while drinking, and a coffee event might take anywhere between 20 minutes to an hour. Stories are told, which might be mythical, rooted in Saami spirituality, or comedic.

Coffee is served with *gáffevuostá*, reindeer cheese. It isn't necessarily specific to the Saami—it exists in other reindeer-herding cultures as well, and perhaps similar cheese also exists in other cultures, made from goat's or cow's milk. The consistency of the *gáffevuostá* is like halloumi, and is meant to keep its shape even when it is put in the hot coffee—though it will become softer. Like halloumi, good *gáffevuostá* should squeak between your teeth when you bite it, but otherwise, *gáffevuostá* does not taste like halloumi.

When making coffee, it is important to make a good fire. Saami fires are made by placing firewood in parallel to each other on top of a couple of perpendicular logs, forming a dense, raised rectangle that will have good oxygen flow but burn slowly. The coffee kettle is always placed on the ground by whichever of the longer sides has the strongest fire going. And as for the cups, it is best if the coffee is drunk out of a traditional Saami cup, a *guksie* (Figure 15).

Figure 15. A *guksie*, a traditional Saami cup used for drinking coffee, carved from wood by Erik Schepers.

Source. Photographed by Erik Schepers, Susteren, the Netherlands, February 2010. Used with permission.

I would like to start a nomadic café. It could travel to Saami festivals, weekend events and markets as a kind of 'pop-up' shop. The coffee would be presented in Saami style, but there might also be a cultural element to it: an exhibition or a mini concert, for instance. I would make coffee using immersion and hand brewing methods.

# References

Nordic Coffee Culture Blog. n.d. 'The Sami Coffee Ceremony: An Interview with Anne Wuolab', Online: nordiccoffeeculture.com/the-sami-coffee-ceremony-an-interview-with-anne-wuolab/ (accessed 24 July 2018).

Schepers, Erik. 2010. 'A freshly carved cup', 27 February. Online: www.flickr.com/photos/schepers/4406455419 (accessed 22 August 2018).

# 22

# Cultural Revitalisation: 'Feeding on the Tools of the Conquerors'—A Sami-American Perspective

Chris Pesklo

The Sami are one of the world's many Indigenous peoples, and one of Europe's few Indigenous people. Numbering somewhere between 25,000 and 250,000, depending on the counting method used, the Sami people (derogatorily known as 'Lapps') live in the northern Nordic countries of Norway, Sweden and Finland, and on the Kola Peninsula of Russia—an area that the Sami call Sapmi. The Sami have a history of coexistence with their Nordic neighbours, but they have also endured forced, coerced and incentivised cultural assimilation into the dominant cultures where they reside. The history of the Sami in their respective Nordic counties is similar to the histories of exploitation of other Indigenous peoples. The borders drawn across the Scandinavian landscape have more meaning to the Nordic countries than they do for the Sami, as families are often on both sides of these government-created barriers.

Approximately 30,000 descendants of Sami immigrants live in North America ('About the North American Sami' n.d.)—an immigrant story that their Sami kin in Sapmi often cannot relate to. In this article, it is hoped that the reader will learn how one North American small business has tried to contribute to the revitalisation of Sami culture outside of Sapmi.

# What is a *lavvu*?

The *lavvu* is a tent that has been used by the Sami people for centuries. To the untrained North American eye, the *lavvu* looks very similar to the Native American *tipi*, but its structure, pattern and even spiritual use are very different. There are other similar structures in the Arctic polar regions, such as the *chum* used by the Nenets and Khanets of northern Russia, each with their own history, but most outsiders know even less about these structures (Figure 16).

Figure 16. The Inga family c. 1896. The photograph was taken at Kanstadfjord on the Hinnøy part of Andøy. A *lavvu* tent is in the background, while a *goahti* is in the foreground.

Source. A Lapp Family, Norway (c. 1895–1900). Library of Congress Prints and Photographs Division Washington, DC 20540 USA. LC-DIG-ppmsc-06257 (digital file from original). No known restrictions on publication. Online: www.loc.gov/pictures/item/2001700768/ (accessed 9 July 2018).

# Cultural revitalisation and the *lavvu* as a cultural symbol

Although the *lavvu* itself has never been targeted for assimilation by the dominant Nordic cultures, unlike religious and other cultural practices, it has been looked down upon by outsiders as a 'backward' or 'primitive' shelter over the centuries. The *lavvu* has always been the domain of the Sami and was not appropriated by outsiders until recently.[1] However, in contrast, the *tipi* has been appropriated by many outsiders, such as the Germans throughout the 1900s, in reenactment groups, to the present day. The *lavvu* has always been in the shadow of the *tipi*—for better and for worse. Despite its being overlooked by outsiders, the *lavvu* had always been a powerful symbol of the Sami for centuries, just as the *tipi* has for Native Americans.

## The *lavvu* v. the *tipi*

The *lavvu* is markedly different from the *tipi* in several aspects; first, the *lavvu* has no smoke flaps at its top. The walls of the *lavvu* are more slanted towards the ground, at about 45 degrees rather than the *tipi's* 55–60 degrees (see Figure 17). The door of the *lavvu* door, like that of the *tipi*, is unattached, but is much larger than its North American counter parts. In North America, one of the largest disadvantages of the *lavvu* is that so many people confuse it with the *tipi*. There have been several occasions where individual Native Americans, upon first seeing a *lavvu*, react with hostility, believing that it is simply a 'badly made *tipi*', but upon learning more, react more positively to their cultural similarity.

---

1    The single exception to this was the creation of the *kohte*, designed by the German, Eberhard Koebel in c. 1930. The *lavvu*-inspired *kohte* was a symbolic tent used by the German Youth Movement (*Die deutsche Jugendbewegung*), later banned during the Nazi era, but brought back after the war and now an important symbol of the German environmental movement, no longer connected with its *lavvu* origins.

Figure 17. A present-day 4-metre (12-foot) *lavvu*.
Source. Photographed by author, Hancock, Michigan, 2011.

## Northern Lavvu – more than just a small business

Northern Lavvu is a privately owned business founded in 1995 that produces Sami *lavvus*. The owner, as well as many of the part-time employees, are of Sami ancestry. Northern Lavvu is presently the only company in the world (Galloway 2014)[2] that commercially produces traditional *lavvus* following the liquidation of the Sami-owned *lavvu* company, Venor AS, the only *lavvu* company in Sapmi ('Tvangsoppløsning' 2014).

### Philosophy

Central to the philosophy of Northern Lavvu are four visions that are closely connected to each other:

---

2    Laura Galloway mentions that Northern Lavvu is now the only company in the world, following the closure of Venor AS. However, a new venture was started recently under Arctic Lavvo in Norway.

1. Materials: The use of natural and environmentally friendly materials, as much as possible, with a minimum of carbon footprint, and avoiding petroleum-based products.
2. Education: Educating the general public about the Sami, our world view, who we are, and how the *lavvu* is part of our world view.
3. Philanthropy: A portion of the proceeds is used to provide material and financial support for North American Sami events.
4. Standard and protection: 'Defending the *lavvu*'—to protect the *lavvu* from commercial and cultural exploitation by non-Sami, so that it is kept within the community, and on Sami terms.

Many manufacturers use petroleum-based fabric materials in their tents, and although it may be cost-effective to use them, these fabrics cannot withstand exposure of heat from an open fire or other heat source. Cotton duck, which is naturally fire resistant (with limitations), has been used extensively for Northern Lavvu tents. These fabrics can be treated using natural elements, such as saline to inhibit mildew staining, but they provide warmth and are partially resistant to fire—the whole purpose of a *lavvu*.

## 'Defending the *lavvu* …'

When Northern Lavvu first started during the mid-1990s, a 'social licence' was 'granted' from several Sami Elders with the understanding that the knowledge of *lavvu*-making would be kept within the community, and not suffer the same fate as the *tipi*—namely, being made by outsiders. 'Defending the *lavvu*' has been a mantra within Northern Lavvu ever since.

There have been a few instances over the years where some non-Sami wanted to use the *lavvu* in derogatory ways—whether intentional or not. One example was when, during the late 1990s, a commercial film company contacted Northern Lavvu and wanted to create a comical sketch, using a 'cheap *tipi*' to be part of a commercial. Northern Lavvu refused this exchange as it would have been demeaning to the Native American culture. It also would have been seen as demeaning by the larger Sami community who would protest such antics. After some discussion, the film company dropped the *lavvu*/*tipi* idea and later used a generic nomadic tent, which looked neither like a *lavvu* nor a *tipi*. Another example is when participants in a local Minneapolis art show wanted to 'make our own *lavvu*', and portray Sami people in a skit, yet without any Sami community input, or direction in this matter. They also mistakenly believed that the *lavvu* is of the same design as a *tipi*. They were discouraged from doing this and moved on to another concept.

In both instances, not only were *lavvus* not provided to these groups, but also they were persuaded to avoid any connection—even remotely—with the Sami culture, as they would have represented it, even if unintended, in a negative way. In both these instances they were persuaded to use other methods of expression rather than the *lavvu*. This is an example of not only educating the public of certain cultural expectations, but also of 'defending the *lavvu*'.

## Northern Lavvu's contribution to the Sami community

Apart from the private business perspective, Northern Lavvu's long-term goal has been to provide philanthropic funds for Sami cultural projects, such as supporting film societies, providing Sami Elders with their own personal *lavvu*, and sponsoring Sami- and Nordic-related events. Although not a major source of philanthropic funds for the North American Sami community, it has financially 'smoothed things over', in regards to providing help for cultural demonstrations, film societies, social events and even for personal emergencies for individuals within the Sami community for a variety of reasons.

However, to raise such philanthropic funds, a commercial perspective is needed, which requires business savvy; something that seems counter to an Indigenous perspective. Indeed, 'business' and 'Indigenous' are often in conflict with each other—and rightfully so. There are many Indigenous peoples all over the world fighting timber, mining, or fishing industries that encroach on Indigenous land and fishing rights.

A recent public example has been the Dakota Access Pipeline protests of the Dakota People of the Standing Rock Tribe in North Dakota in 2015–17. The tribe protested the building of an oil pipeline upriver and under their reservation's water supply, thus threatening the tribe directly. The protests became a global focus for Indigenous rights and were supported by thousands of people for many months, from hundreds of North American Native Tribes, and including non-Natives—but also by several Sami visitors during the two-year conflict. During that time, Northern Lavvu provided both financial and material support in the form of *lavvus*, food, water and fuel to the protesters, who were all in conflict with both federal and state law during that time. There were nearly a dozen *lavvus* set up alongside hundreds of tipis in their camp.

## Business interests vs Indigenous interests

At first glance, 'business interests' and 'Indigenous interests' may seem in conflict; however, they are not polar opposites and can be in alliance with each other. There have already been precedents for this in the past.

A simple mistake in a $147 Minnesota county tax bill resulted in the US Supreme Court's landmark 1976 decision in *Bryan v. Itasca County*, which became the 'bedrock' of the Native American gaming industry (Washburn 2008). Although casinos/gambling were not necessarily part of the history of North American Native Communities, billions of dollars have been raised that directly benefited the majority of tribes that participated in gaming. This success requires knowledge and understanding of their business plan, their customer base, and even the exploitation of the dominant culture.

However, the reverse has also been true. If one is looking for a Native-made, commercially sold *tipi* made by a US federally recognised tribe, one will be hard pressed to find any on the market, as nearly all *tipis* advertised today are made by non-Natives, even in the United States and Canada. The *tipi*—a strong and powerful symbol of Native Americans— is not available commercially in a way that benefits Native Americans. To prevent the *lavvu* from suffering the same fate as the *tipi*, this is where Northern Lavvu's philosophy of 'defending the *lavvu*' comes into effect. Northern Lavvu are always aware of the possible exploitation of the *lavvu* by outside interests.

In Sapmi, many cultural organisations, individuals and (in some instances) corporations, often do get some type of government financial backing in the form of grants or loans of varying degrees, though their funding has always been a source of on-going political debate. In Canada or the United States, any government grants to cultural organisations and individuals, if available, are often very limited, and rarely available for long—to the point of being just lip service. In North America, business-savvy is the only way for Indigenous peoples to step in to fill that financial void, such as the gaming industry.

## The *lavvu* — a 'snapshot' in time

Northern Lavvu's goal has been to reproduce the *lavvu* design as it was during the late nineteenth and early twentieth centuries. There are several reasons for this time frame: English textiles, with their inexpensive cotton duck from colonial India, were reaching the far corners of the globe, including Sapmi. Before the transition period of 1850–1900, *lavvus* were made primarily of reindeer hides; however, during this transition, cotton, and to a lesser extent woollen felt, came into use. This transition period started roughly during the 1850s and into the early 1900s as more accessible and inexpensive British fabric goods became available to the Sami. The 'olive drab' *lavvus* were popular following World War II as this was the material that was readily available following the destruction of residential housing during the war.

## Research

Even though the *lavvu* remains a powerful symbol of the Sami people (see Figure 18), there is still very little in the way of academic research on the subject, and to date none known in the English language (except for the author's manual for the *lavvu* from Northern Lavvu). When Northern Lavvu started research on the *lavvu* in the preinternet era, there were only two main sources of research: the oral traditions of immigrant Sami to North America[3] (who made only one traditional *lavvu* here in North America), and historical photos of the tent structure. The only way to simulate a pre-1900 *lavvu* structure was to build it, experiment, make it into a living structure, and then compare the work with period photos of the *lavvus*. See Figure 16 as an example of this research, among others. There are also movie reels from the era. One such is *Le Vie chez les Lapons* (Life in Lapland) (1908), which is another example of the historical work that we attempt to incorporate into our research into *lavvu*.

---

3    The vast majority of the oral traditions were from Anja Kitti of Toronto, Canada and Ellen Binder of Tuktuyaktuk, Canada during the early 1990s. Nathan Muus, coeditor of *Baiki: The North American Sami Journal*, also had considerable background knowledge of the *lavvu*.

The *lavvus* produced by Northern Lavvu are a hybrid made up of ideas from these oral traditions, photographic evidence, and an application of practical design. With this basic design, plus minor variations in size, colour, and so on, the pattern is a commercially viable product that has been used in a variety of the world-wide environments, that provides for people with differing camping skills, and is cost effective for production. It is with some interest that *lavvu* poles, normally spruce or birch of the northern climates of Sapmi, have been substituted with bamboo in such places as Indonesia, South Africa, Brazil and even Florida. The vast majority of *lavvus* are now going to areas never seen by the Indigenous Sami. Northern Lavvu's consumers have mostly been non-Sami wanting a unique camping tent and, along the way, learning about a Sami world view perspective.

Figure 18. The coat of arms of the Sami town of Kautokeino (Guovdageaidnu), Norway.

Source. Wikipedia Commons. Online: upload.wikimedia.org/wikipedia/commons/2/29/Kautokeino_komm.svg (accessed 2 September 2018).

## Cultural revitalisation and *lavvu* today

When Northern Lavvu started in 1995, there was only one known traditional *lavvu* in North America made by an elder, and one of the very few outside of Sapmi. Today, the *lavvu*—and the Sami world perspective—has spread to every continent on the globe. To date, Northern Lavvu has published the only work in the English language that deals exclusively with the *lavvu*, while some of the proceeds go to supporting Sami cultural events in North America.

Revitalisation of Indigenous cultures will come from many sources and directions, and although commercialisation and business have often been used as weapons to exploit Indigenous peoples, this need not be so in the future. The very seeds of Indigenous cultural revitalisation may actually feed upon the roots of past exploitation—'feeding on the tools of the conquerors'.

## References

*A Lapp Family* (c. 1895–1900). Library of Congress Prints and Photographs Division Washington, DC 20540 USA. LC-DIG-ppmsc-06257 (digital file from original). Online: www.loc.gov/pictures/item/2001700768/ (accessed 9 July 2018).

'About the North American Sami'. n.d. *Báiki*, Online: www.baiki.org/content Baiki/about.html (accessed 9 July 2018).

Arctic Lavvo. Online: www.arcticlavvo.no/ (accessed 29 August 2016).

Galloway, Laura. 2014. 'Eneste lavvoprodusent i USA' [The only Lavvu producer in the USA]. *Ságat*, 6 August.

*Le Vie chez les Lapons* [Life in Lapland], Pathé Baby, 1908, Online: youtu.be/ ZTyoe59qoyw (accessed 29 August 2018).

'Tvangsoppløsning' [Enforced liquidation]. 2014. *Ságet*, 21 August. Venor AS. Online: www.sagat.no/kautokeino-nyheter/2014/08/21/tvangsoppl%C3% B8sning/ (accessed 29 August 2018).

Washburn, Kevin K. 2008. 'The legacy of *Bryan v. Itasca County*: How a $147 County tax notice helped bring tribes $200 billion in Indian gaming revenue'. *Minnesota Law Review* 92: 919–70. Online: www.minnesotalawreview.org/ wp-content/uploads/2012/01/Washburn_FinalPDF.pdf (accessed 29 August 2019).

# 23

# *Sydisdans*: A New Traditional Dance in Sapmi

Nils-Jonas Persson

## Introduction by Åsa Virdi Kroik

I do not remember when I first heard of *sydisdans*. I just remember that suddenly it was there and every Saami knew what it was. In the inland of Scandinavia and Sapmi, where I grew up, events are often arranged in the villages. A local band is hired for one night and people gather from the nearby villages to dance. People may need to travel 100–200 kilometres or more to such events, but the motivation to attend is often very high among local people. Youngsters without a driver's licence or car somehow manage to find their way to the location and back again. South Saami have been dancing with their Scandinavian neighbours at such dance events for generations, and they have developed dances together and integrated influences from the outside. Time for dancing is often integrated in Saami events, like important political meetings or sport competitions, although no competition in dance has ever taken place in a Saami context as far as I know. It was in such Saami contexts that *sydisdans* developed.

In 2015, when the South Saami *joiker* and singer Jon Henrik Fjällgren almost won the popular Swedish national song contest, Melodifestivalen, he took the dancers Nils-Jonas Person and Jannie Staffansson on stage with him to perform a *sydisdans*. Something happened. From being a concept that every Saami (but hardly any non-Saami) was familiar with, *sydisdans* became a word on everybody's lips. The following text is edited from an interview that I conducted, together with Hiroshi Maruyama and Gerald Roche, with Nils-Jonas Persson about *sydisdans*.

***

*Sydisdans*—southern dance—is danced by couples. It's almost like a mixture of foxtrot and swing. The best way to dance it is when there's a lot of speed in the music, a lot of movement. Most of the time, *sydisdans* is a happy dance. It's never sad. But, sometimes, it can be a little more affectionate, a little more sensual. But mostly it is happy. So to me, that's what a *sydisdans* is all about—good fun. It makes people happy, and you can be social. The music for a *sydisdans* can be anything. It doesn't have to be *joik*. It could be country, hip-hop, reggae, or whatever. It works with everything.

Figure 19. Jenny Virdi Kroik and David Kroik dancing the *sydisdans* at a family gathering. The collage gives a sense of the movement of the dance.

Source. Photographed by Åsa Virdi Kroik, Buarkantjahke/Borgafjäll, July 2018.

I don't think anyone knows the origins of the dance, but a rumour says it began in southern Norway, or the middle of Norway. But that's not really known for sure—I guess you could say it's more of a myth. My friend did some research on the topic, and that was the closest she came. And although this dance is new, Saami people probably did have some sort of traditional dance in the past. It might have been part of their shamanic tradition, but it vanished because people lost the deep connection to their shamanic religion after Christianity came and, sort of, made it disappear.

My first encounter with a *sydisdans* was at a wedding here in Amarnäs, where a Saami girl taught me to dance it. Ever since that day, I have danced every single chance I get. You can't really learn a *sydisdans* from a book. There's no school for it. You learn it on the dance floor, with your friends. And since you have to dance with emotion, everyone dances it differently. They have their own style and moves—different spins, jumps and lifts. It depends on the person (see Figure 19).

When we danced on television for Jon Henrik's performance on Melodifestivalen, our performance was largely improvised, but they did give us some directions. So, when we danced on the TV show, they told us that we had to be at specific places at specific times during the song, but they couldn't direct what types of steps or spins we did or anything like that. We were really free in the dancing, as long as we were in the right place at the right time.

Before the performance, I had danced with a particular girl a couple of times—we had met each other at gatherings with Jon Henrik and others. Jon Henrik knows us both. The girl's name is Jannie Staffansson. I have a bit of a name in Sapmi for being a good dancer, so Jon just called me and asked if I wanted to join him. And as for Jannie, she and Jon grew up together, so he knew she was a good dancer. That was my first time dancing on TV, so it was quite nerve-wracking. But it worked out well. Before that, I'd been to ordinary dances in pubs and so on, but nothing like this. The only thing that comes close is that the same girl and I had a clip on YouTube a few years ago (Melodifestivalen 2015).

As for my identity—this dance hasn't made much of a difference to my identity. That's because I already had a very solid grounding in my identity, with the reindeer and so on. But I know that, especially in the southern parts of Sapmi, dancing is very important for people's identity. It's almost as if you are expected to dance. Once you're 10 years old, you need to learn how to dance if you come from the southern part of Sapmi. In the northern part, they don't dance as much. So, for the northern part, the dance doesn't have much connection to identity, but in the southern part there's a connection and there's an expectation that you should be a good dancer.

Now, however, I think the *sydisdans* is starting to become distinctive of Saami culture. I think that in the future we will see more and more of it at special occasions. A couple of years ago, I published some brief instructions about how to dance *sydisdans*, together with a woman from Jokkmokk. We published that in the Saami magazine *Nuorat*, which is produced by and published for young Saami. After we published that article, I noticed a few changes. For example, some people called me and asked if I could hold a class, or teach them. And after that, I also was a leader for a confirmation.[1] And, then we had a lot of staff classes for various businesses. So, a couple of years after the publication of the journal article, I had about 70 youths who came and danced. Now they've really grown up and they still know how to dance. In fact, young people really like the dance—they're really excited about it and they want to learn more about it. So, I think the dance is spreading and its popularity is growing.

Since the TV performance, the reaction has been really good. I vanished for a while immediately after the performance, because I went to see my girlfriend in Norway, and I am not known by so many people there. When I got home to Sweden, the whole thing had settled down, so I missed the immediate reaction after it. But, generally, the opinion has been that it was very good. It was good that we represented Sapmi so well. It felt good to share it with people.

I think the popularity of the dance is somewhat connected to growth in other areas of Saami culture. For example, in my area, people didn't *joik* openly until recently. My grandfather didn't speak the Saami language, even though he knew it, because he got beaten and told that he was not allowed to speak it. They were also told not to *joik*. So it is only, perhaps, 30 or 40 years ago that children began to be allowed to speak the language at school, and public opinion changed so that the language became more or less accepted. So *joiks* have only very recently returned, perhaps in the last 10 or 20 years. For a lot of people, the *sydisdans* is connected to their identity and self-respect and their general feeling about their roots. But, for me, and for others too, it is something modern—something to be proud of because we have it and no other culture has it. So, on the one hand, the popularity of the dance is connected to the return of traditions, but on the other hand, it is also very modern. I think it's a little bit of both.

---

1    The Swedish church organises schools or camps for teenagers to learn more about Christianity and to confirm their baptism. It is very common to baptise newborns in Scandinavia and in Sapmi, and it is a strong tradition for those who are baptised to make their confirmation of those vows as adolescents. Among the Saami, it is common to participate in such camps, and since about the 1980s, there are also special camps only for Saami youth. Apart from priests, there are also lay leaders at the camps, and in the Saami confirmation camps, the leaders are recruited from among young Saami adults.

I think the dance is also a way to reach out to Swedish people and to show them that we exist, that we have traditions, and that we really want to talk about them, and to show people our culture. Even in my neighbouring village, about 200 kilometres away, they don't even know what a Saami is. So, the dance is a way to reach out to the general public and let them know that we exist.

## Reference

Melodifestivalen. 2015. Jon Henrik Fjällgren - Jag Är Fri. Online: www.youtube.com/watch?v=3tfvV-5Wq4w (accessed 27 July 2018).

*Nuorat*. Online: www.nuorat.se (accessed 9 July 2018).

# Conclusion: Indigenous Efflorescence

Gerald Roche

In this book we have sought to introduce the concept of Indigenous efflorescence both as a descriptive label for a real-world process, and as an analytical frame for thinking about that process. Descriptively, Indigenous efflorescence refers to the demographic surge in Indigenous populations, coupled with their increasing political empowerment, economic success and cultural flourishing, all of which have gathered pace over the second half of the twentieth century and into the twenty-first century. As an analytical framework, Indigenous efflorescence involves a commitment to explore these phenomena in a way that is process oriented (rather than product oriented) and future (rather than past) oriented, and, finally, is also positively engaged in supporting Indigenous peoples to deepen and spread Indigenous efflorescence.

In order to provide a rich account and exploration of this process of efflorescence, the contributions to this volume were organised around the themes of *contexts* and *practices* of efflorescence. In looking at the contexts of efflorescence, we drew attention to the economic and political developments that have enabled Indigenous efflorescence, and at how social movements, technological developments, and access to and control over land underpin Indigenous efflorescence. Meanwhile, in looking at practices of efflorescence, we examined how ongoing structures of colonialism continue to condition not only what can viably be *done* by Indigenous people, but also how it *feels* to participate in efflorescence.

In the conclusion to this volume, I aim to create a foundation for future work in Indigenous efflorescence by discussing, first of all, what it means for anthropological theory and practice, and second, how Indigenous efflorescence might continue to spread and grow amongst Indigenous people around the world in the future, and thus how anthropologists working in different contexts might engage with and support Indigenous efflorescence.

## Extending the anthropological engagement with Indigenous efflorescence

What are the implications of the concept of Indigenous efflorescence for anthropological theory and praxis? Perhaps the most important issue anthropologists need to consider is whether or not studying Indigenous efflorescence in any way demeans the deep loss that so many Indigenous peoples have experienced. Here, I am not only referring to the subjective sense of loss and grief, but to the real substantive losses—of land, livelihood, political control, language and culture. The loss of lives. Is it responsible for anthropologists to study and promote efflorescence while the structures that created these catastrophic losses still remain in place? Can it be anything but Pollyanna-ish myopia to focus on positive developments while so much about the Indigenous predicament remains negative? What are the ethical entailments of highlighting Indigenous efflorescence?

I think a starting point must be that an ethical discussion of Indigenous efflorescence must always be framed in terms of the ongoing nature of colonisation and settler academics' complicity within it. Echoing William Faulkner's dictum that 'The past is never dead. It isn't even past', Patrick Wolfe (2006: 388) has famously described colonisation as 'a structure, not an event'. Colonisation is not simply something that happened in the past and is now finished, nor is colonialism a debunked and interred ideology that no longer impacts on policy or daily life. Dispossession from land, the persistence of colonial systems of defining and classifying Indigenous peoples, and the corrosive intergenerational impacts of trauma (Atkinson 2002), among other factors, persist as contemporary realities that maintain colonial structures and ideologies. Acknowledging ongoing colonisation as a constraining context to Indigenous efflorescence is essential to understanding it, and the subjectivities it produces. Furthermore, for those of us who are settler academics, situating ourselves as beneficiaries of colonisation is essential to an ethical approach to Indigenous efflorescence.

A second issue that needs to be highlighted in future work on Indigenous efflorescence is the paradoxical role that the enabling political and economic factors play in its continuation. Whilst greater recognition and the cessation of aggressive assimilatory policies have created opportunities for Indigenous peoples, numerous scholars have drawn attention to the ways in which contemporary practices of recognition also result in the consolidation and legitimation of state power, whilst also subjecting Indigenous peoples to regimes of discipline, definition, classification and regulation that are not only fundamentally disempowering, but also divisive, exclusionary, and reifying (Povinelli 2002; Fraser 2003; Coulthard 2014; Vincent 2017). Meanwhile, although authors such as James Clifford (2013) have argued that the economic conditions of late capitalism have provided opportunities for Indigenous efflorescence, it is also clear that neoliberalism exposes Indigenous people to various forms of violent capitalist exploitation that destroy not only social ties between Indigenous people, but also between people and land. Furthermore, as Glen Coulthard (2014: 171) observes, without 'a massive transformation in the political economy of contemporary settler-colonialism, any efforts to rebuild our nations will remain parasitic on capitalism, and thus on the perpetual exploitation of our lands and labor'. Therefore, although political and economic changes have clearly enabled Indigenous efflorescence to some extent, they are also domains in which both inertia and innovation work towards the continuing domination and marginalisation of Indigenous peoples. These tensions need closer scrutiny by anthropologists working on Indigenous efflorescence.

A final issue that anthropologists need to examine in relation to Indigenous efflorescence is the discipline's well-developed tradition of critical engagement with structures of domination, which has become particularly central to the discipline since the 1980s (Ortner 2016). What are the implications for critical anthropology suggested by a focus on efflorescence? I think it is possible, first of all, to find precedents to the concept of Indigenous efflorescence within the framework of the 'anthropology of the good' (Robbins 2013) or 'positive anthropology' (Fischer 2014), an incipient turn in anthropology that seeks to problematise the discipline's voyeuristic fascination with 'the suffering subject … living in pain, in poverty, or under conditions of violence or oppression' (Robbins 2013: 448). Rather than continuing anthropology's obsession with the powerless (Kulick 2006), and portraying Indigenous people simply as victims, a focus on Indigenous efflorescence provokes us to look at 'the way people understand the good and define its proper pursuit', and thus contribute to a broader project of understanding 'the cultural construction of the good' as something that 'must be imaginatively conceived' (Robbins 2013: 457). One potentially productive field of inquiry along these lines is the theorisation of the sentiment of hope that underlies Indigenous efflorescence, such as the 'radical hope' of the Crow elder Plenty Coups described by Jonathan Lear (2008)—a hope for cultural revival in the face of an apocalyptic 'breakdown of the field in which occurrences occur' (34). We can thus investigate Indigenous efflorescence as a project that entails the cultivation of productive sentiments, quotidian practices, moral and political theory, the creation, maintenance and evolution of social movements, and arenas of conflict around the pursuit of the good.

Such a focus on 'the good' is not incompatible with a critical outlook, especially when the object of critique is shifted to the anthropologist and our complicity in continuing colonisation. Marshall Sahlins (1993: 7), for example, has noted how the anthropological obsession with colonial agency and native passivity effectively achieves 'in theory just what imperialism attempts in practice'. In a similar manner, Joshua Fishman (1985), one of the founders of the study of language revitalisation, examined how tropes of the death and demise of languages—he referred specifically to Yiddish—are often more prescriptive than descriptive, expressing desires more than prediction. For Fishman, to speak of death was to wish it, and he considered one of the roles of scholars in relation to suppressed and endangered languages was to support those languages and their speakers, at the very least by avoiding such laden terminology and misleading, negative imagery.

Leanne Betasamosake Simpson, a Michi Saagiig Nishnaabeg scholar, artist and activist, gives an insight into the subjective experience of scholarly focus on colonial domination and the need to draw attention to the achievements of Indigenous people, saying, 'It's crucial to see all the good work that's going on, because colonialism [works] to obfuscate that, and to keep us in this place where we perpetually feel like we're drowning' (Simpson 2013). As Marcia Langton (2013: 135) reminds us, 'Counting the successes ... sometimes results in a small measure of hope in a landscape of obstacles, bureaucratic monsters and traps'. The concept of efflorescence, then, in drawing attention to Indigenous agency, entails a strategic and critical intervention, and a refusal to participate in the feedback between the actual and theoretical hegemony of colonialism.

It involves a commitment to work towards the production of hope (Hage 2002) and its distribution to those most denied it: anthropology *as* hope, rather than simply the anthropology *of* hope.

## Globalising Indigenous efflorescences

The anthropological study of efflorescence in different parts of the world will necessarily be entangled with the complex ways that efflorescence emerges from broad political and economic developments. Therefore, we must also pay attention to the ways in which those developments are unevenly spread throughout the globe, and how the conditions that enable efflorescence are thus also unevenly distributed. Here, I focus on how uneven political developments, in particular, impact the globalisation of efflorescence, starting with a discussion of Indigenism.

Indigenism refers to the transnational movement to promote the political interests of Indigenous people, including promotion of the universal applicability of the categories 'Indigenous peoples' and 'indigeneity' (Niezen 2003; Clifford 2013). Although originating primarily in the CANZUS (Canada, Australia, New Zealand and the US) countries, and now vigorously supported by the Nordic countries (Finland, Sweden and Norway), this movement has since taken on global dimensions (Merlan 2009), including the creation of legal norms and international agreements that have developed in the constant feedback between local movements and global networks (Johnson 2016).

The uptake of Indigenism, and contribution to the movement, have, however, been globally uneven. One reason for this is the historical legacy of the so-called 'salt water' or 'blue water' thesis, which emerged as part of post-World War II decolonisation regimes in the United Nations (UN), and suggests that colonialism (and therefore indigeneity) only exist in contexts where overseas, noncontiguous territories are dominated by a colonial power (Lightfoot 2016). A result of the promotion of this idea within international forums such as the UN, is that the uptake of Indigenism has been somewhat limited in certain parts of the world. Within Asia, for example, Ian Baird (2016) notes that while in countries such as Japan, Nepal and Cambodia, Indigenism has gained some credence, it is more generally absent from Asian states (Kingsbury 1998). Adherence to the blue water thesis has had some paradoxical outcomes, such as presented by the case of China, which supported such a measure as the UN Declaration on the Rights of Indigenous Peoples, precisely because it claims to have no Indigenous peoples, instead recognising its population to consist of nominally isomorphic 'nationalities', without any having the precedence of indigeneity (Elliot 2015). Nonetheless, although the Chinese state does not support domestic indigeneity, it has, in some cases, turned a blind eye to the growth of Indigenist discourses in certain restricted domains, for example, in association with environmental campaigns focusing on traditional ecological knowledge (Hathaway 2016).

The case of China is indicative of the complex terrain that Indigenism and Indigenous efflorescence navigate in their global spread. This complexity is not only shaped by differing political regimes and their relation to the liberal democratic politics of the CANZUS bloc, but it also varies in response to different aspects of efflorescence, as can be seen in regards to language, through a discussion of how discourses of language endangerment and language revitalisation (and associated practices) have been taken up differently in different contexts.

The concept of language endangerment was first promoted in the late 1980s and early 1990s, and framed specifically as a call to action.[1] The term 'endangered language' was selected to mirror the concept of 'endangered species', and thus draw both methodological tools and moral legitimacy from the global environmental movement. The endangered language movement has sought to raise public awareness of the global scale of language endangerment and loss, and to mobilise resources in defence of linguistic diversity. This program has not only initiated a new field of linguistic research (Austin and Sallabank 2011; Thomason 2015), but has also consolidated into a reasonably well-resourced field of activity backed by large nongovernmental organisations including UNESCO. The achievements of this movement include the description of global patterns

---

1    At the XIVth International Congress of Linguists, in 1987, it was decided that the XVth Congress would take endangered languages as one of its main themes (Wurm 1996). In 1991, in preparation for the XVth congress, a series of articles on language endangerment were published in *Diogenes*, the journal of the International Council of Philosophy and Humanistic Studies (Wurm 1991; Brenzinger, Heine and Sommer 1991; Zepeda and Hill 1991; Kibrik 1991). Some of these articles were also published in an edited volume, published in the same year, titled *Endangered Languages* (Robins and Uhlenbeck 1991). In the same year, Ken Hale, from Harvard, organised a panel at the Linguistic Society of America Conference, on endangered languages, and this was published the following year as a special issue of the journal *Language* (Hale et al. 1992). Also in 1992, a meeting was held with UNESCO to discuss the establishment of a *Red Book of Languages in Danger of Disappearing*. Later that year, at a meeting in Harare, moves were made to establish an International Clearing House for Endangered Languages, which was opened in Tokyo in 1994. The period from 1991 to 1994 was thus crucial for launching the global endangered language movement.

of linguistic diversity and endangerment (Loh and Harmon 2005; Maffi 2005; Nettle 2009; Anderson 2011; Gorenflo et al. 2012; Axelsen and Manrubia 2014), the creation of systems to assess linguistic vitality (e.g. UNESCO 2003, 2011), the global surge in language documentation, the training of linguists and the creation of digital archives to house recordings of linguistic materials. The movement has been successful in internationalising concern over language endangerment, resulting in the global spread of 'discourses of endangerment' (Duchêne and Heller 2008), including to China (Xu 2003), where a centralised initiative to document and archive endangered language has been promoted by the central government since at least 2016, with other, less centralised, efforts going back at least a decade beforehand.

In contrast to this effort to map and record global linguistic diversity, language revitalisation has taken an active approach in fostering linguistic diversity. This involves collaborating with communities to maintain languages that are losing speakers, and also to regain additional speakers, even in situations when the language has ceased to be spoken and exists only in archival records. Language revitalisation as a field of theory and practice essentially combines the call to action of language endangerment with the political vision of Indigensim, focusing on self-determination, empowerment, and service to and collaboration with, rather than the study of, Indigenous communities. As with Indigenism more broadly, language revitalisation has emerged and continues to be based primarily in the CANZUS states and Nordic countries, and is thus entangled with the politics of liberal democracies, decolonisation and human rights (Roche 2018). The political underpinnings of language revitalisation have, to some extent, limited the uptake of its theories and practices globally, in comparison to discourses of language endangerment, which have spread further afield. For example, what we see in China is that whilst discourses of language endangerment, and practices of documenting and archiving languages, are sanctioned at the highest levels, language revitalisation projects typically take place 'off-stage', in the grey space of an amorphous civil society which is neither officially forbidden nor publicly sanctioned.

This book has argued that Indigenous efflorescence is entangled with liberal democracy and late capitalism, and that its uptake and expression vary according to domain (the revitalisation of languages, for example, differs considerably from how control and access to land are reestablished and expanded). In reflecting on this, it seems reasonable to suggest that we should be alert to the possibility of multiple efflorescences,[2] taking place in radically different political and economic contexts, playing out differently in different domains. And, given our focus on the future, we should also be alert to the possibilities of unfolding, becoming, not-yet-occurring efflorescences, waiting to happen in contexts where conditions are at present inimical. We need to reflect on what we can do to support those communities whose time for demographic rebound, greater political enfranchisement, economic enrichment and cultural flourishing is yet to come.

# References


Anderson, Gregory D.S. 2011. 'Language hotspots: what (applied) linguistics and education should do about language endangerment in the twenty-first century'. *Language and Education* 25(4): 273–89. doi.org/10.1080/095007 82.2011.577218

Atkinson, Judy. 2002. *Trauma Trails, Recreating Song Lines: The Transgenerational Effects of Trauma in Indigenous Australia.* North Geelong: Spinifex Press.

Austin, Peter K. and Julia Sallabank (eds). 2011. *The Cambridge Handbook of Endangered Languages.* Cambridge: Cambridge University Press. doi.org/ 10.1017/CBO9780511975981

Axelsen, Jacob Bock and Susanna Manrubia. 2014. 'River density and landscape roughness are universal determinants of linguistic diversity'. *Proceedings of the Royal Society B* 281(1784): 1–8. doi.org/10.1098/rspb.2013.3029

Baird, Ian G. 2016. 'Indigeneity in Asia: An emerging but contested concept'. *Asian Ethnicity* 17(4): 1–5. doi.org/10.1080/14631369.2016.1193804

Brenzinger, Matthias, Bernd Heine and Gabriele Sommer. 1991. 'Language death in Africa'. *Diogenes* 39(153): 19–44. doi.org/10.1177/039219219103915303

Clifford, James. 2013. *Returns: Becoming Indigenous in the Twenty-First Century.* Harvard: Harvard University Press. doi.org/10.4159/9780674726222

Coulthard, Glen. 2014. *Red Skins, White Masks: Rejecting the Colonial Politics of Recognition.* Minneapolis and London: University of Minnesota Press. doi.org/10.5749/minnesota/9780816679645.001.0001


---

2   This suggestion mirrors Francesca Merlan's (2009), that we need to be alert to the possibility of multiple indigeneities.

Duchêne, Alexandre and Monica Heller. 2008. *Discourses of Endangerment*. London: Continuum.

Elliott, Mark. 2015. 'The case of the missing indigene: Debate over a "second-generation" ethnic policy'. *China Journal* 73: 186–213. doi.org/10.1086/679274

Fischer, Edward. 2014. *The Good life: Aspiration, Dignity, and the Anthropology of Wellbeing*. Stanford: Stanford University Press.

Fishman, Joshua. 1985. 'The lively life of a "dead" language (or "Everyone knows that Yiddish died long ago")'. In *Language of Inequality*, edited by Nessa Wolfson and Joan Manes, 207–24. Berlin: Mouton Publishers. doi.org/10.1515/9783110857320.207

Fraser, Nancy. 2003. 'Social justice in the age of identity politics: Redistribution, recognition, and participation'. In *Redistribution or Recognition? A Political-Philosophical Exchange*, edited by Nancy Fraser and Axel Honneth; translated by Joel Golb, James Ingram and Christiane Wilke, 7–109. London and New York: Verso.

Gorenflo, Larry J., Suzanne Romaine, Russell Mittermeier and Kristen Walker-Painemilla. 2012. 'Co-occurrence of linguistic and biological diversity in biodiversity hotspots and high biodiversity wilderness areas'. *Proceedings of the National Academy of Sciences (PNAS)* 109(21): 8032–37. doi.org/10.1073/pnas.1117511109

Hage, Ghassan. 2002. *Against Paranoid Nationalism: Searching for Hope in a Shrinking Society*. Annandale: Pluto Press.

Hale, Ken, Michael Krauss, Lucille J. Watahomigie, Akira Y. Yamamoto, Colette Craig, LaVerne Masayesva Jeanne and Nora C. England. 1992. 'Endangered languages'. *Language* 68(1): 1–42. doi.org/10.2307/416368

Hathaway, Michael J. 2016. 'China's Indigenous peoples? How global environmentalism unintentionally smuggled the notion of indigeneity into China'. *Humanities* 5(3): 54. doi.org/10.3390/h5030054

Johnson, Miranda. 2016. *The Land is Our History: Indigeneity, Law, and the Settler State*. Oxford: Oxford University Press. doi.org/10.1093/acprof:oso/9780190600020.001.0001

Kibrik, Aleksandr E. 1991. 'The problem of endangered languages in the USSR'. *Diogenes* 39(153): 67–83. doi.org/10.1177/039219219103915305

Kingsbury, Benedict. 1998. '"Indigenous peoples" in International Law: A constructivist approach to the Asian controversy'. *The American Journal of International Law* 92(3): 414–57. doi.org/10.2307/2997916

Kulick, Don. 2006. 'Theory in furs: Masochist anthropology'. *Current Anthropology* 47(6): 933–52. doi.org/10.1086/507198

Langton, Marcia. 2013. *Boyer Lectures 2012: The Quiet Revolution: Indigenous People and the Resources Boom*. Sydney: HarperCollins Australia.

Lear, Jonathan. 2008. *Radical Hope: Ethics in the Face of Cultural Devastation*. Cambridge, MA: Harvard University Press.

Lightfoot, Sheryl. 2016. *Global Indigenous Politics: A Subtle Revolution*. New York: Routledge. doi.org/10.4324/9781315670669

Loh, Jonathan and David Harmon. 2005. 'A global index of biocultural diversity'. *Ecological Indicators* 5(3): 231–41. doi.org/10.1016/j.ecolind.2005.02.005

Maffi, Luisa. 2005. 'Linguistic, cultural, and biological diversity'. *Annual Review of Anthropology* 34: 599–617. doi.org/10.1146/annurev.anthro.34.081804. 120437

Merlan, Francesca. 2005. 'Indigenous movements in Australia'. *Annual Review of Anthropology* 34: 473–94. doi.org/10.1146/annurev.anthro.34.081804. 120643

Merlan, Francesca. 2009. 'Indigeneity: Global and local'. *Current Anthropology* 50(3): 303–33. doi.org/10.1086/597667

Nettle, Daniel. 2009. 'Ecological influences on human behavioural diversity: A review of recent findings'. *Trends in Ecology and Evolution* 24(11): 618–24. doi.org/10.1016/j.tree.2009.05.013

Niezen, Ronald. 2003. *The Origins of Indigenism: Human Rights and the Politics of Identity*. Berkeley: University of California Press. doi.org/10.1525/california/ 9780520235540.001.0001

Ortner, Sherry B. 2016. 'Dark anthropology and its others: Theory since the eighties'. *HAU: Journal of Ethnographic Theory* 6(1): 47–73. doi.org/10.14318/ hau6.1.004

Povinelli, Elizabeth. 2002. *The Cunning of Recognition: Indigenous Alterities and the Making of Australian Multiculturalism*. Durham: Duke University Press. doi.org/10.1215/9780822383673

Robbins, Joel. 2013. 'Beyond the suffering subject: Toward an anthropology of the good'. *Journal of the Royal Anthropological Institute (JRAI)* 19(3): 447–62. doi.org/10.1111/1467-9655.12044

Robins, Robert and Eugenius Uhlenbeck. 1991. *Endangered Languages.* New York: Berg Publishers.

Roche, Gerald. 2018. 'Regional perspectives: Decolonizing and globalizing language revitalization'. In *The Routledge Handbook of Language Revitalization*, edited by Leanne Hinton, Leena Huss and Gerald Roche, 275–78. London: Routledge.

Sahlins, Marshall. 1993. 'Goodbye to *tristes tropes*: Ethnography in the context of modern world history'. *The Journal of Modern History* 65(1): 1–25. doi.org/10.1086/244606

Simpson, Leanne Betasamosake. 2013. 'Dancing on our turtle's back'. *IGOV Indigenous Speakers Series*. Online: www.youtube.com/watch?v=28u7BOx0_9k (accessed 9 July 2017).

Thomason, Sarah. 2015. *Endangered Languages: An Introduction.* Cambridge: Cambridge University Press.

UNESCO. 2003. *Language Vitality and Endangerment.* Document submitted to the International Expert Meeting on UNESCO Programme Safeguarding of Endangered Language. Paris, 10–12 March. Online: www.unesco.org/new/fileadmin/MULTIMEDIA/HQ/CLT/pdf/Language_vitality_and_endangerment_EN.pdf (accessed 16 June 2018).

UNESCO. 2011. Background Paper. *UNESCO's* Language Vitality and Endangerment *Methodological Guideline: Review of Application and Feedback since 2003.* Online: www.unesco.org/new/fileadmin/MULTIMEDIA/HQ/CI/CI/pdf/unesco_language_vitaly_and_endangerment_methodological_guideline.pdf (accessed 16 June 2018).

Vincent, Eve. 2017. *'Against Native Title': Conflict and Creativity in Outback Australia.* Canberra: Aboriginal Studies Press.

Wolfe, Patrick. 2006. 'Settler colonialism and the elimination of the Native'. *Journal of Genocide Research* 8(4): 387–409. doi.org/10.1080/14623520601056240

Wurm, Stephen. 1991. 'Language death and disappearance: Causes and circumstances'. *Diogenes* 39(153): 1–18. doi.org/10.1177/039219219103915302

Wurm, Stephen, with cartography by Theo Baumann. 1996. 'Atlas of the World's languages in danger of disappearing'. In *Atlas of the World's Languages in Danger of Disappearing*, edited by Stephen Wurm, with cartography by Theo Baumann, 1–24. Paris and Canberra: UNESCO Publishing / Pacific Linguistics.

Wurm, Stephen (ed.). 1996. *Atlas of the World's Languages in Danger of Disappearing*. Paris and Canberra: UNESCO Publishing / Pacific Linguistics.

Xu Shixuan. 2003. 'Language endangerment'. In *The Language Situation in China* Vol. 1, edited by Li Yuming and Li Wei, 261–70. Berlin: De Gruyter.

Zepeda, Ofelia and Jane Hill. 1991. 'The condition of Native American languages in the United States'. *Diogenes* 39(153): 45–65. doi.org/10.1177/039219219103915304